Empowering Latinas

Breaking Boundaries, Freeing Lives

YASMIN DAVIDDS-GARRIDO

Penmarin Books
Granite Bay, California

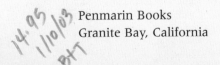

Editorial Offices:
Penmarin Books
2011 Ashridge Way
Granite Bay, CA 95746

Sales and Customer Service Offices:
Midpoint Trade Books
27 W. 20th Street, Suite 1102
New York, NY 10011
(212) 727-0190

Penmarin Books are available at special discounts for bulk purchases for premiums, sales promotions, or education. For details, contact the Pub-lisher. On your letterhead, include information concerning the intended use of the books and how many you wish to purchase.

Grateful thanks to the following:

Barbara K. Bassett for her permission to use her poem "Angela's Word." In Canfield, Jack, Mark Victor Hansen, Marci Shimoff, and Jennifer Hawthorne, eds. 1996. *Chicken Soup for the Woman's Soul.* Deerfield Beach, FL: Health Communications, Inc.: 73.

Steven Carter and Julia Sokol for granting us permission to use excerpts from their book, *Men Love Women Who Love Themselves.* 1996. New York: Dell Publishing, a division of Bantam Dell Publishing Group, Inc.

Claudia Colindres and Third Woman Press for permission to print an excerpt from the book, *The Sexuality of Latinas.* 1989. Berkeley, CA: Third Woman Press.

Visit our Website at **www.penmarin.com** for more information about this and other exciting titles.

Printed in Canada

1 2 3 4 5 6 7 8 9 10   05 04 03 02 01

Library of Congress Cataloging-in-Publication Data

Davidds-Garrido, Yasmin.
    Empowering Latinas : breaking boundaries, freeing lives / Yasmin Davidds-Garrido.
        p. cm.
    Includes bibliographical references and index.
    ISBN 1-883955-22-X
    1. Hispanic American women—Social conditions. 2. Hispanic Ameri-can women—Civil rights. 3. Hispanic American women—Psychology.
4. Sex role—United States. 5. Man-women relationships—United States.
6. Family—United States. I. Title.

E184.S75 D35 2001
305.48'868073—dc21   2001050039

I dedicate this book to the most important people in my life

Mi Mámi

Whose love saved my life

My Husband

Who showed me what a "REAL MAN" is made of

My Daughter

Who is my life and my soul

My Sisters

Who never stopped believing in me

And to my special friends

*Vonni, Xochitl, Dominika, Michelle D., and Michelle R.,
who have loved me, supported me, and never judged me*

I Love You All

Contents

Preface

It all began one fall day in 1997 in my graduate Women's Studies class. The discussion for the day was from our reading for that week, *Borderlands La Frontera,* written by Gloria Anzaldua, a Chicana feminist. As in most of my Women's Studies classes, I was the only Latina in the room and excited that we were reading a book I could closely relate to. The professor asked me to choose a passage from Gloria's book and read it out loud:

> Though I will defend my race and culture when they are attacked by non-Latinos, I abhor some of my culture's ways, how it cripples its women, our strengths used against us, bearing humility with dignity. The ability to serve and claim the males is our highest virtue. I will not glorify those aspects of my culture nor embrace the virtues of submissiveness, guilt and self-sacrifice which have injured me and which have injured me in the name of protecting me. (Anzaldua, 1987, p. 16)

As I finished the last sentence, I heard a voice speak out and say, "submissiveness and guilt? What do Latinas feel so guilty about? They just need to get over that guilt and shame part. That's what is keeping them down—they are allowing it to happen." I looked around the room, waiting to see what the other women would say, but to my disbelief, they were all nodding in agreement. "NO," I said in a strong voice, "It's not that easy, you don't understand what we have to go through." I attempted to explain the virtues of our culture and the many responsibilities Latinas must abide by in order to be accepted and considered good daughters and wives. I described the responsibility of partly raising our younger siblings, not questioning or speaking back to our elders, and placing family loyalty first (even if it doesn't make sense). Even though I struggled to help the other students understand our experiences, they just could not understand. They explained their understanding of the concept, but they did not understand the reasoning behind it. One of the Anglo women asked, "If Latinas believe they are being humiliated by an older relative, why don't they speak up and inform this relative that what they are doing is wrong and humiliating; what's so wrong with telling your family members how you feel?" I told her, "It is seen as a lack of respect." I knew there was absolutely no legitimate reasoning behind my response, and I had no basis for supporting something I knew was wrong. "I know it's wrong," I told the class, "but I am sure there are plenty of ways Latinas are combating this issue and creating solutions for the betterment of our women, and therefore our culture." I promised to research the topic and bring my findings to class in order to educate the women about Latina issues.

As I endlessly searched every university library in southern California, I found absolutely nothing pertaining to Latinas, cultural barriers, or solutions for overcoming them. The more I spoke to Latinas about this topic, the more I observed that many Latinas realized certain cultural traits were wrong but submitted to them in order to avoid friction. Other Latinas were ambivalent to all damaging traits and believed all cultural traits were absolute. When I asked these women if they were happy living this way they all hesitated in answering. No one said "Yes." "I'm all right," said one woman. The others shrugged their shoulders and said, "I don't know. I never really thought about it." When I finally asked them what they would do if they had to choose between their personal happiness and following strict traditional rituals, they all said they would follow traditional rituals because that is what their mothers did.

Due to my personal tragedies, I had dedicated a great amount of time to my recovery, working twelve-step programs and learning how to live an emotionally healthy and prosperous life. I had learned that in order to live a life of truth and love I had to recreate my belief system of what it meant to be a Latin woman. I kept the wonderful cultural traits that I greatly admire such as passion, affection, love, and compassion, but I had to release beliefs that did not place my emotional, spiritual, physical, and intellectual health first. My greatest challenge was living this new way of life without feeling guilty. Given that my mother and sisters are a very important part of my life, I desperately encouraged them to join me in this journey of self-discovery and healing, but they were not ready. It took all the courage I had to continue on this journey without my family understanding why at times I had to do things they believed were wrong. It hurt me at the very core of my soul just thinking that my family believed I was selfish and disloyal. All I could do was pray to God that one day they would understand how important it was to be loyal to myself first in order to survive. Most of the time I was overwhelmed with guilt, but it was the belief in God and the process of my journey that kept me going.

After speaking to many Latinas and becoming more and more frustrated at the lack of information on something I deemed so important, I applied one of my mottos in life: "If what you want has not been created, then it is time for you to create it." And so I began to write this book. I began speaking intimately with Latinas about the sorrows, pains, joys, and loves that being Latina gave them. I spoke, cried, and laughed with Latinas from California to North Carolina. I already knew what challenges (predominantly first-generation) Latinas faced in the United States, but because I was taught in college to find and present unbiased facts, I had to acquire legitimate research to support my beliefs. In order for me to trust research pertaining to Latinas, I needed to know who conducted the research, how it was conducted, and the specific demographics of the sample group. To my surprise, the only research I found on this subject was conducted by a corporation that surveyed Latinas in regard to their attitudes about their heritage and cultural limitations. The study concentrated on Latinas of lower socioeconomic status. The findings were that Latinas did not believe any of their cultural traits were barriers and that they were very proud of their heritage.

Did this research company truly believe Latinas would write the truth about their feelings, especially if it related to their families and the traits that are sacred to them? Did they not realize that many young Latinas believe that the way they are living is truth rather than tradition? It is the only reality they know—they don't realize they have a choice on how to live their lives. Frustrated with the lack of research on Latinas and how our cultural traits negatively affect our quality of life (and therefore our happiness), I decided to conduct my own research.

Believing that traditional research methods would not work for my study, I bypassed anonymous sampling and searched for Latinas who were willing to speak candidly about their experiences. I searched the country for outspoken Latinas who would reveal their true feelings about self-esteem, machismo, sexuality, depression, mental illness, loyalty, and *familia* and how Latinas view these issues differently than other women. I conducted hundreds of personal interviews with Latinas and also established focus groups to discuss these matters. Each group consisted of ten Latinas ranging in age from fourteen to forty. For most of these women this was the first time they had addressed many of these topics in public. At first many Latinas were hesitant about opening up their hearts and speaking the truth, but as soon as I shared my own experiences of tragedy and triumph they let their guards down and shared their stories.

The power and compassion within these focus groups was incredible. Latinas who barely knew each other cried together and wiped each other's tears. Never had I seen so much compassion and openness as I saw with these women. It was the honesty and lack of judgment that allowed them to feel safe and speak about their lives. The greatest truth that I learned from my focus groups is that, regardless of Latinas' socioeconomic and educational levels, they share similar subconscious beliefs, which limit them from developing their true selves.

My goal in writing this book is to raise the level of consciousness of all Latinas and inspire them to reach their full potential. I did not write this book to bash our culture or criticize our Latino men; the Latino culture is filled with love, compassion, and passionate traits that I am proud to embrace. But reality shows that Latinas have the highest rate of dysfunction among all minority groups, including depression, suicide, dropping out of high school, teen pregnancy, drug addiction, and gun possession. Although there are many factors contributing to these appalling statistics, we cannot continue to ignore those aspects of our culture that contribute to them.

It is time we stop blaming the system, our mothers, fathers, boyfriends, and all the other excuses we use to avoid taking personal responsibility for our lives. It could be that there have been many formative influences on our lives, but starting now, it is up to us how we will live our lives. At times we need to teach people how to treat us, only accepting equality and respect—our birthright—in our lives. But remember, in order for you to ask the world for anything, you have to be willing to offer the same in return.

It is my wish that one day all Latinas will believe that the world lies in the palm of their hand and live accordingly!

With all my love,
Tu hermana, Yasmin

Acknowledgments

Throughout my life I have met many wonderful and inspirational people and have been blessed in knowing them. Although it is not possible for me to mention them all, I would like to express my love and gratitude to the following:

First, to my editor, Patricia Hernandez. It is with her insight, support, honesty, and diligent work that I was able to finish this book.

To Mr. Raul Vargas, Dolores, Veronica, and the USC MAAA board of directors, thank you for always extending yourselves to assist me with my endeavors. To my HOPE and HLI sisters, thank you for all your support and encouragement. To Juan Garcia, who believed in me and was the first professor to utilize *Empowering Latinas* in teaching his Multicultural class.

To Claudia Trejos, Irene Ibarra, Martha Diaz-Aszkenazy, and Congresswoman Hilda Solis, the women I profiled, thank you for sharing your courageous stories with the world. To all the women I interviewed for this book and the women in my focus groups, thank you as well.

To Debra and Victoria from Maracas Entertainment, Diana Martinez from L.A. Media, Fred Smith and Steve Potter, thank you for everything you have done for me.

To Congressman Xavier Becerra, Susan Sifuentes-Trigueros, Elmy Bermejo, and Leigh Steinberg for their wonderful quotes.

To my publisher, Hal Lockwood, at Penmarin Books, Brad Manning, Miguel Lua, Jamie from Strike a Pose, Zenaida Mendoza from Nuevoink, and David Dominguez from Imagen Latina, whose efforts transformed my manuscript into a beautiful book.

Last, but definitely not least, I would like to deeply thank my family: My husband, Norberto, who provided me with endless encouragement, patience and love; my mother, who took care of my daughter day and night until I finished the manuscript; my sisters, who allowed me to share their life stories; my daughter, Divina, whose presence makes my day; and my husband's family, Norberto, Rosa, Sandra, Carolina, and Moses, who lent their support in moments of need.

About the Author

YASMIN DAVIDDS-GARRIDO is the daughter of Latino immigrants, raised in a predominantly Hispanic neighborhood east of Los Angeles. Strongly influenced by her experiences as a first-generation Latina in America, she has done extensive research on Latino culture, with an emphasis on how issues of machismo and self-esteem affect Latinas.

Yasmin has beccome an empowerment specialist who teaches women, particularly Latinas, how to take personal responsibility for their lives, happiness, and self-esteem. Her simple message is, "People will only treat you the way you allow yourself to be treated; if you want others to respect you, you need to begin by respecting yourself first—that means standing up for yourself and not allowing yourself to be mistreated by anyone." She believes Latinas have great untapped talent within themselves that they do not recognize. Yasmin's mission is to make them aware of these talents so that they may capitalize on them. Yasmin has dedicated her work and her life to improving Latinas' quality of life, and she is a highly sought inspirational speaker.

Yasmin graduated from the University of Southern California in 1995 with a degree in Business Administration: Entrepreneurship. After a marketing stint with Philip Morris, she went on to receive her master's degree in Women's Studies, specializing in Latina issues. To broaden the scope of her study of women, she attended the University of Cambridge in Great Britain, where she studied gender roles in a variety of ethnic groups. Since 1989, she has counseled thousands of young Latinos of both sexes and has been an advisor to over 750 Latinas from junior high school to the university level on subjects ranging from drugs and violence to self-esteem and goal setting.

Ms. Davidds-Garrido serves on the board of directors of HOPE (Hispanas Organized for Political Equality) and is a graduate of their HOPE Latina Leadership Institute. She has been an integral member of the San Diego State University (SDSU) Associated Council, SDSU Finance Board, and SDSU Associated

Executive Committee. As a member of the board of directors of the University of Southern California Mexican-American Alumni Association, she has helped to provide Latino/a students with over one million dollars in scholarships. As a strong political activist for Latina issues on both the state and national level, she assisted in chairing the committee for "Latina Action Day" in Washington, D.C., in which Latinas from all over the country met for three days with national legislators to discuss the national Latina agenda.

Yasmin and her husband, Norberto, an offensive lineman for the Arizona Cardinals, made history for both women and professional sports when he became the first NFL player to add his wife's last name to his jersey. Yasmin, her husband, and their two-year-old daughter, Divina, live in Chino Hills, California.

A Family Shattered

I thank God for my tragedies, for through them I have found myself and my purpose in life.

When people ask me to describe myself, I say I am an empowered Latina—a Latina who knows she can provide for herself financially, emotionally, and spiritually. I am proud of who I am, not just of what I've become but of my process of becoming. Being a Latina survivor is what I am most proud of.

As a professional, an educator, a member of numerous community boards, an NFL wife, and a mother, I do not look like someone who has been through tragedy after tragedy, and I never will. No one I have contact with today can possibly imagine what my life was like as a child and young adult. I've been knocked down both literally and figuratively, but there is nothing in the world that could ever keep me down. In spite of the odds, I never allowed my soul to die. I learned how to take care of myself and, more importantly, why it was necessary for me to put myself first. I share my story of survival and success here because it is time that Latinas learned how to find strength within themselves and take control of their lives—because all women have an exquisite and powerful wellspring of strength, especially Latinas.

From a very tender age, I knew precisely who was in charge. In my family, when my father said we had better do something, you better believe we did it, even if it didn't make sense. My father was the ruler of his castle—that's what he called our house—and rulers were not to be questioned, for that would be a challenge to his authority and a sign of disrespect. When he was good, my father was very, very good, giving us everything we could ever want. But when he was bad, he was terrible, doing whatever he felt it took to maintain respect, power, and money, which he believed were essential to life, at least to his life.

My father and mother immigrated to the United States from Ecuador and Mexico, respectively, in 1968 with two hundred dollars in their pockets and a determination to create a better life for their future children. With nothing more than elementary school educations, they began working in factories at a time when the American dream was attainable to anyone who was willing to work hard for it—educated or not. My father made twenty dollars a week and my mother fifteen dollars. Mother's check would automatically be saved in the bank, and they would somehow survive on my father's pay. Meat and fresh foods were a luxury for them, and most days they ate chili beans with tortillas. Christmas was the only time they splurged and purchased a bucket of Kentucky Fried Chicken—they were too tired to even cook a meal for themselves.

When my mother was eight months pregnant with her first child, Dad was horrified to learn that she wasn't allowed to sit at her factory job, and so, in order to give her feet a few minutes of rest, she would pretend to need to use the bathroom. Miserably, however, employees were allowed only four minutes maximum to relieve themselves. My furious father decided then and there that, although the sacrifices would be immense, he would never again work for someone else or allow his family to. He would not be disrespected by anyone ever again.

So in 1970 his entrepreneurial adventures began. With seven hundred dollars of their savings, my father went to a wholesaler and purchased some stereos and radios. He took a blanket from home, stood in the vendors' line at the Azusa swap meet, and made thirty dollars on his first day. He must have been the happiest man in the world. Within five years, he expanded his business by opening a retail electronic store and a record store and investing in a number of other ventures. By 1977, he had become a millionaire, owning a myriad of businesses: retail stores, gift shops in Holiday Inns, and businesses along the Mexicali border. In less than a decade, my father had gone from impoverished and vulnerable to wealthy and powerful. He had everything a man could ask for, including a faithful and hard-working wife and three beautiful daughters.

My father insisted that his daughters be educated, so we were sent to Catholic schools, where we were expected to excel, which we did. We never disobeyed Dad. He was a strict disciplinarian, using both words and fists. We were given lessons in everything—from ice skating and baton twirling to ballet and piano—so many classes and activities that my older sister developed stomach ulcers. There was, however, abuse in our home, but I managed to cope, partly because I believed everything in my household was normal, and partly because everyone around us confirmed that. We were the family other families envied. Our friends loved to come over because my father would give them money. My school's principal and staff visited often because he gave them stereos. My father loved to give, because with giving he earned respect.

We had a luxurious lifestyle, but given to us by a man who would build us up one day and break us down the next. We lived under his complete control (except for the times my mom covered for us), and he planned to make sure that his daughters were respected above all else. Because he created us, he felt he owned us. He tried to protect us from the dysfunctions of the world, yet he actively cultivated dysfunction in our own home with everything from fits of rage to alcoholism. I was proud of being my father's daughter—I did feel protected—but what I didn't realize was that my protector was also my abuser. I wasn't yet able to see that sometimes our most important influences are also our worst abusers, and that is why we should never depend solely on one person to help us define ourselves.

Although we were well-to-do, my father instilled a very strong work ethic in us from an early age. My sisters and I never had what could be called an ordinary life. While most kids were sleeping in on weekends, my seven-year-old sister (who was two years older than me) and I would wake at 5:00 A.M. and head outside in our pajamas with footies to carry heavy boxes full of electronics into trucks leaving for the swap meet. One of us would carry the merchandise to the truck while the other waited inside the truck to stack it up. Neither of us ever wanted to work inside the truck because, if the boxes were not organized correctly, they could shift or fall. God forbid that should happen, because whoever was responsible for the stacking was going to get it from Dad. My older sister always felt the need to protect me, and whenever possible she would, but for some reason or other I was the one who always got into trouble.

The only times we could really relax were when my father left on his business trips. Thank God he had weekly trips, because those were the only times the ache in my stomach would cease. When he was gone, we all felt free, free to just be who we wanted to be, not who he wanted us to be. As soon as we heard his truck pull up, we'd all run to the window to see what kind of mood he was in, which we could always tell by his facial expression. Often my mother, sisters, and I would even get down on our knees and pray to God to bring him home in a good mood. If he came home cranky, somebody would inevitably get hit or yelled at. To make things even more confusing, half the time he'd come home mad, ready to take it out on one of us, and half the time he would come home with a diamond jewel for my mother and more money for us. The hardest part was that we never knew what to expect from him; we just had to wait until he walked through the door. I promised Jesus so many things just to bring him home happy. It was as if I lived two lives—one full of happiness when Dad wasn't around and another full of fear when he was.

My mother was the perfect wife (or what macho Latino men consider perfect), but my father had mistresses all over the country. He had illegitimate children with who knows how many women and consistently denied their existence to my mother, my sisters, and me. In fact, he prided himself on us, his primary family. Everyone who knew about my father's affairs was sworn to silence. If anyone told us anything about his other life, he would make sure they paid for it one way or another. Growing up, I always knew my father had other women, but I would never dare question him for fear of what he would do to me for being disrespectful. Funny how the concept of disrespect seemed to be twisted for him; to question him about his mistresses was considered disrespectful, yet what he was doing to us, his family, he felt had nothing to do with disrespect. My maternal grand-mother would tell my mother, *"Déjalo, es hombre, y hombres son de la calle; al cabo a tí no te falta nada."* ("Leave him alone, he is a man, and men are of the streets; anyway, you have all you need.")

We girls were only allowed to talk to other girls and would be punished if seen talking to boys. Dad believed that all men wanted just one thing, and no man was going to get it from one of his daughters. He told us that he would provide us with the most expensive lifestyle he could afford, so that no man would ever be able to impress us with money. Ironically, though, he lured women with his money, power, and status. Many were "charmed" enough to sleep with him. I didn't realize it then, but now I see that my father was preparing us for men like himself. He saw how money and power wooed women. Some women just wanted the easy way out, he believed.

When I was twenty, everything changed. Our world collapsed, and during the next two years all I had been brought up to believe in, everything I thought I knew about family—responsibility, loyalty, and honesty—was turned on its head, *patitos para arriba* (feet in the air), leaving me profoundly changed. In retrospect, the trials and tribulations, many of which were terrifying, formed the foundation of what I now consider to be my life's work—helping women, particularly Latinas, to live full and satisfying lives, independent of all of our deeply ingrained traditional, cultural, and familial expectations.

In 1986, my mother and father finally separated after years of dysfunction. Their marriage had ceased to exist emotionally for years, and my mother finally had had enough. She asked Dad to move out after being confronted, yet again, by one of his many mistresses. He agreed to leave the house, but only after warning my sisters and me that, although he would not live with us, he would continue to command and direct our every move. We would not have expected any less from him.

Because my mother had decided that she no longer wanted to be part of the everyday activities of the family business, she and Dad came to a contractual settlement, which gave him complete control in return for a monthly stipend for my mother, my sisters, and me. For five years my father kept to his monthly monetary obligation, but that ended one day in October 1991.

I was living in San Diego, attending San Diego State University, when my twenty-two-year-old sister, Judy, called me. Infuriated over what he perceived to be a threat to his indomitable status in her eyes, our father had confronted Judy's boyfriend, Conrad, and had threatened him with violence. Although Judy was frightened by my father's rage towards Conrad, she was also furious that once again my father had threatened us with violence. My father was a tyrant when it came to his daughters' social lives. Doling out threats, directed at any potential date and at us, he rationalized his behavior by claiming, again, that he was only trying to protect us. Behind his back, and with the consent of our mother, we managed to meet and date boys, and we honestly thought that eventually he would realize we were growing up and relinquish his power to control us. Instead, he turned on us after the incident with Conrad, vowing to disown the family. He wouldn't even take our phone calls. My mother, Karina, and I could not understand why he did not want to speak to us; we thought he only had the problem with Judy, but we were wrong.

I tried to contact him on a daily, almost hourly, basis, but his employees had been instructed to tell us that he had nothing to say. Even my little sister, Karina, who was twelve, tried to call him, only to be disappointed by his refusal to speak to her. My father completely stopped providing for his family financially. My mother, two sisters, and I had always depended on him, and his abrupt action left the family in a state of emotional and financial chaos. We were threatened with the loss of our home, our cars, and our dignity in one fell swoop.

Within the next three weeks, my mother was hospitalized after suffering a nervous breakdown, and Karina was notified by the private school she was attending that unless she paid past-due tuition she would not be able to return. Judy, the only one of us with a steady income, gave every last penny to save our assets, so to speak. My own part-time job funded my food and utility expenses, but not my rent or tuition. Our situation seemed totally without hope.

As the weeks went by and we gathered what was left of our emotional strength, we decided to fight back. The contract my parents had drawn up stated that if, at any time, my father stopped providing for us financially, the businesses would auto-matically be transferred back to my mother. We knew that Dad was breaking the law, and Judy knew that it was imperative we hire an attorney and take Dad to court, a difficult mission with-out any money. Finally, though, we found an attorney who was willing to accept the case, with the provision that his fees be paid immediately upon the sale of our house.

In early December, we received notice from our attorney that because a minor, Karina, was involved, our case was considered a priority and had been given the only available date that month, December 24th. On Christmas Eve of 1991, one of the most frightening days of our lives, we took legal action against the man we had always counted on, always trusted to protect us, and—although often difficult—always loved. The situation seemed almost absurd. We never thought we would have had the courage to take such an action, but being forced to fight for our survival, we felt there was no other choice. The alternative meant losing everything we owned and homelessness.

When we arrived in court, Dad was already there with his attorney, someone who had been hired at the last minute because Dad never believed we would actually go through with it. The judge asked Karina and me to wait outside, only allowing Judy to enter the courtroom to testify. Judy walked straight in, focusing on Mom's face, and never glanced at Dad, although she could feel his stare burning through her body. She sat on the wit-ness stand with her lips quivering as she answered questions concerning the burden of instant and unexpected financial responsibility. When Dad took the stand, Judy dared to look at him and sadness swept over her. He had allowed his pride and machismo to take things too far. Moments later, that sadness turned into anger as she listened to him shamelessly lie about the nonexistent thousands of dollars he had given us over the last few months. In fact, Judy could not stop herself from vocalizing her disgust, shouting, "He's lying!" over and over. The judge eventually asked her to leave the courtroom.

We were all waiting impatiently in the hall when Mom walked out and shakily declared that the judge had ruled in our favor. We were, naturally, ecstatic. Dad had no proof of making any alimony payments, and we had proof of mortgage, insurance, and utility payments with copies of the cancelled checks from Judy's checking account. The judgment was further supported by the fact that Dad had broken the legal agreement he had signed a few years back. But what infuriated the judge most was Dad's malevolent decision to leave my mother and little sister with no source of income, placing the entire responsibility on Judy. We were temporarily granted 70 percent of the family businesses until a future court hearing. Dad was given two hours on the 24th of December and two hours on the 25th to remove his personal belongings from the premises of the businesses awarded to us. He didn't react violently; he was utterly expressionless.

Out in the hall, Dad made a beeline for the public phone. He had previously arranged for his loyal employees to remove the entire inventory from the various sites should the judgment go against him. Although my heart was now numb to sorrow, my body was pumping adrenaline. Judy and I reacted quickly and rushed to the phones ourselves to call Conrad and Joe, the men we were seeing, in hopes that they would hightail it to our main retail location and stand guard.

This particular store, which specialized in electronics, was located in a shopping center in the Los Angeles suburb of Baldwin Park. When Joe and Conrad arrived, they surprised my father's employees carrying box after box of merchandise out of the store and loading it onto a big truck. A physical confrontation ensued, and by the time my mother, sisters, and I arrived with our lawyer and the police, my father's employees had taken off.

We spent that Christmas Eve in the shop, awake and in fear that my father would return for some sort of vengeance. He had threatened us so many times and had even vowed to kill us if we ever antagonized him. We also knew that taking him to court was far beyond his threshold. The next morning, Christmas Day, Dad came with his mistress and illegitimate children to collect his personal belongings. With tensions as high as they were, it was no surprise that a fight erupted between Conrad and Dad, and they brutally beat each other in the back alley. Then suddenly, my father's business partner appeared with a gun, and in order to protect my father, he shot bullets in our direction. I jumped to cover up Karina, and we all rushed inside the store, where an infuriated Joe grabbed the gun the business kept for protection and ran back out, looking for Dad and his partner.

Not long afterwards, a police helicopter began hovering over the scene, and the crime unit arrived by the truckload. Six streets were blocked off while they searched for Dad. Within an hour, he was found hiding behind a house and was arrested and hand-cuffed. As he stood there waiting for the officer to open the back door of the car, he looked over at my mother, sisters, and me—the family he had created—with nothing less than hate in his eyes. Although we were surrounded by fifty police officers, we were terrified, certain that he would explode, knowing that as soon as he had the chance, he would kill us all. Judy and I felt somewhat protected by our boyfriends, but we knew there was no stopping Dad. We had to be prepared to fight back.

The court charged my father as an accessory to attempted murder but later dropped the charges due to lack of evidence. After being released, Dad had the police drop him off right in front of our shop. He wanted us to see him and for us to know that we did not win.

2

The Choice to Survive

*God grant me the serenity to accept the things I cannot change,
the courage to change the things I can, and the wisdom to know
the difference.*
—The Serenity Prayer

From the day Dad disowned us until January 1992, I was in a
state of numbness. My mind and body would not allow me to
feel pain. I needed to be strong, not only for myself but for the
emotional and physical protection of my family. I had survived
three months of torture, and I thought I was ready to start my life
again. Unfortunately, I was mistaken. Little did I know that several tests were yet to come.

One day in February, I woke up early for school. As I
attempted to rise from my bed, my body wouldn't move. I felt
absolutely no physical strength in any area of my body. I tried to
lift my head, and it hurt. I tried to lift my leg, and pain shot
through it. I began to lift my arm, but it felt so heavy that it fell
back down onto the bed. I looked at my hand and moved my fin-
gers slowly—it hurt when I tried to move them with any speed.
I lay there terrified, not knowing what had happened to my
physical strength, my energy. I used everything I had to sit up,
arms and legs barely responding, while feelings of desperation
washed over me. I wanted to scream for help, but who would I

call out to? What would I say? I knew I wasn't paralyzed; my muscles would grudgingly respond if I tried really hard.

It took me three hours to leave the house that morning, when it usually took me thirty minutes. I cried in frustration and pain. I never knew my body could hurt so much for no explicable reason. Getting through the next few days was miserable. I dragged myself out of bed in the morning, and I cried in the shower. I cried because I hurt; I cried because the only time I didn't hurt was when I was sleeping. I went to see a university-affiliated doctor, who ordered dozens of tests. He found absolutely nothing wrong with me, and rest was prescribed. But I knew my ailment would require more than rest.

A few days later, anxiety and panic descended on me. I was so physically exhausted I had trouble making it to class. I had no interest in socializing with my friends or doing any of the fun things I used to do. No one seemed to understand me, telling me to "just get up and stop being so lazy!"

"Lazy!" I responded. "I wish I were just lazy; at least I would be able to control my body and get up. I can't even walk around school without crying because my body hurts so much!" I decided to seek help somewhere else and went to a university psychologist. I spilled my guts about the events of the past few months and was immediately diagnosed with posttraumatic stress disorder. Everything I had experienced had wreaked havoc on my mind and body, and my body had managed to prolong the effects of my tragedy for as long as it could, proving that our bodies are capable of performing miracles of self-preservation. The doctor told me there was nothing I could do but let it play itself out, and with time the effects would go away.

For five months I lived in complete agony. When I was alone in my apartment I turned off all the lights, disconnected the phone, and cried for hours. I didn't really know why I was crying, but I remember the pain of feeling as though my heart was being ripped apart—a sorrow that I cannot explain. My friends began to worry about me and would visit with the intention of cheering me up, but I had no interest. I was just a heart pumping in a hollow body. My soul had been shattered into little pieces, and I couldn't find the physical or mental strength to pick up those pieces and put them back together again. As summer came, my depression worsened, seriously compromising my full-time summer job. I needed to work to survive, but physically I could no longer function. Finally, I began to realize that the emotional torture I was feeling was the betrayal of my father; I was grieving the loss of my father's love.

All of my life I had been against drugs. Friends of mine used them, but they always knew not to offer me any because I refused to take part and usually ended up crying and begging them not to do that to themselves. Soon I'd be crying for myself.

On July 3, 1992 (I'll never, ever, forget that date), I was lying in bed, feeling as though I couldn't handle another day. I had attempted to see doctors, but without insurance I couldn't afford the endless $60 office visits, let alone the cost of prescription medications. I was totally frustrated. Collapsing was not an option either. My mother had just been released from the hospital, and Judy had finally reached the end of her rope as well, taking time off from work for emotional distress, even though her paycheck was vital for us to keep our house. Karina was desperately in need of the mothering her own mother could no longer provide.

I gave myself two options. I could either lie in bed and hope to die, or I could do whatever it took to make myself get up, go to work, and function as a sister, mother, daughter, employee, and student. I chose the latter and made the decision to turn to methamphetamine, also known as "speed," in order to "medicate" myself.

"Since when do you use speed?" my friend Michelle asked when I begged her to go with me to a former classmate's house to make my first purchase.

I was adamant. "Don't ask, don't advise, don't lecture. I have to do this. Please just come and get me and we'll go."

When we got there, we went directly to a back room that was used to handle all of the drug transactions. The woman shook out what looked like a teeny amount of white crystalline powder onto a mirror and lined it up with a credit card. I looked at the line in desperation. I needed it. I wanted it to survive. I took the straw, snorted the line, and within seconds felt something amazing. I felt like I was coming out of a haze, like I'd had shock treatment. Not only did I feel highly alert, the pain in my body now seemed secondary. It was an inconvenience, not a burden. Speed made me feel like I was on top of the world. I felt all-powerful; I was mighty and full of strength, ready to take on anything. I felt like there wasn't a person in the world who could hurt me, not even my father. I had convinced myself that I was going to use speed only to get over these tough times. But speed very nearly destroyed my life.

In no time I was hooked. I did it in the morning, afternoon, and evening. I did it to go to work, and I did it to stay up at night. I knew it was wrong, but it gave me the false sense that I had control over my life, which was exactly what I craved.

Before the ordeal of the previous few months had begun, I had applied to the University of Southern California (USC). One month into my drug use, I received a letter from USC granting me admission, along with a financial aid package consisting of grants and loans totaling $21,000 for the year. There was no way that I could pass up the opportunity to attend one of the most prestigious universities in the country. Although I knew I was in no shape emotionally to take on this new challenge, in my eyes, education meant salvation.

In September 1992 I began my new life at USC. Only Judy and a few friends knew I was using speed. It wasn't difficult for me to hide it, because to the outside world I had everything together. Anyone knowledgeable about my drug use was completely disassociated from my school friends. My roommate, George, had transferred with me from San Diego State, and we had been friends for years. Despite our closeness, however, he didn't suspect for a minute that I was on drugs. My room was connected to a bathroom, so every morning it was easy for me to privately do a line of speed in there, then I'd walk out through my room, meet George at the front door, and walk to school to our first class. George knew that I had gone through tragic family problems and admired me for staying so strong. To him, I was the same Yasmin he had known for years. I'd head home after classes and do another line so that I'd have the energy to study, staying up until three or four o'clock in the morning, although I often had to read things over and over forgetting what I had just read.

After a few days, I got a job at the USC M.B.A. Career Services Office. Completely numb to my pain and desperation, I was able to deal with my new school, my new job, and my new life. Nonetheless, in spite of the new job my sense of self-worth was completely shattered. How had I become so weak? How could I, someone people admired for abstaining all these years, become reliant on illegal street drugs? This powerful sense of vulnerability was so emotionally intolerable that I could not discuss my drug use with anyone except those who already knew. So I continued to live my life as a closet user and convinced myself that I would stop using speed during Christmas vacation, when I didn't have to go to school and I could sleep it off. When December came along, I went to my mom's and was determined to rest and sleep and do whatever it took to stop using speed.

From December 21st through the 24th, I slept and slept and slept, comforted by the idea that I had made it through the rough times and that my body and mind would be ready to go back to normal. On December 25th, I woke up, sure that I had slept enough and that I would feel good, but boy, was I wrong. All the feelings of insecurity and hopelessness I had experienced before I started doing speed came back with a furious intensity. I trembled with fear and anxiety and once again became utterly immobilized. It took less than ten seconds for me to make the decision: I ran to the bathroom and did a line. This time was different, though. I was terrified, knowing now without a doubt that I no longer controlled the drug—the drug controlled me. I wanted to stop. I really wanted to stop, but I couldn't; I had become an addict.

In January, I returned to school in worse shape than I had ever been. Feeling out of control only made me want to do more speed, thinking that the more I did, the better I would feel. So I doubled the amount I was doing, and I now obsessed over doing as much as it took to make me feel good again. But the more I did, the worse I felt. As much as I tried to get the powerful feeling back, I couldn't. I didn't know where to go; I didn't know who to turn to. I was so ashamed. I felt like a fake, nothing but a fake. Was I the strong, powerful woman who could handle it all, take care of it all? Or was I a weakling who couldn't even get out of bed in the morning for fear of facing the day?

By March I was completely out of control. I was often too sick to go to work, and I was missing more and more classes. Within a few weeks, I walked into the USC M.B.A. office and told my boss I had to quit. I took some diamond jewelry that my father had given me and pawned it for $600. I figured this money would serve as a substitute for my work income until the end of the semester.

As the end of the semester came along, I could do nothing but cry. I cried out of desperation, cried out of depression, cried because my life was worse than it had ever been. When it was time for finals, I couldn't make it to class without breaking down. On the day of my accounting final, I was so depressed and physically weak that I didn't even show up. The next day I went to see my professor, who took one look at me and told me not to worry; he wasn't going to make me take the final; he would just assign a final grade on the work I had already done. He certainly didn't know I had destroyed myself doing speed; he just took one long look at me and knew something was terribly wrong. My overwhelming sense of shame caused me to believe that if professors and others knew what I was doing, they would never respect me again.

Between January and June of 1994, I secretly and frantically looked for professional help. However, without health insurance, I couldn't afford anything but a free counseling session. Prior to this time, I never realized what low-income people who had no health insurance had to go through. I was crying out for help but could not get any. "Can't you see?" I begged them. "I need help. I'm not asking for free help. I will pay you once I graduate. I only have eighteen months until I graduate with a business degree from USC, and I will start making payments with my first paycheck." My father had raised me to know that there were no free rides. Everything had a price. I begged for a loan to pay for rehabilitation treatment.

"Sorry," they said, "we do not have any loan programs. The only way you can go into rehabilitation is through private health insurance or state-provided MediCal." MediCal! That was it! I would go to the state and ask them for temporary help with health insurance. My anxiety was minimized now that I had some hope. I went into the Los Angeles County Social Services Center and filled out about twenty forms. I sat there for most of the day waiting for them to call my name. Finally, six hours later, they called me.

"Are you pregnant?" they asked.

"No."

"Are you under the age of eighteen?"

"No."

"Then there is nothing we can do for you."

"But I'm a student who desperately needs some help. Isn't there any way the state can help me?"

"Only if you're pregnant or a minor."

I could not believe that in order for me to receive MediCal, I had to be pregnant. I thought that it was supposed to be a good thing to go to college and not get pregnant—in my case, I would have been better off if I was carrying a baby. The rejections exhausted my mind and depleted my soul; each time I was turned away my hopelessness grew into deeper feelings of self-destruction.

By the end of May, my depression had deepened even more, and I had become manic. I decided to write a letter to Oprah Winfrey. I honored and respected her for being a survivor. When she talked about her life, I felt her pain. She had gone through so much and survived. It was because of Oprah's life story that I believed I still had some hope for survival and that one day I would become the successful woman I had always wanted to be. I thought that if Oprah read my letter, she would understand me and help me. Then, in one of my very frequent moments of cynicism and hopelessness, I thought about it again and decided not to write the letter. I knew there were probably thousands of people who wrote her letters asking for help. What made my situation any different?

The semester was over, and it was time for me to move out of my USC apartment. The drugs had overwhelmed my immune system, and it was taking me three times as long to do even the most menial tasks, like packing and moving out. The situation with my family had gotten worse. We had lost our house and only had a few weeks to find somewhere to live. Judy was at her wit's end. The pressure of being economically responsible for our family caused her to stay up night after night trying to figure out how we were going to survive. She also believed she needed to stay up in order to protect our family from physical harm. When I arrived home, Judy had not slept for three days, paranoid and terrified that my father would come and kill the family. She had reached a state of delirium, and I stayed up most of the night with her, trying to convince her to sleep while I guarded the house. Finally, around 3:30 A.M. she took a nap; I sat there in tears staring at my poor sister, hoping all of this torment would end soon. I was so happy to see the daylight. I woke Judy up and took her to the hospital, so she could get a doctor's note for missing work. When the doctor came in to see her, he asked if she really would shoot her father if he broke into the house. "Hell, yeah," she said. "I would shoot anybody who broke into our house and tried to hurt my family."

The doctor told her he was going to have to call the police. He claimed that she was a threat to society, and she would have to be retained until she no longer felt that way. My sister and I took one look at each other and ran. Neither one of us could believe that the doctor had reversed the situation and made my sister the potential assailant. If anything, it was her courage that saved us. She was the only one who ever had the guts to stand up to Dad. The rest of us—my mother, Karina, and me—couldn't even look him in the eye. He had engendered so much fear in us that one stare from him had the power to immobilize us. Shortly thereafter, Judy went on disability. The whole tragedy had completely robbed her of her physical and mental capabilities. Her anger towards my father kept her sane, but it was pain and agony that consumed her soul. I knew she had unintentionally blocked her pain. It is always easier to be angry at someone than to allow yourself to feel the pain of their betrayal. She couldn't see it that way, but I could.

During the prior semester I had applied for a summer internship at one of America's most successful enterprises, the McDonald's Corporation. I had been awarded the internship and was to begin my corporate training the first week of June. The night before my first day of work I couldn't sleep. I was understandably nervous about being able to function normally at the job and terrified that the management would be able to tell I was high on drugs. I had worked hard for an opportunity to work for such a huge company, but I was a mess, riding an emotional roller coaster. All night I waited for the clock to read 5:00 A.M. so I could get up and get ready. I was panicked that I might oversleep and be late my first day, so I didn't sleep at all. I thought it was safer that way. At 6:30 A.M., I began driving up the 101 Hollywood freeway. The lack of sleep and my manic episodes had reached their highest peak, and I begged God to please let me die: "Just let my car malfunction and wreck. I'm done. I can't take it any more." I didn't have the courage to take my own life, but I was telling God that I would rather die than continue living in misery. I had finally hit rock bottom. Things had been bad, even intolerable. But now, finally, I saw death as my only alternative. There was no more "pulling through" or overcoming anything. My life was no longer worth living. I was completely exhausted—physically, emotionally, spiritually. In my mind, there could be nothing worse than how I was feeling.

Whether by the grace of God or by my own last gasp to survive, I pulled off the freeway. Within a few feet was a pay phone. In a state of foggy consciousness, which even to this day I can't explain, I got out of the car, tears streaming down my face, trembling, insane. I had no idea what I was doing or what I should do, but I got out and walked to the phone. Barely readable, written over with graffiti, and adorned with old chewing gum and sticky horrible substances, was the number of a suicide hotline. I dialed. "Disconnected due to insufficient government funds," a recording told me. "God help me, God help me, God help me." I kept saying it like a mantra, over and over. I fished through my wallet and found the number of a rehabilitation clinic. They kept me on hold for twenty minutes while I watched cars whizzing by, full of people who had a life, who had hope, who had a plan. Twenty minutes felt like twenty hours. Numb and crazed at the same time, I went back to my wallet, searching through business cards and numbers written on torn pieces of paper, resources that all had turned me down over and over again. Two-thirds of the way through my useless stack of people to turn to, I found the home number of a therapist whom I had spoken with by phone at the Beverly Hills Women's Clinic. After having been turned down so many times, I had regarded her kind words—like those of so many others—with cynicism. Oddly, though, I remembered that she had given me her home number that day, although it was against the rules. It was 6:55 A.M. when I called her.

"Who is it?" she answered.

"It's Yasmin," I said, shaky and feeling as if anything I said would come out sounding like gibberish. "I spoke to you over the phone a while back. You gave me your home number in case of an emergency. . . . I'm sorry to bother you, but I don't know who else to call. I need help so badly. . . . Please help me!" I was sobbing so hard I could barely speak. "I don't want to live like this anymore. If I have to feel like this all the time, I'd rather die. Please, Laura, help me. I've tried everything to get help, but nobody will help me."

She was silent for a few seconds, took a deep breath, and told me, "For the past seven years I have been teaching yoga at 6:00 A.M., and I've never missed a class. Something strange happened this morning. . . . My alarm didn't ring. I know I set my alarm clock last night. This morning I could not understand why my alarm didn't ring, but now I do understand. If my alarm had gone off as it always does, I wouldn't have been here to receive your call." I knew down deep in my heart that this was no coincidence. "Where are you? Stay put. I'll be right there."

I had never felt God's presence as deeply as I had at that moment. For the first time in my life, I had experienced a true miracle. I did not know this woman. I had never even met her, but I knew God had intervened so that she could help me. She arrived within fifteen minutes and took me back to the Beverly Hills Women's Clinic. We searched through the clinic references for eight hours, calling many different rehabilitation centers and asking them to take me in. "No insurance, no money, no service," is what one clinician told us.

Finally, we found a center that was willing to give me a $5,000 loan if I could get a cosigner and $500 cash ($250 payable on check-in and the other $250 two weeks later). For a thirty-day stay, the price was incredibly low. I hadn't been able to find a rehabilitation center for less than $10,000 until then. Although my sister was on disability, she was still considered a full-time employee, and I asked her to cosign for me. Neither one of us knew how I'd pay her back, but she didn't even think twice before saying yes. I now had a cosigner, but how was I going to come up with the $250 due when I checked in? The only thing I had left of any value was my furniture. I called George, and after telling him that I would explain everything later, he agreed to buy it for $250 if he could pay for it in biweekly installments. It was a start.

For so long now, every time I neared my goal of entering rehabilitation one obstacle after another had hindered me. I was tired of hitting brick walls. My energy was completely depleted, but I felt clearly that this was my last chance. I had to find the money. I called my ex-boyfriend, Joe. We had broken up, and I hadn't spoken to him for almost a year. He didn't know about my drug problem, and I didn't want him to know. He had always thought so highly of me; he had always respected me for not doing drugs. I was too ashamed to tell him why I needed to borrow the money, and I made up a story about having to go away to a depression clinic. He agreed to lend me the money and to be repaid in biweekly payments from George.

On June 12th, the day before I was to enter the recovery center, I was terribly anxious. I knew I was going to get better, but I was terrified. That night my family had a dinner in celebration of Judy's graduation from college. Although my friends and family surrounded me, I felt totally alone and detached. While they sat around the table happily laughing and talking, I prayed to God that one day I could be happy again. My mother instinctively knew something was very wrong with me and would have been horrified if she knew the truth. Before going to bed, I went to her room and told her, "*Mámi*, I need to go away for a while. I need to deal with what's happened to me because of *Papá*. I'll be back in a few weeks." She didn't really understand what I was talking about, but she comforted me and told me she loved me. She made me a *té de manzanilla* (manzanilla tea) and held me in her arms until I fell asleep.

The next morning, I awoke from a half-sleep at 5:00. I packed my things and woke Judy, who had offered to drive me to the recovery center in Laguna Beach, an hour away from Glendora where my mother lived. After driving through the hills of Laguna, I thought we had somehow made a mistake when we reached the address I had written down. Instead of the cold, intimidating institution I had pictured in my mind, the center was a beautiful mansion, surrounded by flowers and greenery and with a breathtaking view of the Pacific Ocean. First Step, which had only just opened within the past few months, had been founded and funded by a wealthy businessman whose brother had died from a heroin overdose. I couldn't believe how blessed I was to have found Laura and this program. Judy checked me in and signed all of the loan papers, and I was admitted with the promise that I would pay the remaining $250 within the next fourteen days. God knows how I was going to get that $250, but that didn't matter; all I wanted was to feel safe, nurtured, and taken care of. For so long I had played this nightmare of a game, and it was finally over. I slept fourteen hours the first night.

Rehabilitation was nothing like I thought it would be. There were only nine residents, who were in there for addiction to everything from alcohol to heroin, speed to marijuana, plus the counselors and a doctor. The patients ranged from the CEO of a Fortune 500 company to a sixteen-year-old trying to kick a heroin habit. Some people truly wanted to be there, and others had been forced by the court. I learned that drug use crosses all economic and racial lines and that the rich just do more expensive drugs than other people; the poor do whatever they can get.

Beginning on my first full day there, I was expected to be ready for class at 8:00 A.M. Daily counseling sessions lasted from 8:00 A.M. until 3:00 P.M. and consisted mainly of intense, enlightening, and often painful discussions concerning our addictions. For those of us who wanted to learn, workshops were provided on everything from how childhood traumas can affect addiction to how some people are genetically predisposed to addiction. I learned so much at First Step. We talked about real issues— issues that people on the "outside" deemed too sensitive for discussion. We all shared our stories of trauma, and we learned that everyone had their own unique background and their own unique reason for turning to drugs and/or alcohol. Although there were arguments, even the occasional screaming match, our group was bonded not only because of our similar circumstances, but because most of us realized the gravity and enormity of what we were trying to do.

Two weeks passed, and the other $250 came due. I was told that if I couldn't come up with the money, I would have to leave. I was still very weak emotionally, and I certainly wasn't prepared to go out and face the world yet. I sat in my room, crying and pleading to God to take care of me because I didn't know what I was going to do. My roommate came in and casually tossed a package on my bed, which had arrived that morning in the mail. Glancing at the return address, I recognized the name of a friend I hadn't seen in over a year. I ripped open the brown paper, hoping at least for something that would cheer me up. A note attached to the outside of the box gave me no indication of what I would find inside. She simply wished me well, delivered some news about mutual friends, and wrote that she hoped her care package would provide me with a bit of comfort. Inside the box I found a teddy bear, packages of chocolate and cookies, a paperback novel, photos of us in happier times, and an envelope with $700 in cash. After an initial shriek of surprise, it took me more than an hour before I could speak again. It was unbelievable, truly and amazingly unbelievable, and I knew it was God's second miracle in as many weeks. When I was at the end of my rope, God had once again saved me. There was no way that my friend could have known how desperately I needed the money. Nobody but Judy and my counselors knew of my financial problems.

After forty days at First Step, my counselors and I felt I was ready to go home and begin a new life. I started working two weeks after leaving the center, and shortly after that I began the fall semester at USC. My friends asked, "How was your summer?" And I could only answer, "Full of life-changing experiences."

As the months went by, I felt much better emotionally, but I continued to feel lethargic and depressed. Because my internship with the McDonald's Corporation provided me with medical insurance, I decided to again see a doctor about my condition. Given that my health insurance now covered all of my medical expenses (a luxury I had never appreciated to the degree I did then) the doctor decided to run various tests, and after a lengthy evaluation I was diagnosed with an organic chemical imbalance. It was determined that I had had a predisposition to chemical imbalance since birth, but the actual shift did not occur until my body was hit with posttraumatic stress. The horrendous emotional strain of the year before had resulted in a chemical change in my brain that had left me feeling sick, frustrated, confused, and utterly exhausted. I was given prescription medicine to treat my condition and, within weeks, finally got better. It was that simple. If I had had medical insurance, or if I'd somehow been able to pay for my medical tests, I would have been diagnosed and treated and would never have had to self-medicate with methamphetamine.

Eventually I chose to open up to certain people and tell my story, and my confidence level about my experience grew with time (at the time of this writing, I have eight years of sobriety). As time progressed, I experienced some major realizations, and I thank God for my tragic experience. Although it might sound strange, I thank God for allowing me to hit rock bottom and experience things most people don't experience in a lifetime. . . . I now appreciate love, genuine people, and life for life's sake. I have learned to believe that God does everything for a reason, and I believe that God put me through these experiences to help me acknowledge the reserve power I have. It was through my pain and agony that my courage to survive emerged. Now I truly believe that there is nothing in this world I cannot handle. I thank God that I found my inner strength at such a young age. Now I can use it to help other women, other Latinas, find theirs.

It has been nine years since I last saw or heard from my father. People occasionally ask me how I feel about him and whether I would ever speak to him again. I have forgiven him, and although he did many terrible things, I thank God for him. I understand that many of his own frustrations were brought about by his dysfunctional upbringing and our culture's value system, and I cannot look at him from a one-dimensional perspective. Much of what I am today is because of him. Success was never an option with Dad; it was a given. He taught me that there was no such thing as "the unachievable." There was always a way to make things happen if you wanted them badly enough.

My father believed that because of his power and money he could own women, and his experiences proved it. On the other hand, he was also dedicated to making sure that no man ever owned his daughters. He always demanded that we become educated and independent. He'd often say, *"Ustedes van a estar preparadas para si un dia sus esposos les maltraten ustedes cojen sus hijos y se van. Van a estudiar para que nunca vayan a depender de un hombre."* ("You will be self-sufficient in every way so if one day your husbands treat you badly you can take your children and leave them. You will be educated, so you will never have to depend on a man to take care of you.") Without a doubt, my father gave me many of the positive attributes that I carry within myself today, one being determination, which I now put to use helping Latinas to break through the cycle of oppression.

Millions of Latinas suffer from depression and low self-esteem, for they believe that is the life they are meant to live. We Latinas have been conditioned to believe we must put everyone's needs before our own. Yes, we all have a certain responsibility to our loved ones, but we also have that same responsibility to ourselves. We were not meant to live the life of another or for another. God created us so that we can make the most and best of ourselves and be prime examples to others. We each have a responsibility to God and to ourselves to live our lives to the fullest, in the way that we desire. Many of our mothers did not believe they had a choice and ended up living their lives for their parents and by the traditional rules. I am here to tell you that you *do* have a choice and that it is *your* choice.

No money is worth your soul and happiness. Money never comes that easy. When it does, there is usually a high price to pay. Many women pay that price every day because they believe that as long as they are good and obedient, someone will take care of them for the rest of their lives. That price is too high, and there are never any guarantees. Breaking free from a controlling father, husband, or boyfriend can be one of the most courageous acts a woman can ever take to save herself. Although breaking free can seem impossible, I personally promise that it's not. The rewards of personal freedom are monumental, and you can never experience them until you break the chains.

Latinas are fearful of change, for they believe that their families will not accept them. I believe that, at first, Latino *familias* will have reservations about their daughters, granddaughters, sisters, and nieces emerging into beautiful, strong, independent women, but I truly believe that in time they will come to realize that, "The flower that blooms through courage and strength is the most rare and beautiful of them all."*

Adelante mujer!

---

*Mulan, 1998. Burbank, CA: Walt Disney Pictures.

3

Facing the Truth About Our Traditions

Most myths are ways of keeping us out of touch with our own strength, confusing many generations of women.
—Erica Jones, *What Do Women Want?*

During a wonderful time in my life, the planning of my wedding, my fiancé, Norberto, asked me, "Will you take my last name?"

I thought about it for a second and asked, "Would you take mine, too?"

"Of course," he replied. So we decided that we would carry both our last names by hyphenating them—Davidds-Garrido. This decision was exciting for us and of great significance to me. Norberto knew that keeping my maiden name was important to me, so his compromise was the ultimate act of love and respect for me and our upcoming marriage.

Unfortunately, not everyone shared our delight. When Norberto phoned his parents to tell them the news, his mom freaked. *"¿Que? Eso no está bien. Tu eres el hombre y ella debe de llevar tu apellido,"* she cried. ("What? That is not right. You are the man of the family, and she should carry your last name.")

She demanded to speak to me, and once I got on the phone she sternly explained how family traditions worked. "I had Beto as a gift for his father," she said. "He has carried his father's name with pride for twenty-four years, and now you want to take that away? What are you, a *macha?*" In Mexican tradition, *macha* refers to a woman who wants to take a man's role.

"I have also lived with my last name with pride for twenty-five years," I explained. "Why should I have to give it up? Norberto and I are adults who love each other, and we are proud of this decision."

Norberto's father grabbed the phone and said, "How dare you disrespect our family like this?" "No, *señor*," I told him, "how dare you disrespect me like this." He then told Norberto, "If you take her last name, you will no longer be my son!"

I was devastated and angry. Norberto and I thought his parents might have a slight problem with our new last name at first, but hoped that they would eventually accept our decision. We were both taken aback by their extreme reaction, and it was painful. We all want to be loved and accepted by those who are important in our lives, and Norberto's parents were an important part of our future together. I wanted desperately to be accepted by my future in-laws . . . but at what cost?

I cried for hours. It hurt me deeply that something Norberto and I were so proud of had turned out to be something disgraceful to his family.

My husband, Norberto Davidds-Garrido, is the first player in the National Football League (NFL) to honor his wife's last name by wearing it on his jersey next to his. This is a great source of pride for both of us. When reporters ask Norberto why he took my last name, he always says, "Because I respect her."

Can a man's decision to honor his wife cause family ties to be destroyed? Unfortunately, the power of pride can be abused in our culture and converted into what I call *orgullo tóxico* (toxic pride). In our culture, pride is a beautiful trait that our fathers, mothers, brothers, and sisters live by. It unites our families and carries with it a certain level of respect. But when this very same *orgullo* is taken to extremes or used against our own mothers and daughters, it becomes destructive to our *hermanas*, to our culture, and to ourselves; it becomes toxic.

Although our religion, families, and culture continue to be the center of our universe, we cannot allow them to completely define who we are. The time has come for us to open our eyes and see what is really going on around us. Although many of us continue to deny it, *machismo* (robust manliness) still lives strongly within our culture. It might not look like the familiar stereotype of the strong, *macho* man not wanting his wife to work and expecting his dinner to be hot and ready the moment he walks in the door from work, but it still exists. A different kind of machismo is lurking in our lives today, leaving Latinas emotionally empty and exhausted.

Be wary of a man who tells you he is all for the empowerment of Latinas. Yes, there are wonderful men who truly are, but there are many others who are only supportive of Latinas becoming independent and self-sufficient as long as it is not their Latina. These men talk the talk, but behind closed doors, they do not walk the walk. They say they believe in equality but still expect their wives to make all the sacrifices—like being the one who stays home from work when the baby is sick. These men like it when their women work and earn good money as long as it is not more than they earn. They like their Latinas to be outspoken . . . but not too outspoken. They want their women to be independent . . . but not too independent. In other words, they want to be able to control the income, independence, and outspokenness of their women. It's still about control and machismo; it's just a more modern version.

The old-school machismo is still very evident in our parents' generation and ours, too. Our parents and family members do not question machismo, because they believe it is normal—it is all they have ever known. But I am here to tell you that it is not normal, and it is definitely not healthy. Machismo eats away at the self-esteem and dignity of Latinas. It takes away their identities and makes them believe that their husband, boyfriend, or father is their identity. If you ever wanted to do something that you knew in your heart would be good for you, but stopped yourself from doing it because you did not want to disappoint your "man" (whether boyfriend, husband, or father), then this *machista* attitude (a male sensibility of entitlement to certain privileges that it is believed women should not have) is controlling you. Believe it or not, Latinas treat men as though they are superior because, at a subconscious level, they truly believe it.

Through my research, I have found that one of the main reasons Latinas have not "made it" in the world is that after being controlled so well by their fathers, boyfriends, husbands, and brothers, they have no self-worth, no self-respect, and no energy to take on the challenges of the outside world. I have rarely met a Latina, besides myself, who says, "I believe I can conquer the world." (By "conquering the world" I don't mean I am here to take on the world; I mean that there is nothing this world can hand me that I cannot handle. I will conquer anything that comes my way!)

It saddens me to see so many Latinas negate themselves, their needs, and their wants in order to please the men in their lives only to end up depressed and feeling unappreciated. There is this universal feeling that no matter how much we do, it will never be enough. It is always the Latina who has to sacrifice her dreams, her time, and herself in order for another family member to pursue his dream. It's always the Latina who waits for the right time to go back to school, pursue her career, or live out her own dream; unfortunately, she waits forever. While we Latinas watch our sisters of other ethnicities educate themselves and choose careers, we as a group have stayed in the background, perpetuating our own lack of fulfillment.

The Long Legacy of Machismo

When I ask *machistas* why they believe men should have certain privileges that women do not, there is always a stunned look in their eyes. Not one man I have ever asked has been able to offer me a legitimate answer. The two most popular responses I get are "That's just the way it's always been" and "That's what the Bible says."

Of course that's the way it's always been! These *machista* traditions and our Bible were created and written by men for the convenience of men. Jose Luis Segundo, Ph.D., a Latin American theologian and expert in scripture, wrote:

> Sacred scriptures have developed within specific cultures. These cultural forms are suspected of being at the service of the controlling interest of society. And we certainly have a long history of a culture made, at least in its most specific forms, by men, although women have had an enormous influence on culture. Women's influence has not been direct in the formulation of

written text. These usually have been written by men. In this sense we can be suspicious, and, in fact, we can confirm our suspicions. We must begin to suspect in a systematic way that the books made in cultures where men are in control reflect male interests. There may be a feminine influence, but this influence is as it were hidden, oppressed beneath male influence, and is not apparent.[*]

To protect their own status and power, men have always taken great care to ensure that women remain subservient. But things are very different now than they were hundreds of years ago. The time has now come for Latino men and women to take a fresh look at the many rules and cultural devices that work against half the members of our society.

At the heart of machismo is a false concept about men. When men had to fight with a sword and spear, hunt enormous animals, and lift the stones on which civilization was built, there was some justification for the notion that a man's physical strength was a special gift, an offset to the more mysterious ability of women to reproduce humanity. Women's power was private, miraculous, and associated with divinity. Men's power was clear and obvious—the ability to lift a heavy stone signified manliness. But is physical strength still such an important characteristic that men should continue to claim superiority because of it? If we had to make a choice, would we not say that giving life is more of a superior characteristic than being able to lift the heaviest stone? Why does this ancient and outdated system of judging a person's value still apply at the start of the twenty-first century? The answer is that it is deeply ingrained in our culture to the extent that everything about our culture encourages men's elevated status.

The simple truth is that machismo defines people by their physical strength, as if this were the deciding factor in what defines a person's importance. In so many ways, Latino culture convinces us that as women—"the weaker sex"—we cannot take care of ourselves physically or emotionally. It teaches us that we must depend on our brothers, fathers, or husbands to protect us from harm. Therefore, we tend to believe that we cannot take

---

[*]Tamez, Elsa. *Against Machismo*. Costa Rica: Meyer Stone Books, 1987: 8.

care of ourselves in this difficult world and that we need a man to protect us. This is one way that Latinas automatically feel inferior to men. I have a simple solution for this problem—instead of putting your young Latina in ballet, put her in karate when she is five years old so she can grow up confident, strong, and capable of defending herself!

Our culture perpetuates myths that are often destructive to Latinas. For example, every young Latina is told it is dangerous to look an unfamiliar man in the eye. The myth is that since man is naturally the aggressor, he is likely to get the wrong message and think she might want him. He'll think she's easy or, even worse, a whore! He may even attack her! But on the other hand, there is nothing wrong with a man checking *her* out and giving *her* the eye; after all, women are not the aggressors!

This is ridiculous. As a certified women's self-defense instructor, I know this myth is absurd. A woman should always look a man in the eye to show him that she is not afraid—even if she is—and that she is confident in her ability to protect herself. "Fake it if you have to," I tell the women in my class, "but don't let him think you're weak, because then you will be a perfect target."

The sad part about all this is that many of us actually believe we are weak and in need of a man's strength to keep us safe. We have been taught that our men know how to protect us better than we know how to protect ourselves.

Living in the Shadow of Legends

Latino culture comes fully equipped with a variety of feminine icons, either celebrated for their purity or slandered for their lack of virtue. Sex roles and societal expectations are very strict and very clear. If a woman rebels or stands up for herself, she is a bad woman and a bad influence on other women. If a woman doesn't sacrifice herself in favor of the male, she is selfish. If a woman is not a virgin when she marries, she is dirty. But the same rules do not apply to men.

A male friend of mine, a Catholic, commented to me that the woman he marries will have to be a virgin. "Are you a virgin?" I asked.

"No," he said, not realizing the direction I was heading.

"Then how could you ask a woman for something that you can't offer in return?" He was speechless, uncomprehending. I said, "Doesn't the Bible say to treat others the way you would like to be treated? Doesn't that also mean to expect from others only what you can and are willing to offer?"

"You ask too many questions," he snarled, and then walked away.

An aspect of machismo philosophy is that men have "needs," including the all-important need for sex, and that it is our duty as women to sexually please them. Yet Latinas are expected to deny any and all aspects of their own sexuality. The more I speak to Latinas about sexuality, the more I hear them say that they do not enjoy sex. Some are even proud of their lack of sexual desire because they believe it makes them trustworthy in their boyfriends' or husbands' eyes. Their mentality is "If my husband realizes that I don't really like sex, he'll never have to worry about me sleeping with another man."

Wives and girlfriends who seem to enjoy sex too much are a threat—they are perceived to have the potential to betray their men. Men who enjoy sex are seen as healthy and powerful—truly macho. Women who have sexual encounters with different men become *mujeres del gusto*—women who like pleasure—and pay a very high price in the machismo culture. They are labeled as *sucias* (dirty women) and relinquish themselves to a lower status, losing all respectability and becoming known as *mujeres de la calle* (women of the street), no better than prostitutes.

Why is it that Latinas are forbidden to enjoy natural feelings of ecstasy? Why is it expected that an orgasm will lead a Latina to betray her family and culture? What is it about the freedom of sexuality for a Latina that so threatens many Latino men? Perhaps it began with Doña Marina.

THE LEGEND OF *LA MALINCHE*

The Spaniards called her Doña Marina, or *la Malinche* (the captain's woman), a name given to her because of her close relationship with Hernán Cortés. But to many Mexicans, *la Malinche* is considered the "Mexican Eve," a mother to the Mexican race, but also a traitor who turned her back on her own culture.

Marina was a well-educated Aztec whose ill-fated family circumstances resulted in her becoming a slave. During the Spanish Conquest of Mexico, she was given to Hernán Cortés who soon recognized her unique talents. Because she spoke Mayan and the languages of other non-Mayan Indians, Marina was able to act as a translator between the Spaniards and the Indians, and she became a valuable asset to Cortés. In time, she became one of his closest aides, and with her words rather than Cortés' army's weapons, she convinced the Indians that surrendering to the Spanish was their best and only choice. Today, historians recognize that her actions saved thousands of lives because she gave Cortés the opportunity to negotiate rather than slaughter. Marina later bore Cortés a son, who was known to be the first child of the Mexican race. Though frequently compared to the Virgin Mary, la Llorona, and even Medea, Marina is despised by Latinos.

Today, to be called a *Malinchista* means that you are a traitor. Marina's house still stands on Calle Higueroa in Mexico City, where people throw rocks and malign her name, even though she's been dead for nearly five hundred years. Some Mexican feminists claim that *la Malinche* continues to be at the root of the general disrespect Mexican men show Mexican women, as expressed in the country's high rates of infidelity and domestic violence.

The legend and legacy of *la Malinche* remains powerfully negative to Latinas—even after five centuries! While monuments and museums in honor of Cortés are numerous and celebrated, Marina's house serves only as a monument to the alleged inherent evil and dishonesty of women.

THE MYTH OF *LA BUENA MUJER*

In the machismo culture, the ideal role of a woman is *la buena mujer* (the good woman), who is based on the example of perfection—the Blessed Virgin Mary. We all know one: our mother, grandmother, aunt, or even sister. *La buena mujer* is all about unquestioned self-sacrifice, purity, and unspoken tolerance. She represents a life of taking care of everyone except herself, never expecting the same in return. *La buena mujer* lives only for others, in the shadow of the men who surround her: father, boyfriend, husband, son. When she marries, her husband instantly becomes the single object of her devotion. The reward for giving her body and soul completely to her husband is a certain degree of respect and her husband's protection. But why does a woman need to surrender herself to her husband and family to earn respect? Do surrender and respect have anything to do with each other? A man does not need to sacrifice anything to earn respect; he automatically secures it, just by being a man.

Motherhood is idealized in the Latino culture. The mother is considered the core of the family, yet the father is considered the head. *La mujer* is the one who holds everything together while *el hombre* is the one who takes all the credit.

In our culture, it is expected that a mother should devote her *entire* self to her family, and it is this expectation that subordinates and dominates Latinas. A macho man believes that all of his needs should be met by his woman. Not only does he expect her to run a home, care for children, and cook food, he also expects her to fulfill his sexual and emotional needs but is rarely willing to offer the same in return.

Within this family structure, *aguantando* (tolerating or enduring) is crucial. Mother is expected to be a self-sacrificing saint. She exists to fulfill her family's needs yet does not believe that she has a right to impose her needs, pains, or frustrations on her family. Her silence only serves to enhance her role as a martyr. Mother is supposed to be a superhuman who can perform miracles on behalf of her family. Her utmost reward comes from seeing her children grow and from knowing that she is meeting her husband's every need. Her capacity to give is endless, and she expects nothing other than seeing her family thrive. She lives purely through others and, in turn, is dehumanized. She never learns how to live for herself; in fact, she has no sense of self.

The role of *la buena mujer* destroys self-worth. It represents a value system that equates obedience with perfection. The price that *la buena mujer* pays in her attempt to be the ideal woman is the loss of her voice—the voice she would use to speak of her pain, her dreams, her hopes for herself. And when a woman loses her voice, she loses herself. No matter how heroic a woman's intentions might be, to live entirely for another is to deny her own existence. The most disastrous part of being *la buena mujer* is that, sooner or later, a woman is faced with an emptiness she cannot explain, as illustrated in the poem "La Buena Mujer," by Elsa Tamez.

La Buena Mujer

And then began the years
Of silence, the years
My mouth would open
And no words would speak,
My mouth locked tight.
And a loneliness grew
That I couldn't name.
I looked for it
In my husband's eyes.
I looked for it
In my children's eyes.
I looked for it
In supermarkets.
I looked for it
In the oven.
I looked for it
In the dustpan.
I looked for it
In the sink.
In the TV.
In the washing machine.
In the car.
In the streets.
In the cracks.
On my linoleum.
I polished
And cleaned and cared for everything silently. I put on
my masks, my costumes and posed for each occasion.
I conducted myself
Well, but an emptiness grew
that nothing could fill. I think, I think,
I hungered for myself.[*]

---

[*]Tamez, Elsa. *Against Machismo*. Costa Rica: Meyer Stone Books, 1987:134.

A 1997 national survey on Latinas and depression showed that, compared to other women in the United States, Latinas have the highest rate of depression. When *la buena mujer* examines her life, without recognizing and admitting what cultural obligations have done to her, she is left with confusion and disappointment, usually blaming herself for not being *"buena"* enough.

Just as the ideals of machismo have been taught to generation after generation of Latino men, the role of *la buena mujer* has been taught to women for hundreds of years. Until Latinas realize the danger of tolerating machismo belief systems and take action to break through these boundaries, they will never truly be free.

Making Changes: How Do We Even Begin?

Without support from the family, Latinas often break down and give up their efforts to grow or break free. We all know that our family's support is crucial for us to move ahead in the world. Unfortunately, you need to prepare yourself because you might not receive the support you so desperately want. Even so, it is very important that you do not give up! You must be ready to accept the fact that your family might not understand that you are trying to stand up for yourself and improve your lot in life. They might see it as a sign of rebelliousness and react angrily or even shame you for trying to change "tradition." But if you know deep down in your heart that you want to live a better, fuller life, you must be strong. At times you might experience a wonderful, liberating feeling from something as simple as saying "no" to something you have always said "yes" to, even though you didn't want to. You might run to share this feeling with a family member only to have that person make you feel guilty. This will happen. But believe me when I tell you it is only part of the process, and sometimes things have to get worse before they get better. So many of our grandmothers, mothers, and sisters live in a state of denial and probably will continue to, because it is the safest thing to do. But when we Latinas begin to choose to make the world our world, to educate ourselves, and to break free of our culture's stifling restrictions and imposed roles, we will become a huge force to be reckoned with.

An undeniable aspect of the machismo attitude is that in order for the *machista* behavior to exist, there needs to be some-one willing to accept this behavior. By definition, one doesn't exist without the other. Most *machista* men will never voluntar-ily change their attitude toward women; it's not convenient for them. Machismo is such an essential part of so many Latino men that taking it away would be like taking away part of their very being. I cannot imagine a *machista* man getting up one morning and thinking: "I've been too much of a *machista* to my wife and daughters; from now on I will only expect from my wife what I am willing to offer."

Sadly, even Latino boys as young as six or seven years old have expressed thoughts about women to me that mirror exactly what their grandfathers, uncles, and fathers think. Their entire community has instilled in them a sense of superiority that, once securely established, is very hard, but not impossible, to unlearn. Boys are not born *machistas*; they are directly and indirectly taught to embrace that attitude. Although there are more Latino men now than ever who have discarded negative ideas about women, even the smallest degree of machismo can have a nega-tive impact on a woman's sense of self-worth. Any man can acknowledge and change his *machista* behavior, but most men will never do it until Latina mothers, sisters, daughters, and wives demand it.

When I speak of Latinas taking control of their own lives, many *machista* men tell me, "You women already have too much power; you let men think they have the control, but you women are the ones who really have it." If that were true, why is it that Latinas still get beaten by their husbands? Why is it that the rate of depression among Latinas is five times that of Latino men? If Latinas hold so much power in their households, why is it that a large proportion of Latinas, when divorced, immediately fall beneath the poverty level while Latino men increase their qual-ity of life? Worst of all, why is it that when a Latino cooks, cleans, and does the dishes, he is seen as a wonderful man—a keeper—yet, when a Latina does the same work, she is seen as just doing her job?

● Latinas accept machismo from family members and most men because that is what our culture tells us to do. But when Latinas allow this, they are contributing to their own self-degradation. How then do we start doing what we need to do for ourselves? How do we begin to realize our own individual potentials?

First, we need to believe that we are worth fighting for. Even if you don't believe it now, you will start believing it by the time you finish this book. We need to realize that when our talents and needs are ignored and our self-worth is buried we cannot perform successfully in a competitive society. Low self-esteem, minimized status, and emotional struggle carry over into whatever we attempt. We need to realize that it is not normal to experience these feelings, and it is not healthy to live a life dictated by the standards of others, including our outdated Latino traditions. It wasn't until I left the family home to enter college that I realized I had been living in a house saturated by my father's macho pride. My mother was completely subservient, and I'd always assumed that it was normal for a father to have the final say in all matters.

In our own Catholic Church, women are not allowed to be priests, only nuns, who are at the bottom rung of the hierarchy of the church. There are some people within the church who embrace change, however. In an interview, Father Gustavo Gutiérrez of St. Mary's in Phoenix, Arizona, commented on Latinas and their oppression within the community and the church. He said that although he wished it weren't true, the oppression of Latinas is real and obvious. He also called on Latino men to be sensitive to what the whole society is losing because of this oppression.

By the year 2005, one out of every five American women will be a Latina. We are a force to be reckoned with. We are capable of influencing politics and social policy to a degree we've never even considered. Our mothers couldn't teach us this and our fathers wouldn't, but we, as a social force of huge importance, should be helping to form educational programs for our children, acting as a major influence on the media, forming legal policy, and running corporations. We are artists and governors, attorneys and designers, doctors and judges. The first step is simple

realization: the minute we begin to question how our own culture's traditions have held us back is the minute we realize what
we are actually capable of doing. It is difficult to break away from
machismo oppression, but we have an obligation to ourselves and
to the women of the next generation to act now. The rewards of
personal freedom are worth the frustration and the effort twenty
times over.

According to an old saying, traditions are meant to be broken, and my greatest hope is that Latinas will value themselves
enough to seek out the many sources available to them. The
resources section in the back of this book lists many organizations and resources that can help Latinas find their rightful place
in both Latino society and the world at large. We are all blessed
and special souls with talents meant to be shared. Without our
invaluable input, this country will always be less than what it
could be. Without discovering and pursuing what you can be—
to yourself and society—your life will be only a fraction of what
it was meant to be.

4

A Crisis of Self-Esteem

Character cannot be developed in ease and quiet. Only through experience of trial and suffering can the soul be strengthened . . . ambition inspired, and success achieved.
—Helen Keller

Recently, at a nightclub in Los Angeles, I had the opportunity to help a woman change her perspective of herself and her life. I was out dancing with my husband and some friends when, across the room, I noticed a young Latina crying. I approached her and asked what was wrong. Her head hung in shame as she described the situation to me. Her boyfriend had been dancing and kissing another girl openly on the dance floor. Through the tears, I could see the insecurity and desperation in her eyes.

I grasped her hand and looked her directly in the eye. "You do not deserve to be disrespected in this way," I said. The woman pulled her hand away and said, sadly, "But he's all I have. No one has ever loved me the way he loves me. He makes me feel like I am worth something."

I took her hand again and said, "You do not need a man to make you feel good about yourself. You need to recognize how great you are, because you feel it inside yourself, not because someone from the outside tells you so. If you depend on others to tell you what your worth is, you will forever be confused and dependent upon them. Look at you; you are a beautiful 'Latina Queen!'"

The woman's face lit up, and she proudly lifted her head. "Do you really think I'm beautiful? As beautiful as a queen?" she asked.

I answered, "Yes, you are beautiful, not only physically but deep down in your soul. All Latinas were born to be queens of their own destiny. We have complete power over our throne, which, metaphorically, is our life. We have total power over our thoughts, actions, and beliefs. We alone can choose how we will be treated. Would a queen allow a man to treat her the way your boyfriend has treated you tonight?" I asked.

She responded, "No way!"

Filled with a renewed sense of hope, she hugged me and told me that no one had ever spoken to her like I had. She thanked me for making her feel valuable, with or without her boyfriend. She also asked me why I had taken the time to approach a stranger and offer help.

"Because most of us do not know we are queens," I explained. "We act as servants to others and forget that the most important person in our lives is ourselves. When I say 'Latina Queen,' I am referring to a person who recognizes her inner beauty and takes control of her own life. Unfortunately, most women do not view themselves this way. Regrettably, we were taught to believe that our worth comes from the outside world. Society dictates that our only measure of worth is what we do for others, not what we do for ourselves."

My husband and two of his male friends were watching as I spoke to this woman. They signaled for us to join them. As we approached, I realized that Norberto's friends were preparing to hit on her. They saw a lonely, vulnerable woman and thought she would be an easy target. Feigning concern, the guys asked if she needed anything. She said "no" and immediately turned her attention back to me. She asked my husband, "Do you know how lucky you are to have her? What Yasmin told me tonight will stay with me forever. She's made me feel so much stronger and worthier."

Annoyed by the woman's interest in me, rather than in them, the men continued to pursue their pick-up routine. They peppered her with silly questions, but, much to their dismay, they couldn't get her attention. Instead, she continued on about the magnitude of our conversation, and how it had impacted her. Rejected, the guys finally stopped trying and later told me they thought she would surely go back to her boyfriend. "They always do" were their exact words.

"She might," I replied, "but at least this time she's aware that she's worth something."

The events at the club that night have caused me to reflect, many times, on the messages we are sending to young Latinas. A single spoken "you're beautiful" can have such an enormous impact on the way a person feels about herself. Shouldn't Latinas already know that they are strong and powerful? Why don't they recognize this? How can a comment from a stranger, like myself, be a woman's only sense of worth? How can the concept of a "Latina Queen" be so foreign to a young Latina?

The Hidden Realities Latinas Do Not Know

In December of 1999, the Coalition of Hispanic Health and Human Services Organizations (COSSMHO) released this startling news about Latinas:

> The four most serious threats to American girls today are pregnancy, depression, substance abuse, and delinquency. Alarmingly, Hispanic girls rank highest in rates of depression and suicide, along with teen pregnancy, substance abuse and self-reported gun possession.

We must open our eyes to the huge crisis in our communities involving young Latinas. One in three of these young women reports seriously considering suicide, the highest rate of any racial or ethnic group. It has been proven that many of these girls not only plan but actually attempt suicide. While most people are unaware of the crisis, others choose simply to ignore it.

The only way to help these Latinas, and to decrease the high rate of suicide, is to understand the root of the problem. Through focus groups, personal interviews, and data analysis, I have conducted my own research involving young Latinas, targeting identity issues such as self-esteem. While I have found many commonalities with current research on Latinas and depression, I have also discovered disturbing patterns relating to this identity crisis among these young girls.

My studies (which have included viewpoints from conservatives and liberals, from varying economic and social classes, from different countries of origin, and from a variety of educational and generational backgrounds) have shown that young Latinas, like girls from other ethnicities, are faced with the general pressures of assimilation into American society. In order to help their own people cope with this difficult process, Latinos have established a set of traits to create a strong intracultural unity; however, I strongly believe that many of these traits actually do more harm than good, often with terrible consequences.

Early adolescence is a critical period of transition for all girls, regardless of their ethnicity. Researchers have described this passage as the "goodbye to girlhood crisis." It has been documented that between their ninth and fourteenth birthdays, girls tend to lose self-confidence, and their performance in school declines. They become less physically active and neglect their own interests and aspirations. One might think this transition would be less complicated for Latinas because of their strong family bond, but the truth is just the opposite. The family bond poses countless challenges that can hinder a Latina's independence, including specific cultural expectations with respect to gender roles and family responsibilities, discriminatory attitudes by mainstream Americans, and pressures from acculturation. These challenges can create an overwhelming amount of pressure for young Latinas, and without support from family, friends, and the community, they can lead to depression.

In 1998, a survey by Dr. Veronica Martinez, a self-esteem specialist, reported that 27 percent of Hispanic girls described themselves as feeling moderately to severely negative about their lives. In a similar survey, which I conducted, 60 percent of Latinas felt that they did not have control over their own lives. When I discussed these results with friends and colleagues, most were not aware of the high percentage but admitted they were really not surprised.

Depression, suicide, loss of control: What can we do to help? Latinas must be taught how to have control over their lives. We cannot wait for our society to change, for our parents to understand, or for our boyfriends to support us. We have to empower our Latinas; teach them how to take responsibility for their lives and how to overcome harmful cultural traits. The first step in this process is identifying and understanding ourselves and creating a positive self-image.

THE CONSTRUCTION OF SUBCONSCIOUS BELIEFS

Self-esteem is the measure of confidence that we have in ourselves. Our level of self-esteem is directly influenced by the messages we receive, and have received, from our families and others while growing up. These messages have been communicated to us verbally and nonverbally. A message, either positive or negative, if constantly repeated during childhood, will be internalized and will become ingrained in the mind as a subconscious belief. When the messages are negative, then our perception of ourselves will be negative; this is where low self-esteem comes from.

In my focus groups, many Latinas have expressed that they believe it is important to instill a positive self-image in their daughters, even though they do not have a positive self-image themselves. I often ask, "How can you instill something in your daughter that you don't have?" Usually, the room is silent, so I answer my own question: "You have to pay attention to yourself, recognize your own self-worth, and learn to love yourself."

My focus groups are comprised of bright, passionate women who are full of love and want to provide the best for their families. Their main problem is that the love and compassion is always for their families and never for themselves. These women are aware that loving themselves and having high self-esteem is important for their own emotional well-being, but they haven't taken the time to reflect on themselves, to understand who they truly are. Many Latinas have rarely given much thought to what their passions and ultimate goals are in life. When I ask them what their needs and wants are, most reply, "I don't really know, because I haven't thought about it before now." But when I ask them what their husbands, boyfriends, fathers, and children's needs and wants are, they can quickly rattle off a list.

If one does not know who she is, or what she needs, then she lacks a sense of identity. Many of the Latinas in my focus groups have spoken about how they feel they "should be," a notion that was ingrained in them while growing up. Many have received mixed messages of who they "should be" as well. These messages have been subconsciously internalized, and as a result, a system of beliefs has been established. For example:

Melissa had been taught throughout her childhood that sex was something to be shared only with her future husband. She learned that women who had sexual experiences without being married were considered whores. She also learned that it was acceptable for men to have many sexual experiences with different women because they have sexual needs to be fulfilled. As she told us her story, she said, "I love my boyfriend very much, and I want to share with him that wonderful sexual intimacy everyone talks about. But when we have sex, I tense up and my emotions shut off completely; I just end up going through the motions to get it over with. I can't let myself be free and enjoy sex. When I think about letting myself be sexually free, I feel dirty and ashamed; I feel like a whore. In my mind, I know I am a sexual being, and I have the right to be sexually free, but when the moment comes for me to do it, my body and my emotions won't let me."

Melissa is experiencing something very common among Latinas, as well as among women from other ethnic cultures. From birth, women have been programmed to believe everything their culture dictates about what is "right" for women. When a Latina gets older and realizes that these beliefs are wrong for her, she tries to change but finds she can't. These imposed cultural beliefs have become her beliefs. As Christiane Northrup, M.D., author of *Women's Bodies, Women's Wisdom*, explains:

It is important to understand that our beliefs go much deeper than our thoughts, and we cannot simply will them away. Many beliefs are completely unconscious and are not readily available to the intellect. Most of us aren't aware of our own destructive beliefs that undermine our health. They don't come from the intellect alone, the part that thinks it's in control. They come from that other part that in the past became lodged and buried in the cell tissue.

Breaking free from these beliefs is not easy and requires creating a new belief system. The shame of sexuality is only one of the many negative messages Latinas have received while growing up. Other messages include being loyal to family before being loyal to oneself; that taking care of others is more important than taking care of yourself; and that one must respect one's elders even if they do not respect you. All of these negative messages can have a monumental impact on one's identity and self-esteem.

So how do we change these imposed beliefs that we know are not good for us? First, we need to get in touch with our subconscious beliefs, and then we need to understand where they came from, how they were developed, and how they have affected our self-esteem.

Latinas frequently measure their self-worth against the approval they receive from their families. Consequently, many have refrained from doing something they felt was important because their families would oppose it. One Latina teen recently said, "If my family does not want me to do something, I usually don't do it, because they know what's best for me. They tell me what is good for me or is not good for me because they love me." Clearly, this girl would rather avoid conflict and gain her parent's approval than make an independent decision.

In a study conducted by research analyst Sonya Ryar, Ph.D., young Latinas were asked if they would ever consider doing things that were different from the things their friends and family did. Almost all answered, "I don't like to do things that make me different from my friends and family." For these young Latinas, being different is not an important characteristic, and it is clear that, for the most part, being different is discouraged throughout the Latino culture. The idea of a woman's independence is not fostered, a situation that greatly hinders self-esteem, because independence is self-esteem's most important component. Latinas must shed the identity that has been forced upon them by their parents and their culture; they must find their true natures, their "Latina Queen" personas.

SEXUALITY: THE SHAME THAT BINDS US

Monica was a twenty-seven-year-old mother of two and a lawyer. By all outward appearances, she was strong, confident, and very intelligent. She seemed to have broken down all of the negative cultural influences that plague other Latinas. She appeared powerful and in control at work, and at home she appeared to be a loving wife and mother. On the outside, it looked as though she had it all.

We had been friends since we were children, but we never seemed to agree on issues concerning Latinas. Then something happened during the course of our discussions that changed Monica forever.

One day she and I were sitting on her sofa, and she told me, "I don't believe in all that oppression stuff. I grew up Latina, and I have lived my life to the fullest. I never internalized any of those submissive messages that other Latinas claim to have internalized. If they don't like what they learned in the past, then they should get up and just do something about it." I tried to explain to Monica that many Latinas don't know that they are being affected by these early negative messages. She replied, "How can they not know. That's impossible!"

In order to demonstrate my point, I suggested we play a game. I began, "As educated Latinas, we know that each one of us has different roles we take on at various times. We have the ability to shift our consciousness into whatever role is needed at a particular time of the day without even thinking about it. For example, there is Monica the mother, and there is Monica the attorney. Monica the mommy puts on her mommy hat when she needs to and the same for Monica the attorney."

"I understand," Monica replied. "And I agree."

I stood up and asked Monica to rearrange the furniture in the living room. She looked at me like I was crazy but played along, following my directions. When she was done, I pointed to the chair on my left and said, "Will Monica the mommy please sit here and pretend she is doing her mommy role." Accordingly,

Monica sat on the chair and pretended to be putting her babies to sleep. She sang to them and gave them each a kiss goodnight. Then I asked, "Can Monica the attorney sit on this chair to the right and pretend she is doing her attorney role?" Monica got up, sat on the chair, and pretended to argue a case in court.

Monica was truly enjoying her role-playing and was switching in and out of her roles with great ease. I posed the final question: "Can Monica the sexual being please come sit on this sofa?" Baffled, Monica paused for a few seconds. She sat down, then lay down on her back, and then sat up again and replied, with some alarm, "I don't think she exists!"

Appalled by this discovery, Monica sank back into her chair. She truly believed that she was in touch with herself and that she knew every aspect of her being, but she had never thought of herself as a sexual entity. "Yes, I have sex with my husband," she said, "but that's it. Sometimes it's okay and other times I just lie there and wait until he's done." Monica confessed that she never thought of sexuality as an actual part of her being. Frustrated, she explained, "I was taught that sex is just something you do with your husband when you get married, and that's it. There's nothing else related to sex. It's just something you do with your husband out of obligation."

I could sense Monica's discomfort, but before I changed the subject, I asked her, "If you were ever to divorce, do you believe sex and your sexuality would cease to exist?"

Without hesitation, she answered, "Yes."

I asked, "Do you think that is right?"

"No," she said, "but that's just what I was taught it was supposed to be."

"That's my point," I said. "You, too, have internalized your early messages about sexuality, which have turned into your beliefs." Monica admitted that she had never thought about it that way, and I assured her that most of us don't.

For many women, sexuality constitutes the last frontier of self-acceptance and self-love. Many Latinas can describe themselves as loving mothers, wives, and competent professionals, yet when asked about their sexuality, they express self-doubt and shame. Sex is a taboo subject in traditional Latina households; the topic is simply not discussed. Regardless, sexual messages are still conveyed in the household, and these mixed messages include duty, self-worth, control, and shame, but not pleasure or female gratification. No one is born thinking sex is either bad or good. Rather, the Latino culture and society as a whole define our attitudes towards sex and sexuality.

Below are some examples of the messages that are given to young Latinas. These recurring messages eventually become beliefs and shape our attitudes toward sex in our adult lives. Are any of them familiar?

- Although sex is dirty, it's not so dirty for men. Sex, in fact, is good for *los hombres*. Boys are supposed to be sexually curious and sexually experienced. They were made biologically different from girls, and therefore they have sexual needs girls don't have. *Buenas mujercitas*, however, are supposed to be neither sexually curious nor experienced. Girls aren't supposed to "want" sex or have any interest in it until they are married.
- Female genitalia are dirty and the natural cause of female shame. Male genitalia, by contrast, are magnificent, the natural source of male pride.
- Although sex is dirty, it is permissible for women to be sexual under certain conditions: in matrimony, for the purpose of procreating, and *para darle el gusto a tu hombre* (for giving pleasure to your man).
- Although sex is dirty, and it's best if women don't enjoy it, sometimes even sexual pleasure is permissible. Again, certain conditions must be met. A *mujer* can have sexual pleasure only as long as her husband has equal or greater pleasure.

With all of these rules and negative connotations about the female body, it's no wonder Latinas have a hard time getting in touch with their sexuality. Latino culture allows Latinas only two options: Follow the rules and never truly experience sexual pleasure and freedom, or break the rules and live in shame.

Personally, I created my own alternative: To be in touch with my sexuality and never to live in shame. You can do this, too, if you recognize that you are the master of your own sexuality and your own life.

Sexual Shame   Shame is one of the most powerful emotions a human being can ever experience because the feeling lies at the core of the self, the soul. Shame can cause a person to feel as though her very birth was a mistake. Again, shame is most often created by those negative actions and verbal messages we received growing up, those same messages that become our internal beliefs that we keep hidden in our subconscious. The situation becomes dangerous when shame is internalized and, over time, becomes toxic to the body, mind, and soul. The result is self-repression, and the only way to overcome this is by creating a whole new belief system. Guilt can sometimes feel like shame, but be careful not to confuse the two—guilt is what one feels when one has done something wrong, or made a mistake. Guilt is outside of us; we can go back and repair what we did wrong, forgive ourselves, and go on. Shame, however, is a deeply rooted feeling of inadequacy that is difficult to reverse.

THE TRUTH ABOUT SEXUAL ABUSE

Sexual abuse is occurring in all of our communities, and this grim reality must be brought to the attention of all women. The National Institute of Sexually Abused Children reports statistics showing that one in every four girls has been sexually molested by the age of eighteen. That means one in every four girls you know. Sexual abuse is a horrible crime and, given the fact that it is an extremely sensitive issue, many of our families would rather not discuss it. Nevertheless, if we do not educate Latinas about sexual abuse, they will remain vulnerable, and we will not be able to protect them from this crime. Eighty-five percent of sexual abuse against girls and boys happens in their own homes by their own relatives. The culprit is usually a father, uncle, cousin, brother, or other close member of the family. Due to the nature of the crime, sexual abuse is rarely reported to police.

In my own research, I have found that sixty-five out of every one hundred Latinas (aged fourteen to forty) who took part in my focus groups have been sexually assaulted by a family member. Twenty of them had told a relative about the abuse; the other forty-five girls had never shared their secret shame of molestation until the day they shared it with the group. Out of the twenty girls who had told a relative about the abuse, nine were not believed, six had relatives who prohibited the abuser from entering their homes, and five had relatives who empathized with them but later pretended it had never happened. Not one girl reported the incident to authorities or pressed criminal charges against the perpetrator.

Throughout the sexual abuse portion of my focus groups, the girls and I discussed the fact that sexual abuse is taboo. We cried as some told their stories and rejoiced when the shame was not a secret anymore. These young girls had never been able to open up to anyone about these issues; the feelings of shame were just too intense. Sexual abuse is not unique to Latino culture; it crosses racial, class, and economic lines, and we cannot continue to go on ignoring it. By doing so, we are allowing ourselves, and our daughters, to be victims. It is an extremely difficult and sensitive topic to broach, but it must be done for the well-being of our children. The following hypothetical situation might help you to address the issue with your daughters or sons.

A Mother Talking to Her Daughter About Sexual Abuse

"Hijita, I need to tell you something very important. I love you very much, and it is very important to me that you always feel safe. When God made you, he gave you your body, which is yours and only yours. Nobody else has the right to touch you in a way that makes you feel uncomfortable, especially in your private areas. (If she does not know where her private areas are, show her.) If anyone ever wants to touch your private parts, no matter who it is, they are doing something that is very wrong. If anyone ever tries to do anything to you that makes you feel uncomfortable, you do not have to do it, no matter who it is. If they tell you that it will be your little secret, you tell them 'no,' and you come and tell me what happened. If they tell you nice little girls do whatever it is they're told, you tell them 'no,' and you come and tell me. If they threaten you by telling you they are going to hurt somebody you love, you tell them 'no,' then come and tell me. What they tell you is not true; they are only trying to scare you into doing what they want. When I am around you, I will always protect you and not let anything like that ever happen to you. But when I am not around, I need you to be strong and to protect yourself. And if for some reason something does

happen to you, don't ever feel it was your fault. It is very important that you come and tell me so I can protect you and make sure it never happens again. No matter what happens, I will never get angry with you or blame you. Remember that this body is yours. You have permission to say 'NO' to anyone who tries to touch you where they shouldn't—this includes strangers, friends, or family."

After you speak with your children, hug them and tell them you love them. Make sure you relay this message to your children at least once a year. The more they hear it, the more they will understand it and believe it.

CREATING A NEW BELIEF SYSTEM ABOUT YOUR SEXUALITY

Before you can take steps to empower your sexual being, you need to understand that your feelings about your body and your sexuality are not entirely accessible to you intellectually. Many of your feelings are stored in your body and in your subconscious. In order to change subconscious beliefs, Christiane Northrup, M.D., author of *Women's Bodies, Women's Wisdom*, suggests that one must go through the following three steps of spiritual truths:

- **Step One:** *I must admit I am powerless to change my belief about my sexuality with intellect alone.*
  You must admit that this belief is not healthy and that it is making parts of your life unmanageable. Your belief won't go away if you beat yourself up over it or try to force yourself to change it with your intellect alone.

- **Step Two:** *(I must come) to see that a power greater than myself can restore me to peace with my sexuality.*
  This "power greater than yourself" is a part of your inner guidance and bodily wisdom. Acknowledging that you have access to a power greater than your own intellect is a very positive step toward actually getting in touch with that guidance.

- **Step Three:** *(I must make) a decision to turn my will and my life over to the care of my inner guidance, my divine wisdom.*
  This step bypasses the intellect entirely. It is a leap of

faith that acknowledges the fact that we all have inner guidance available within us and that that guidance has the power to remove our harmful beliefs. The words "make a decision" are extremely important. In order for a woman to change her belief, she has to make the decision to do it and to commit to the process.

These three steps were taken from the twelve steps of Alcoholics Anonymous. Participating in twelve-step meetings and working the steps around beliefs, fear, or anything you have found your intellect to be powerless over, can be very empowering.

Affirmations for Creating a Healthy Sexual Being   Affirmations are any positive statements that we make. Too often we think in negative messages such as "sex is dirty," therefore perpetuating our negative belief system. Changing a negative message into a positive one such as "sex is beautiful when shared with someone you love" will shift our consciousness into a new way of thinking. Below you will find an exercise to help you with this process. Note that you must make your statements in the present tense, such as "I am" and "I want."

Find a quiet place where you can be alone for at least ten minutes every day. Sit or lay down, whichever is more comfortable for you, and close your eyes. Try to concentrate solely on your breathing. Visualize the particular messages regarding sex that you received when you were little. Try to remember the messages as clearly as possible. Pick the messages that made the strongest impression on you. Who is giving you this message? What are they saying? How are they acting? Are they giving you verbal or nonverbal messages? Now open your eyes. For every negative message you remember, write down a positive message that dismisses the negative one. For example:

- *Negative message: Mujeres* who have sexual feelings are dirty.
  Affirmation: *Mujeres* have the right to sexual feelings and are sexual beings.
- *Negative message:* You must have sex with your husband anytime he wants, no matter what.
  Affirmation: I don't have to do anything I don't feel comfortable doing. The decision to have sex is a joint decision.

LATINAS AND MENTAL HEALTH

When Rebecca was a teenager, she suffered from headaches and, at times, claimed to hear voices. Her family took her to a number of different medical doctors (that is, doctors who only work with ailments of the body, not the mind), but they could not find anything physically wrong with her. The voices began to increase, and she reported that a voice was telling her it was God and asking her to return to heaven. Her family then took her to a priest, hoping that he would be able to provide an explanation for the voices, but the priest only said that she was a very religious girl. Five weeks later, Rebecca committed suicide. Although hearing voices can mean different things to different people, it has also been proven that hearing voices is a strong indicator of schizophrenia—a psychotic disorder that causes one to hear, see, or feel things that are not there.

On May 3, 2000, Congresswoman Grace F. Napolitano introduced a bill to Congress titled "The Latina Adolescent Suicide Prevention Act." In a Washington, D.C., press release, Congresswoman Napolitano stated:

> Findings from the Hispanic Caucus' Report on Hispanic Health in the United States prove that Latina adolescents lead girls of all other ethnic groups in rates of suicide, alcohol and drug abuse, depression, pregnancy, and self-reported gun use; therefore, I will introduce a bill—the Latina Adolescent Suicide Prevention Act—which will provide more mental health care services targeted at teenage Hispanic girls, so they don't end up on the path to suicide.

This bill is a milestone in the fight for mental health among Latinas and is the first step toward saving our youth. However, we must recognize that within our communities mental disorders are perceived as shameful, and the existing belief is that one must be really *loca* to seek a therapist. In order for these programs to be successful, our communities must recognize that mental illness is not a sign of weakness, but a genuine illness.

Ninety-five percent of the one hundred Latinas who took part in my focus groups had either directly experienced, or someone in their family had experienced, some type of deep depression. Out of the 95 percent, 90 percent never sought professional help. Depression was never discussed in their households, but everybody knew something was wrong. "Everybody knows something is not right with that person," said one young Latina, "but nobody dares to talk about it." In a personal interview with Carmen Valdez, a mental health expert working predominantly with Latina families in San Diego, she stated:

> A lot of Latino/a families suffer because they do not know how to recognize an entity of mental health. Others suffer because they do not believe their depression is true or real. When a Latino/a teenager and his or her family come to see me due to this teenager's feelings of depression, his or her parents tell me, *'No tiene nada, se está haciendo tonto; nada más que es flojo.'* ('There is nothing wrong with him/her; he/she is just playing dumb. He/she is just lazy.') I clearly tell them that my diagnosis suggests their teenager is suffering from clinical depression, but the parents do not believe me.

Additionally, in the Latino culture, one is expected to keep one's personal affairs private. This is yet another debilitating aspect of our culture. When someone does not speak out about their problems, more often than not, he or she will internalize their problems, resulting in everything from headaches and body aches to more serious physical illness. Dr. Northrup explains that our thoughts are energetic forces that create the physical basis for our health and our individual lives. If we don't work through our emotional distress, we set our mind and body up for physical distress because of the biochemical effects that suppressed emotions have on our immune systems. Because of our internalization, many Latinas eventually begin to have symptoms of depression that, if not treated, usually progresses into serious depression.

When young Latinas begin to have symptoms of depression, they usually do nothing because they have never been educated about mental illness. And if they do know a little bit about the symptoms of depression, and perhaps are bold enough to ask a family member to take them to a psychologist, many times they are shamed by the family member and told "no" because, for heaven's sake, they are not *loca*.

Not too long ago, my seventeen-year-old goddaughter called me and asked me if I could take her to a psychologist. "Whatever you do, don't tell my mom," she said. When I asked her why, she began crying and said, "I've been feeling really depressed lately, and I feel like I can't talk to any of my friends or family about the

Miguel Lua

It's imperative, Mrs. Rodriguez, that you put aside some time exclusively for yourself.

Depression Questionnaire

The following depression questionnaire is for you (or anyone you love) to fill out to help determine whether you are suffering from depression. This questionnaire is not intended to be a diagnosis. If you are feeling depressed, please consult a mental health expert.

Use this questionnaire on a weekly basis to track your moods. Changes of five or more points are significant. The eighteen items below refer to how you have felt and behaved during the past week. For each item, indicate the extent to which it is true by writing the appropriate number in the space indicated, using the following scale:

0 = Not at all
1 = Just a little
2 = Somewhat
3 = Moderately
4 = Quite a lot
5 = Very much

1. I feel no hope for the future   _____
2. I feel unhappy   _____
3. I feel tired   _____
4. I feel like a failure   _____
5. I do things slowly   _____
6. I feel agitated and can't stay still   _____
7. It is difficult for me to concentrate on things _____
8. I feel guilty about everything   _____

way I'm feeling. I told my mom that I was thinking about seeing a psychologist, and she freaked. My mom started crying, telling me that what I was feeling was not her fault and that all I wanted to do was go talk bad about her to the psychologist. I told her that it had nothing to do with her, and she said that, anyway, I was not crazy, and only crazy people see psychologists. Sometimes I wonder if I am crazy; sometimes I feel like just ending it all." Other

9. I have difficulty making decisions   _____

10. It takes great effort to do the most menial
tasks   _____

11. The pleasure and joy has gone out of my life   _____

12. I feel trapped   _____

13. Without trying, I have lost or gained weight   _____

14. I feel depressed even when good things
happen to me   _____

15. I feel nothing; no emotions   _____

16. I either sleep too much, have insomnia,
or keep waking up   _____

17. I spend time thinking about how I will
kill myself   _____

18. I have lost interest in things that used to
be important to me   _____

Total   _____

Score Your Depression Questionnaire

54 and up	Severely depressed
36–53	Moderately–Severely depressed
22–35	Mildly–Moderately depressed
18–21	Borderline depression
10–17	Possibly mildly depressed
0–9	No depression likely

If you scored anything above a 9 and there is no major
turmoil presently in your life, you should contact a mental
health specialist.

young Latinas have shared similar thoughts about their parents'
disapproval of their intent to see a therapist or psychologist.

According to Dr. Rios—advisor to the U.S. Public Health Services Office on Women's Health—depression is not new for Latinas; it is a natural byproduct of *aguantar* (to tolerate or endure).
Every day I see Latinas who are living in a state of depression and
do not even realize it. What these Latinas need to know is that

there is a better way of life and that they, too, can live a life of happiness. Until Latinas begin to recognize how depression and other mental illnesses are taking control of their lives, the situation with our young girls will continue to get worse.

It is extremely important that we educate parents about mental illness. We cannot rely on them to educate their children about something they do not understand and are reluctant to even talk about. We need to be the ones who take an active role in either educating ourselves, then educating our parents, or taking steps to educate everyone at once. Being educated about mental illness cannot only save a family member's life, it can protect an entire family from unnecessary pain.

Symptoms of Major Depression   Not all people with depression will have all these symptoms or have them to the same degree. If a person has four or more of these symptoms, if nothing can make them go away, and if they last more than two weeks, a doctor or psychiatrist should be consulted.

- Feeling hopeless, helpless, worthless, pessimistic, and/or guilty
- Persistent sad or "empty" mood
- Fatigue or loss of interest in ordinary activities, including sex
- Irritability, increased crying, anxiety and panic attacks
- Difficulty concentrating, remembering, or making decisions
- Disturbance in eating and sleeping patterns
- Substance abuse (alcohol, prescription drugs, and so on.)
- Persistent physical symptoms, or pains that do not respond to treatment
- Thoughts of suicide; suicide plans or attempts

Danger Signs of Suicide

- Statements about hopelessness, helplessness, or worthlessness
- Preoccupation with death
- Loss of interest in loved ones

- Visiting or calling loved ones
- Making arrangements; setting one's affairs in order
- Giving things away
- Talking about suicide

If you recognize these symptoms in anyone you know, please contact the Suicide Hotline; the phone number is located in the resources section in the back of this book.

Many times, depression comes as the result of low self-esteem. When someone does not believe in her ability to achieve success nor simply value her existence, it is easy for her to lose a sense of all purpose in life, falling into a deep depression, which could later lead to suicide. As research shows, negative self-esteem has proven to be one of the strongest contributors to depression. Disturbing patterns have shown how a Latina's identity crisis can lead to lack of self-esteem and then depression. It is when gender expectations and cultural challenges hinder Latinas from developing their independence that they usually take one of two routes: rebelling through gang activity, theft, and so on, or falling into depression and beginning to self-medicate through drugs. It is only in understanding and treating mental illness, understanding the need for independence, and taking responsibility in nurturing that independence that depression rates among Latinas will decline.

5

A New Perspective of a Latina's Relationship with God

As we search for our internal force, we should remember our spiritual connection, which is the true source of our strength.
—Anonymous

I receive what I consider to be a surprising amount of opposition when I mention that my work is devoted to empowering women, even if it's subtle resistance. I especially find resistance when I mention to Latinos that I am dedicated to strengthening Latinas. Often, I am even stereotyped as a "militant feminist" or a "man-hater." I tell my accusers: "How can I be a man-hater if the two most important figures in my life (besides myself and my daughter) are men—God and my husband."

While I consider myself a feminist, I am also aware that many people have the impression that a feminist is an angry woman. For the record: I am not angry; I am simply reclaiming my birthrights as a human being, aggressively. Why is it that when a man asserts his rights he is seen as a hero, yet when a woman asserts hers she is seen as radical? I'll never forget the day a radio spokesman in Charlotte, North Carolina, called me a "bitch" on his radio morning show. As he talked about the Carolina Panthers and their Sunday win against the 49ers, he nonchalantly said,

"Did you see Carolina Panthers' right tackle, #76? He no longer has his own name on his jersey; he now has his wife's name too. His wife must be a real you-know-what to *make* him take her last name. She must be a bitch!"

Each day I become stronger when it comes to dealing with controversy and criticism. I have been able to keep my strength through the power of my relationship with my higher power, who I choose to call God. For me, God is my spiritual father. For others, God might be female or mythical; some people worship Buddha or Allah. Regardless of faith, though, people around the world spend an enormous amount of energy trying to prove to others that their God is the right God. Of course, in the end, the specifics are not as important as the reality that one God loves all. God is a supernatural power, and however you choose to imagine him, her, or it, is a personal choice—it is yours and yours alone.

Catholicism as an Institutional Control System

Through my life experiences, I regained my faith in God, and I learned how to reclaim my worth. It was not through Catholicism, or any other institutional religion, that this miracle occurred. As a matter of fact, it was through Catholicism that I first knew shame. I first recognized the control that the church holds over its people while I was attending Catholic school. The notion of God was used to instill fear. There were also innumerable rules that were so strict no human could be expected to abide by all of them.

I was taught that there were certain roles that boys and girls played, and if I deviated from my role, God would know and would punish me. It often seemed to me that unless I behaved just like the Virgin Mary, I wouldn't be good enough to win God's approval. In order to be considered a good girl, I had to be quiet, submissive, and obedient, and I could not ask questions that were considered improper. This is one way Catholicism coerces young girls to mute their voices.

With all the rules, regulations, and a shame-based value system, how was I supposed to grow up being a confident, outspoken, risk-taking woman? At first, I guess I wasn't. A confident, risk-taking woman is the opposite of the "good Catholic woman"; a good Catholic woman is a self-sacrificing woman. I had a very hard time believing, though, that God would want me to sacrifice my life for someone else. He was supposed to love me! Latina mothers often have a very difficult time letting their children become adults and live their own lives for this very reason. These mothers have sacrificed everything for their children and when their children leave, they feel empty. Not being able to claim our identity and live our own lives defeats the purpose of us being in this world. When we are complete, we can provide a much healthier type of support to our husbands, children, and communities.

Many researchers have been critical of Catholicism. These writers contend that the church has encouraged Latinas to embrace an existence of self-denial and passivity by offering feminine images that are rigidly defined. Women are viewed as virgin, mother, or wife, which reinforces a state of social, psychological, and economic dependence. Catholicism splits feminine images into the good woman, represented by the Virgin Mary, and the bad woman, symbolized by the sinful Eve.

Religion usually offers symbols that elevate men to a superior status. These symbolic forms are internalized and passed on from one generation to another, playing an important role in how men see themselves and how women see men. This became the model that made oppression acceptable. The hierarchy of the Catholic Church has, as a rule, excluded women in the development of religious policies and laws, all of which directly affect women. Although many Catholic women cannot consciously accept that religion has had a repressive impact on our lives, it undeniably has.

LA VIRGEN DE GUADALUPE

Because there is evidence to show that religious images have a strong influence on the development of female identification, I am presenting to you images of a powerful Virgin Mary, a *Virgen María* who is all-powerful in mind, body, and spirit. One who can truly take care of herself physically, financially, and emotionally.

Miguel Lua

La Virgen María *empowering Latinas to get an education.*

Finding Your Higher Power Through Spirituality

As I became older and more educated, I lost faith in institutional religions, especially those that base their faith directly on the Bible. The idea that someone would live directly from what a book told her, rather than using her own mind and common sense, seemed absurd to me. Although there are many parables in the Bible with which I agree, there are many other passages I strongly disagree with. The idea of Original Sin, for example, makes no sense to me at all. How can a pure innocent child who has just entered the world carry a sin? I believe God is a wonderful being who loves every child he puts on our earth; he

Miguel Lua

La Virgen María *empowering Latinas to pursue their own career.*

would never burden a baby's soul with sin that he or she hadn't committed. Is a child responsible for his parents' actions? Now, I must say, if you want to baptize your child with a big *pachanga* (a huge party), then go for it; but make it a celebration of your beautiful child's innocent soul.

In my opinion, the Bible was written by men for men. It is terribly upsetting to me when I see religiously dedicated women allowing themselves to be abused by their husbands because the church does not look favorably on divorce. Could it be that these women actually believe that God wants them to be beaten and abused? This is the second, and equally as important, way that Catholicism can victimize women—by denying them the option of leaving men who are destructive to their minds and souls. Until Latinas really understand the impact the Catholic institution has

Miguel Lua

La Virgen María *empowering Latinas to protect themselves from harm.*

had on them, they will continue to ignore their pain, tolerate abuse, and deny their unique power and spirit.

It took me eight years to truly find God in my heart again. When the tragedy of my father struck our family, I literally felt as though my soul died. I felt an ache in my heart and an emptiness in my soul that could not be filled. It wasn't until my recovery from addiction that I truly found my higher power. It was not through religion that I found my higher power, it was through spirituality. To me, spirituality means faith in oneself as a higher power. The most divine way to live is to use our spiritual connection as our guiding force in life. Spirituality means seeing the truth, value, and beauty in all of life. It is a journey inward, which then connects us to all living forces. When you look at a newborn infant and feel a sense of peace, you are living through your spirituality.

When you know who you are from the inside out, and you value yourself for who you are (and not by what you have), you are living through spirituality. "Spirituality is not religion, for it does not depend on which church you belong to or the religious philosophy you follow. Religion is the way, the rules and regulations used to approach the concept of God. Your spiritual connection brings you peace, fulfillment, happiness, and abundance because it enables you to overcome the limitations of the physical mind and body by putting you in touch with the true source of power—the spirit of God."* I share a special relationship with my higher power: There are no rules, regulations, or shame. My God loves me just the way I am.

God Made Us to Be Strong, Powerful Women—What Are We Waiting for?

My higher power is my strength and my might. He is the one who gives me force, yet brings me peace. It is through my experiences, both tragic and joyful, that he helps me recognize that all experiences in life are purposeful. What I do today may not have meaning until a later time. But everything does happen for a reason. Every positive and negative experience in our lives is a message. It is what we do with the message that makes it worthwhile. No matter what tragedy or triumph we experience, we should always seek the deeper meaning of everything; our higher power has purposely put us through that experience so that we will gain wisdom and peace of mind.

God loves us just the way we are, because he created us. He gave us powerful minds and physical abilities to do extraordinary things. We are the ones who impose self-limiting conditions and traditions on ourselves. With the power that God bestows on us, we should fully govern ourselves. We do not need permission, or approval, or definition from the outside world. I know and believe that it is only God who can help me understand myself. He is my higher power who gives me the strength and courage

---

*Vanzant, Iyanla. *Tapping the Power Within*. New York: Harlem River, 1992: 20.

when I feel the world is against me. It is He who carries me through the pain when my body and my mind cannot take it anymore. It is He who fuels me with force when I have used it all up. When my in-laws rejected me for being a strong woman, when the media demonized me for wanting some worth, it was He who restored my heart and my soul.

My faith in my higher power empowers me to believe that even when traditionalists criticize me for creating my own traditions, even when people I love betray me, and even when I wonder if it's all worth it, I know there is not one entity, circumstance, or a combination of both formed against me that will succeed.

As my relationship with God has grown, and as my research has proven, there is one distinct difference between an empowered Latina and an oppressed Latina: identity. An empowered Latina has an identity that cannot be given or taken away by anyone or anything. It cannot be created by money, power, family, or a man. It is created by her own personal beliefs, morals, and values—not her husband's or her family's, but her own. Certainly the empowered Latina takes that which she finds meaningful from her family, her ancestors, and her mate, but she does not adhere to other people's expectations of what she should think and who she should be.

It is time for us to acknowledge the truth about our lives and ourselves. Our lives are a declaration of the choices we've made. We are strong, powerful Latinas; what are we waiting for? Are we living the lives we want to live? God wants us to live our lives to the fullest. If he didn't, he wouldn't have made us so strong and beautiful. If our traditions have conditioned us to believe that we are bitches if we think we are powerful, then call me a bitch, because I know I am all woman with all the power in the world to do anything I choose. Neither my husband, family, nor anyone else can put limitations on me, only myself.

Why is it that Latinas forget that God wants us to be happy? Why is it that Latinas forget that God has made us powerful and divine? Latinas have put tradition and destructive religious beliefs before their love of God and fail to recognize His enduring strength. God is on our side in this quest to be all-powerful, but if we choose pain and suffering then that is what we will have. If we are willing to put up with the disrespect that has been forced on us, we can only expect it to continue. If we choose to do what others want, even though we know better, God won't intercede on our behalf.

We are all on a journey of self-discovery. Some of us live in confusion, others in pain. We must each set out on a personal quest to find the treasures that will heal our lives. We must tear ourselves away from negative beliefs and behaviors. Sometimes we will hurt deeply; other times we will experience immense joy. We must also allow ourselves the time to grieve—to feel all of the feelings we have never allowed ourselves to feel because we feared they would overwhelm us. It is only then that we will release the negativity and connect with our soul and higher power. We will experience anger, fear, and love, sometimes separately, and, at times, all together. Then, we will rest to regain our strength and will rise again with a new sense of resolve. Most significantly, we will be rewarded as our lives heal. This is true for all women. Every woman can experience a heroic journey; any woman's life can be a quest for importance and dignity. It's up to you.

THE PROCESS OF SELF-DISCOVERY

The following ten steps are designed to help you with the process of spiritual self-discovery. Ultimately, it is your decision whether to yield to a new way of thinking or to stick to the old. It is your journey—nurture it!

Awareness You must understand and accept that there is a strong powerful force (your higher power) that will guide you through your tragedies and lead you to your joys. This power is not Christian, Jewish, Catholic, Hindu, or Islamic. It has no denomination. All that matters is that this higher power allows you to feel safe, secure, and powerful. Remember, in spirituality there is no such thing as an angry or fear-provoking God. Your higher power is all loving, nonjudgmental, and serene.

Willingness You must be willing to open your heart to whatever comes your way, whether it be joy, pain, frustration, love, or anger. Often, we must let our guard down before we can really feel our emotions. For some of us, it's nearly impossible to risk giving in to emotions. Imagine (or even better, do) three things that give you peace and joy. This is living from the soul.

Intuition   Trust your intuition; it's the voice of your higher power. Your intuition is the source of your deepest personal truth, and it will serve as a very good guide through any journey. Don't be afraid to go with a gut feeling and work from there. It might come to you through an inner voice, meditation, your art, music, writing or sports; it is different for everybody.

Lie down, close your eyes, and allow your whole body to relax completely. Do not hold on to any one thought; let them all drift in and out of your mind. Now, slowly allow your intuition to manifest itself in a specific area of your body. A "feeling" in this area will often signal that your intuition is at work.

Acceptance   Give yourself permission to explore your true feelings about religion, God, and spirituality. Ask yourself the following questions:

- Do your religious/spiritual beliefs come from within your soul, or are they just something you learned and never questioned?
- Do these beliefs encourage you to be who you truly want to be, or do they hold you back?
- If your beliefs hold you back from living the life you want to live, have you ever questioned the source of these beliefs?

Truth   Live the truth, your truth, not what you learned as being the truth but what your mind, body, and soul tell you the truth is. If we continue to accept outside ideas about how we should live our lives, we will fail to hear the voice of our intuition, our soul, and our higher power.

Close your eyes and relax. When you are at peace, ask your intuition to show you an image of your truest self. You must accept any image that comes forth, for it carries an important message. This is something that takes practice. You may not see anything at first, or you may not understand the message, but in time, it will become clear. You may practice this as often as you like; new images will appear, all of which have meaning.

Choices   Choose to have people in your life that honor you and your spiritual process. Individuals who project negativity will only frustrate self-discovery. Can things in your life be creatively reorganized so that you can spend more time with positive people, doing positive things? The first steps are always the most difficult, but investigating your choices makes them familiar.

You have the power to change any negative aspect of your life. You do not need money, a better opportunity, or luck. It is your willingness and commitment to yourself to live a better life that make change possible.

Love   Be open to receive love, especially from yourself. Understand that your higher power, speaking to you through your intuition, will never cause you to feel tense, pressured, or full of doubt. Your higher power will only bring you love, awareness, energy, and joy. Allow yourself to be who you truly are; if you do not know who you are yet, be who you always wanted to be. The important thing is to avoid being what others want you to be. Find activities in life that make you feel proud, and then make sure to take part in these activities as often as you possibly can.

Immediacy   Think of today as the first day of the rest of your life, and live as if it was the last day of your life: If you have made mistakes, learn from them, and then vow never to make them again. In the end, your past is just dust in the wind. If you are always living on a "schedule" (which I am guilty of), make some time to do something spontaneous and new, as if it might be the last chance.

Embrace the world   Latinas have been taught to fear the outside world, and this has limited our lives and experiences in profound ways. The world is full of marvelous possibilities. What are your greatest fears? Why do you fear them? Do you know where your fear stems from? When you think about it, most of our fears come from tradition and what our families and friends encourage us to fear. Your intuition is your most trusted and useful tool.

Face your deepest fear   It is only then that the fear will vanish. Until we recognize and accept that our deepest fears are immobilizing us and impeding our journey of self-discovery, we will not be able to free ourselves.

Do what you fear most, and I promise the fear will go away!

Dealing with la Familia

What is right for one soul may not be right for another. It may mean having to stand on your own and do something strange in the eyes of others.
—Eileen Caddy

In February 1993, I was at the height of my depression, living day to day, just trying to stay sane. One evening, in my dorm room at USC, I received an urgent call from my mother. She was hysterical, telling me that my older sister, Judy, was moving out of the house. Frantically, she tried to explain that she could not make it alone with my little sister and claimed that she needed help with the rent. My mother demanded that I move out of the dorm and back into her house. Immediately, as I felt the pressure of her request my muscles began to tense. I wanted to help my mother, but I knew that moving back home would be a drastic mistake.

Rent was not the real issue; my mother receive enough money to pay it without my help. The real issue was that she did not want to be alone. In the past, she had relied on my father, my sister, or me to look after her. Years of constant dependence on others made her feel as if she truly could not survive on her own.

"Mámi, no puedo moverme contigo ahorita," I said, desperately trying to compromise with her. *("Mámi,* I can't move back in

with you right now.") I promised I would go home on weekends to help with my little sister and that I would give her some money to help out financially. I could not bear the thought of moving home and knew it would only enhance my depression. At that time I needed to establish my own boundaries in order to keep my sanity and until I did this, I could be of little emotional support to either my mother or my little sister. I begged her to understand.

"Tu dices que quieres a tu hermanita tanto, pero ni siquieras quieres ayudarnos. Entonces tu no la quieres como dices," she said to me. ("You say you love your younger sister so much, but you do not even want to help us out. You must not love her like you say you do.") Her harsh words stung like a hot arrow through my heart. How could my mother say that I truly did not love my little sister when she meant the world to me? After we hung up, I began questioning myself. I knew my mother was distressed and would say anything to persuade me to move back home, but was she right? Was I a terrible daughter and sister? How could I do this to the people I loved most?

A few minutes later, the phone rang. It was my sister, Judy, who sounded uptight. She had obviously spoken to my mother and was upset with my decision to stay in the dorm. Judy was older than me and had always been at home to take care of our mother and sister; she felt it was now my turn to help them. She was aggravated by my selfish behavior. Trying not to break down in tears, I repeated to her what I had just told my mother, that I was willing to give up my weekends and come home and that I would somehow find a way to earn extra money to help support her financially.

Hopelessly, I cried to Judy, "Please tell me, why do I have to live there?"

Judy responded angrily, "You know Mom can't handle Karina by herself. She has to have one of us with her to help. I can't believe you won't do this for your mother. What kind of daughter are you? Don't you have any respect?"

Sobbing out of pain and guilt for what seemed like an eternity, I finally managed to hang up the phone. My family thought I was being selfish, and they were angry and upset with me. But deep down in my heart, I knew that I could not move home. It would not benefit any of us. I was confused and could not stop crying.

My head was throbbing. I needed some support, so I picked up the phone and called a dear friend of mine. Still upset and barely able to speak, I managed to explain the situation. "Am I that bad?" I asked her.

"No," she replied. "You need to do what is best for you. It's not like you are abandoning your family. You are offering your mother an alternative, which is money and weekends with her. Your mother and sister want you to do what they believe is right for you, but only you know what is right for you. Moving home is not going to solve any problems. You are a good person, Yasmin, a very good person. Don't let your family or anyone else ever make you feel like you are not."

Her warm words and encouragement helped ease my pain. I tried to pull myself together, to stop crying, and to think clearly. My family believed I was not loyal to them, and that hurt me deep down in my soul. In the past, I may have given up and out of guilt let my family make decisions for me, but this time it was different. Moving back home was not an alternative; it would perpetuate my mother's dependence on others and would intensify my depression.

I made my decision to stay in the dorm even though my mother and sister were strongly against it. I set my own boundaries and stuck to them. It was not easy to stand on my own against my family's wishes, and for a very long time I felt like a horrible daughter. In my mother's eyes, I had abandoned her.

It has taken many years for my mother to realize that I was not neglecting her. My decision helped her become independent, and today she thanks me. My mother now lives with me and helps me raise my little girl because it is suitable for both of us. If you ask her, she will tell you she's not afraid to live alone.

Breaking Away from a World of Guilt

"Loyalty before all" is a vital aspect of the Latino culture. At a very young age, we are taught to be loyal to our family, without question. This tradition has been passed down throughout the generations; our parents never questioned loyalty to their parents, our grandparents never questioned loyalty to their parents, and so on.

I have had the opportunity to discuss this tradition with a significant number of Latino parents and asked them if they would do something for their parents that they felt was not practical, solely out of loyalty to their family. A large majority of the parents said "yes." When I asked them why they would do something that they did not truly believe in, the recurrent answer was, *"Por respeto a nuestros padres y familia."* ("Out of respect for our parents and family.") To not do what is asked of you by your family and culture is considered disrespectful.

While I consider myself a very loyal person, I recognize that a decision made solely for the sake of loyalty, with no consideration for practicality, can be dangerous. To help demonstrate the difference between loyalty and practicality, and loyalty for the sake of loyalty, consider the following hypothetical situation:

Jessica, who lived in California, had just graduated from high school and had been accepted to two universities. One of them was in her home city of San Diego, California, and the other was across the country in Pennsylvania. The two schools were equal in caliber, and both had offered her a full scholarship. Jessica had always dreamed of going away to college. She wanted to experience living in the dorms, joining college clubs, and meeting different people from around the country. However, her dad was adamant about her staying close to home, and she knew he would probably not allow her to go to college in Pennsylvania. When she approached her father about her desire to go to the Pennsylvania college, he said, "No, no tienes porque irte tan lejos. Aqui tienes escuela cerca de tu casa. Mejor aqui te quedas." ("No, there is no reason why you need to go so far away; you have a school here, close to home. You will stay here.") Jessica was distraught. She did not want to disobey her father, nor disappoint him, but she knew this was her only opportunity to go away to college.

What do you think Jessica should do? If Jessica were to make her decision based on the practicality versus loyalty method, she would create a list weighing why she should and should not attend school in Pennsylvania. The list would look something like this:

WHY I SHOULD GO
1. I will meet new people from all over the United States.
2. I will see and learn about things I would never have the chance to in San Diego.
3. I will become more independent and get to choose where I will live, who I will live with, and learn things about myself that I never knew.
4. I will get to explore the world and myself at my own will.
5. I will be living my dream.

WHY I SHOULD NOT GO
1. Dad will be mad at me.
2. Dad will believe I was disrespectful of him.
3. Dad and Mom will think I am not loyal to my family, because I left them.
4. Dad and Mom will think I don't love them.

If you go over the two lists, you will see that there are enough practical reasons in the "why I should go" column to determine that Jessica should attend college in Pennsylvania. Now that Jessica has thought this through, she could sit down and discuss her decision and the practical reasons behind it with her parents. She could explain to her father that she is not disobeying him and that she does not mean any disrespect toward her family or her culture. She could tell them that even though she would be physically away from home, her heart would always be with her family. She could reassure both her parents that she loves them very much and thank them for raising her to be a strong person in character and mind. Finally, she could ask for their blessing and hope that one day they would understand why she had to do this for herself.

On the other hand, if Jessica made her decision based on the loyalty, she would ignore the practical considerations and decide to go to her hometown college for the sake of her parents. You can guarantee that Jessica would later resent her parents for not allowing her to live her dream.

In a situation like Jessica's, what would you do? Have you ever truly wanted to do something that you knew was good for you, but your parents or family members did not agree? If so, try writing it down, using the practicality versus loyalty method.

WHY I SHOULD DO IT

1. _____
2. _____
3. _____
4. _____
5. _____

WHY I SHOULD NOT DO IT

1. _____
2. _____
3. _____
4. _____
5. _____

Then analyze your list. Do you have enough good, practical reasons in the first column to outweigh the second column? If not, then you must realize that there are not enough practical reasons to violate the loyalty to your parents. If that is the case, you may have to compromise, keeping in mind that this was most likely not the best choice for you now, or in the long run.

If you do have enough good, practical reasons in the first column, then you should consider what effect this action will have on you and your future. If you believe this action will benefit you, then you need to communicate with your family and try to establish a basis of understanding for going forward. Remember, the best solution will always balance practicality and loyalty.

Use the practicality versus loyalty method to help break away from the world of guilt. Realize that it will be difficult to create mutual understanding between you and your family, and it may take a considerable amount of time as well. Your family may not wish to compromise. Remember my situation. I decided not to live with my mother, but I promised to give her money and to stay with her on weekends. At the time, my mother felt this was the wrong solution; I, however, felt it was a practical balance. It took many years and many talks with my mother before she came to realize that this was the best solution to our problems at that time.

Respeto— *Respect Only*
Those Who Respect You

When growing up, my Latina friends and I were taught by our parents to be *mujercitas educadas* (educated girls). This referred to being educated in character and had nothing to do with actual time spent in school. There were unwritten rules of what an educated girl did and did not do. Aside from the common characteristics of being *educada*, such as saying *gracias* and *por favor*, the most important trait was *respeto*—respect for your elders, no matter what!

Recently, I asked a focus group of young Latinas whether they were taught the virtue of *respeto*. Without hesitation, they all yelled, "YES!" Carolina said, "I was taught to respect *a toda la gente mayor* (all older people). Laura agreed, "I was taught that I must respect all my elder relatives, even if they didn't respect me. My parents told me that in time my older relatives would learn to respect me, but I must do the right thing and show respect toward them, no matter what." The other girls agreed with Carolina and Laura and continued to comment on how answering back to any of their elders indicated a serious sign of disrespect.

I asked the girls what they thought about this virtue of respecting elders, even if they did not respect them. Carolina replied, "I don't even think about it, that's just the way it is." Laura added, "It's a family thing, all the elders help one another take care of the kids; therefore, the kids have to respect them as if they were our parents."

Laura brought up a good point. In the Latino culture, it is customary for the extended family to assist in raising, educating, and disciplining one another's children. An aunt, uncle, or even a cousin may have a say in the upbringing of a child. This multi-family discipline is often taken too far and can be devastating to a young Latina. Because Latinas are taught to respect their elders, no matter what, they are subjected to both mental and physical insults from their parents, and, at times, from any number of adult, extended family members, with no recourse. These insults violate the young Latina's self-respect and whittle away at her self-confidence. The end result: a young girl with very low self-esteem who begins to believe that it is appropriate and natural for an elder to mistreat her.

Many of our parents allow this tradition of *respeto*, because they, too, were treated this way and have come to accept it as normal. Therefore, they do not recognize the danger of this devotion. Cathy's story demonstrates the harmful effects that an extended family member can produce by using insults to discipline a child:

Cathy, who was fifteen, was at her Tía Monica's house helping to take care of her three little girls. Tía Monica was teaching Cathy how to braid her daughter's hair, but Cathy was having a difficult time keeping the braid tight; it kept falling apart. After the third attempt, Tía Monica got frustrated and yelled at Cathy, "¿Que no sabes como hacer nada? ¿Que tipo de madre vas a ser si ni siquiera puedes hacerle trensas a la nina? Quitate, Quítate, que no más me estás estorbando." ("Don't you know how to do anything? What kind of mother are you going to be if you cannot even braid her hair? Just move, you are in my way.") Cathy felt humiliated and insulted. She was taught never to talk back to family members, so she just lowered her head while tears rolled down her face. When Cathy got home, she told her mother what had happened. Her mother did not defend her, but just shushed Cathy by saying, "Ya conoces a tu tía. No le hagas caso." ("You already know your aunt, don't pay any attention to her.")

In this typical scenario from a Latina's life, Tía Monica had the right to discipline Cathy in whatever way she pleased simply because she was an adult. She took out her personal frustrations on Cathy, patronizing and insulting her unnecessarily. In the Latino culture, out of *respeto* for her elders, Cathy had no choice but to allow this punishment and emotional abuse.

The situation between Cathy and Tía Monica could have been resolved diplomatically. Cathy could have felt confident enough to say, "Tía Monica, there is no need for you to speak to me in that manner. It hurts me when you yell at me and insult me. Please do not ever speak to me that way again." Unfortunately, many Latinos feel that resolving the matter in this way demonstrates blatant disrespect to elders.

We were taught that another virtue of being a *mujercita educada* is self-respect. To me, this concept is contradictory. How can we maintain our self-respect when our culture hands adults the right to treat the young with contempt? The obvious problem is that the scornful behavior of our elders perpetuates a negative self-image, and therefore the possibility of loving ourselves greatly diminishes.

As Latinas, we must recognize these cultural barriers and break through them in order to define our own success. We must stand up for ourselves and refuse to be insulted by our elders. We must communicate with our parents and family members, and if they do not understand, then it is up to us Latinas to choose how we will or will not be treated. We must redefine *respeto* to mean "respect only those who respect you."

SETTING BOUNDARIES: WHERE OTHERS STOP AND WE BEGIN

"No" may be the most powerful word we ever teach our Latina youth, and it is a word many of us must learn to use ourselves. "No, I do not want to play doctor," "No, I do not want to get in the car with you," and "No, I do not want you to touch me there," are all statements we hope our little Latinas would say in the appropriate situation. If we teach our children to speak out and say "no" when they feel threatened, they will learn to protect themselves for the rest of their lives. This will prepare them as young adults to stand up for themselves and enable them to say things such as "No, I will not be spoken to in that manner," "No, I will not be disrespected," and "No, I do not want to sleep with you."

Saying "no" is the first step in creating our own boundaries. A boundary is a limit that defines us and separates us from others. It defines what we will and will not accept in our lives. Boundaries give us control over our decisions and let others know that we are in control of our lives.

It is critical that every one of us establishes our own set of boundaries, especially in relation to our family. Family boundaries will help us identify where the family ends, and we, the individuals, begin. Yes, we are part of our families and have a responsibility to them, but most importantly, we have a responsibility to ourselves. If we cannot take care of ourselves, then we cannot take care of our families.

Angela's Word

When Angela was very young,
Age two or three or so,
Her mother and her father
Taught her never to say NO.
They taught her that she must agree
With everything they said,
And if she didn't, she was spanked
And sent upstairs to bed.

So Angela grew up to be
A most agreeable child;
She was never angry
And she was never wild;
She always shared, she always cared,
She never picked a fight,
And no matter what her parents said,
She thought that they were right.

Angela the Angel did very well in school
And, as you might imagine, she followed every rule;
Her teachers said she was so well bred,
So quiet and so good,

But how Angela felt inside
They never understood.

Angela had lots of friends
Who liked her for her smile;
They knew she was the kind of gal
Who'd go the extra mile;
And even when she had a cold
And really needed rest,
When someone asked her if she'd help
She always answered Yes.

When Angela was thirty-three, she was a lawyer's wife.
She had a home and family, and a nice suburban life.
She had a little girl of four
And a little boy of nine,
And if someone asked her how she felt
She always answered, "Fine."

But one cold night near Christmastime
When her family was in bed,
She lay awake as awful thoughts went spinning through her head;
She didn't know why, and she didn't know how,

But she wanted her life to end;
So she begged Whoever put her here
To take her back again.
And then she heard, from deep inside,
A voice that was soft and low;

It only said a single word
And the word it said was . . . NO.

From that moment on, Angela knew
Exactly what she had to do.
Her life depended on that word,
So this is what her loved ones heard:

NO, I just don't want to;
NO, I don't agree;
NO, that's yours to handle;
NO, that's wrong for me;
NO, I wanted something else;
NO, that hurt a lot!
NO, I'm tired, and NO, I'm busy,
And NO, I'd rather not!
Well, her family found it shocking,
Her friends reacted with surprise;

But Angela was different, you could see it in her eyes;
For they've held no meek submission
Since that night three years ago
When Angela the Angel
Got permission to say NO.

Today Angela's a person first, then a mother and a wife.
She knows where she begins and ends,
She has a separate life.
She has talents and ambitions,
She has feelings, needs and goals.
She has money in the bank and
An opinion at the polls.
And to her boy and girl she says,
"It's nice when we agree;
But if you can't say NO, you'll never grow
To be all you're meant to be.
Because I know I'm sometimes wrong
And because I love you so,
You'll always be my angels
Even when you tell me NO.

—Barbara K. Bassett

My Boundaries for the Type of Man I Want To Marry

The boundary exercise below is intended to set boundaries for an intimate relationship. It could be changed to fit your particular needs. Please use it, treasure it, and check with it when you feel lost.

My Needs in a Man
These are the things that you must have in your man no matter what.

1. Honesty
2. Strong communicator (or willingness to learn how to communicate)
3. Very affectionate
4. Not intimidated by my assertiveness
5. Supports my quest as an empowered Latina
6. Similar values as mine

My Wants in a Man
These are things that you would like but can live without.

1. Treats me like a queen
2. Has same beliefs as I do

What I Will Not Accept from a Man
1. Disrespect

The following is the story of a Latina who has not yet set personal boundaries:

Diane was a wife and mother of three. She had spent most of her married life immersed in meeting the needs of each member of her family. She never had time for herself, and when she did manage a little time, she did not know what to do with it. When her youngest child was seven, Diane began to feel extremely tired and burnt out. She was having a very difficult time functioning on a daily basis and meeting her

2. Cheating
3. Violence
4. Abuse of drugs or alcohol
5. Demeaning women

What I Am Willing to Accept

1. Almost anything that is not in my "not accept" list

What I Am Willing to Give

1. Honesty
2. Lots of affection
3. Commitment
4. Communication
5. Respect
6. Support
7. Lots and lots of LOVE

What I Am Not Willing to Give Up

1. Time with my friends
2. Time for myself
3. My career

Usually, the "I Need" list and the "What I Am Willing to Give" list coincide with each other. Be careful not to ask for something you are not willing to offer, and vice versa. He should not ask you for something he is not willing to offer you.

family's emotional and physical needs. Within a short period of time, she began to feel very depressed. Not knowing why she felt depressed when she had such a great life, she decided to spend some time doing things she enjoyed. The more she thought about it, though, the more she realized that she did not know what she liked or enjoyed doing. Everything she did was somehow connected to making her children or husband happy; therefore, she did not know how to truly make herself happy. Feeling lost in her own body, she soon fell into an even deeper depression and eventually needed to be hospitalized and treated. Her

husband and children could not understand why Diane was so
depressed when nothing negative had happened in their family. They
were lost as to how to help her.

Since Diane had not determined the boundaries in her life, she was not able to distinguish where her family's needs ended and where her needs began. She was so preoccupied with her family that she did not recognize her own personal issues. In turn, her body and mind reacted to this self-neglect through sickness and depression.

Cases like Diane's are prevalent among Latinas who often get caught between what they feel they are obligated to do and what they feel is good for themselves. If we want to prevail, it is imperative that we set healthy mental, physical, emotional, and spiritual boundaries for every aspect of our lives. Otherwise, like Diane, we can get caught up in other people's problems, constantly worrying, and leaving ourselves little energy to deal with our own health.

Our ancestors did not have the choice to live emotionally healthy lives. Survival was their primary goal, and every action was taken as a group toward that objective. In survival situations, people work together, pooling their strengths in a team effort to better their chances of existence. This is evident not only in the Latino culture but in cultures all over the world. In ancient times, the concept of boundaries did not exist, and with good reason.

The future is here, though, and it is time for Latinas to help our culture evolve. We must embrace our individuality and learn to distinguish our own boundaries from those of others, especially those of *la familia*. Too often, Latinas find themselves trying to decipher what is, and what is not, their responsibility. Out of a desire to do the right thing and to avoid conflict, many of us end up taking on problems that do not belong to us.

There are always a tremendous number of questions in my Latina study groups when discussing boundaries. Someone recently posed the question, "Can I set limits and be a loving person at the same time?" The answer is "yes." You must take the time to nurture and take care of yourself. If you love yourself and are a happy person, you will spend less time worrying and have more time to love and care for others.

Another student asked, "What if my husband or my friends get upset or hurt by my boundaries?" It is likely that our families and friends will sometimes confuse setting boundaries with being selfish; therefore, we must be able to differentiate between the two, and discuss the differences. Relationships with families are so important, that, at times, we passively comply and ignore our own needs. If no boundaries are set, in the end we will find ourselves angry, unhappy, or, like Diane, physically and mentally ill.

Once we have set our boundaries, we must abide by them. Warning: people will test our limits in order to see how serious we are about them. Adhering to newly established positions is a difficult task, particularly for Latinas who often hold on to feelings of guilt and shame. However, it is important to release this guilt.

Isolation is another common fear among Latinas who believe that setting boundaries will separate them from the people who love them. Out of fear of being alone, many stay in harmful relationships. In order to combat this fear, we must be truthful with ourselves and open up to those who will support us. We Latinas need to expose ourselves to new teachings and information in order to overcome the negative images embedded in our culture about boundaries. Latinas need to build a network of support and realize that we are not alone in the fight against the old messages and against the guilt involved during the process of change.

I encourage all Latinas to set their individual, healthy boundaries and to find the courage to abide by them. We cannot change how others think, nor can we control their reaction to our new set of individual limitations. However, if the reaction is negative and people do not wish to respect your boundaries, you may wish to limit your interaction with them or choose to stay away from them for good.

7

Taking Back the Power That Belongs to Us

Believe in yourself—you are a beautiful Latina Goddess with more power and strength inside yourself than you can ever imagine. The only way you will ever know your true potential is if you take the risk of finding it.

Luz was a precocious little girl, full of hopes and dreams for her future. At just five years old, an age when most children are occupied with dolls and toys, she said to her mother, *"Mámi, un día yo voy a ser la presidente de una compania muy grande. Soy como mi pápi, tengo las ganas."* ("Mommy, one day I am going to be the president of my very own big company. I am just like my daddy. I have the will.") Luz's father was a successful entrepreneur, and although Luz was just a little girl, she aspired to follow in her father's footsteps.

Luz's parents were extremely proud of their ambitious little girl, who was always at the top of her class. For her tenth birthday, Luz's parents gave her many gifts, but the special one that stood out above the rest was a snow cone machine. Immediately, Luz set up shop on the sidewalk in front of her parents' house and began selling snow cones for ten cents apiece. Her little snow cone business fueled her dreams about one day running a real business and provided her with the extra confidence needed to succeed. Luz truly believed that she had the ability to accomplish anything, and this was reflected in everything she did, including schoolwork and extracurricular activities.

At twelve, Luz's body began to physically develop. Unlike her girlfriends, Luz was embarrassed by the attention her new curves attracted. She tended to shy away from boys, while her girlfriends, on the other hand, were completely preoccupied with the opposite sex. Luz began to notice the changes in their mindset. The girls didn't want to fantasize about their futures with her anymore. They told her that boys did not like girls who were overly ambitious. Day after day, the girls fawned over the boys, giggling and batting their eyelashes as they vied for attention.

Embarrassed by her friends' behavior, Luz continued to act independently. Her independence, however, eventually resulted in the loss of several friendships. The boys poked fun at her when she participated in class, calling her names like "Goody Two-shoes." After school, they told her she couldn't play sports with them because she was a girl. Luz turned to the few girlfriends she had left for support, but their only advice was to let the boys think that they were smart and strong—boys didn't like girls who competed with them.

Acting dumb and naïve to attract a boy seemed like a ridiculous notion to Luz. But, like most children, she just wanted to belong. Luz let go of her independent spirit and began to blend in with the crowd. During high school, she began to talk less and pay more attention to her looks. She acted coy around the boys, letting them think that they had all the right answers, even when they were wrong. Luz was no longer the outspoken, capricious little girl selling snow cones; now she was the pretty, popular girl with lots of friends.

Although publicly Luz had stopped discussing her thoughts of success with her friends, privately she still fantasized about owning her own company. At night, in her dreams, she envisioned herself running the company, holding meetings, speaking to people in public arenas, tackling all of the everyday office tasks and challenges, and enjoying the luxuries that success had brought her. Luz's dreams were still alive, but they had faded in her quest to fit in.

After high school, Luz went on to college and studied business. It was there that she met Thomas, the man she would later marry. While they were dating, Luz kept quiet about her aspirations, fearing her ambition would scare Thomas away. She wanted to wait until after she earned her business degree to discuss her plans. Then, she hoped, their relationship would be secure. She also felt that having a degree in business under her belt would help her gain the confidence she needed to obtain her goals.

Graduation came and went, and still Luz didn't tell Thomas about her future plans. She was too busy planning their wedding to let him in on her secret hopes and wishes. Shortly after their beautiful wedding celebration, Luz became pregnant. Halfway through the pregnancy, though, Luz began to get bored at home; she had nothing to occupy her. Finally, she decided it was time to discuss her career objectives with her husband. She told Thomas she wanted to start a business and that, with his help, she could handle both the baby and the company.

Thomas held strong opinions regarding parenting and believed Luz should stay home with their child until he/she began school. Luz agreed that one parent should be home with the child but argued that it did not have to be the mother. She felt that Thomas could alter his schedule to help with the baby. The dispute went on for several weeks until Luz, tired of arguing and not wanting to jeopardize their marriage, put her dreams on hold and agreed to stay home full-time with the baby.

When the baby, Carlitos, was three, Thomas told Luz he wanted another child. He wanted Carlitos to have a sibling close in age so that they could play together. Luz told Thomas that while she adored little Carlitos, he was almost in preschool, and this would be the perfect time to set up her business. Thomas was not thrilled with the news. A few days later, at a family gathering, Thomas put Luz in an awkward position, telling everyone at the party that they were going to try to have another child. Everyone was overjoyed and congratulated Luz for being such a dedicated wife and mother. Succumbing to the pressure of her family and husband, Luz once again put her dreams on hold to have another baby.

During her pregnancy, Luz began to have a recurring dream. She dreamt that she finally owned her own corporation and was happy and successful. She felt content in the dream until three men dressed in business suits appeared to inform her that she was no longer controlling the company. Brazenly, they told her that due to her lengthy absence it had been auctioned off and now belonged to new owners. In the dream, she pleaded with the men, explaining that she needed time to take care of her family, but they wouldn't listen, telling her that ownership had already been relinquished. "It's over," they said.

Every time she had the dream, Luz would wake up in a cold sweat with a pain in her heart. The nightmare continued throughout her pregnancy and for many years after, intensifying and becoming more realistic each time it occurred. Luz chose not to discuss the dream with her husband or anyone else. She kept the nightmare locked inside her soul.

Luz had her second child and life continued to roll on. Finally, the day came when Luz's children were both in school and she had time to herself. She began reading novels about powerful businesswomen and began to envision herself as one of them. She could still see herself running a company, yet now she pictured herself as a much younger woman. Luz felt it was too late, that she was now too old to start her own company. She thought she had lost too many years having babies. On top of that, she felt too tired at the end of the day after shuttling the children around and making sure her husband was fed to entertain her long lost dreams. Luz was giving up.

A few weeks later, after dropping the kids at school, Luz was driving through her old neighborhood. She pulled up to the house that she grew up in, got out of the car, and walked directly over to the spot of her old snow cone stand. She began to cry. Sadness rushed over her, leaving an empty feeling inside. The memories of her happy and fulfilling childhood enveloped her, and she cried out to God, "Why did you abandon me when I needed your strength to pursue my dream? Why did you let me give up my dream in order to please Thomas? Now I have no energy to start my life over, and no will to persevere."

In her mind, Luz heard the voice of the Lord answering, "You have received from me the gift of power, will, and strength to fulfill your dreams; it was your choice to misuse this gift. At birth, I bestowed upon you unlimited power to use as you pleased. That power was meant for you to live a full life, not to distribute among family and friends. Reclaim this power, and you will find renewed strength to pursue your dream."

The message was loud and clear. The power she once held inside was meant for personal use, not to serve others. In order to bring back the feelings of happiness, along with the confidence she once had as a child, she needed to use that power to take control of her own decisions. Luz held the reins to her life, not Thomas or her family. Overcome with energy, Luz drove home to share her revelation with Thomas. She prayed for his support, but even without it, Luz had made up her mind: she would finally follow her dreams.

Thomas was shocked when Luz confronted him with her news and her plans. He wondered whether he really understood this woman standing in front of him, frantically babbling about a company she intended to start. Was this the same woman that he had been married to for all of these years? He was speechless but deeply impressed by her conviction.

Hours passed as Thomas sat and listened to Luz explain the plan she had devised to regain her power. First, she made a list of all the people and things that were influencing her and her decisions. She listed her parents, children, friends, and also chores such as housework and grocery shopping. She told Thomas she would confront every person on the list and ask for support and help. She then tackled each of the chores on her list and discussed the household changes that would have to be made.

They reached an agreement. In order to free up some time for Luz, Thomas would now take on half of the family responsibilities such as planning birthdays, doctor appointments, etc. Luz agreed to dress the children and take them to school in the morning, but Thomas would bathe them and put them to sleep. They also agreed to hire someone to help with the children and the housework.

With this agreement in place, Luz began her company and her new life with Thomas and the children. She thrived on the challenges, loved running the business, and welcomed the changes in the arrangement at home. Thomas, on the other hand, quickly began to miss his old lifestyle. He longed for the days when Luz was waiting for him to return from work with dinner on the table. He missed relaxing in front of the TV with his wife at his disposal. He vocalized his frustrations and begged Luz to give up the company in order to have a normal family life like they had had before.

Angrily, Luz replied to his incessant whining, "For fifteen years I have lived my life for you and made my decisions based upon your desires. I put my dreams on hold to make you happy, and you never even thought twice about it. I was not happy living my life that way, Thomas. I have finally found myself, and I am not willing to give this up. I am not asking you to give up your life for me, like I did for you. All I am asking for is my fair share of life. You have your own personal life and career, and I want mine, too!"

After careful thought and constructive discussion, Thomas accepted Luz's career and realized that Luz, too, deserved happiness. Today, Luz and Thomas are both proud of her multimillion dollar corporation called "Taking Back Your Power," a motivational and inspirational training facility dedicated to teaching instructors how to facilitate empowerment seminars. Luz thanks God every day for showing her the truth that every one of us has the power to accomplish our dreams.

Miguel Lua

You used to work before you were married, didn't you, Mámi?

Personal Power: What Is It?

Each of us has power over our lives. We have the power to make decisions such as where we would like to reside and what type of career we would like to pursue. Most people, however, particularly women, misunderstand this power and do not fully utilize it. These people let others make their decisions for them and, as a result, lead unhappy lives. A person who recognizes her true potential draws on this power and uses it to make decisions for herself in every aspect of her life.

Personal power comes from within, and when you embrace it, you feel as though there is nothing in the world you cannot handle. It helps you recognize that everything in your life is a choice, and it reinforces the truth that you have complete control over each and every one of those choices. While we may not have control over the events that occur in our lives, we *do* have control over how we react to these events. You, alone, are in control of your destiny.

Negativity can impact our peace of mind. It can affect our outlook on life and cause us to make bad decisions. Negative people are all around us, and it is extremely difficult to avoid their influence. However, personal power will help shield out negative energy and help us maintain a positive perspective. Personal power is directly related to the love we have for ourselves; it is not driven by ego or material possessions. The more we learn to love ourselves, the more power we have to shape our own futures without being manipulated by others.

Personal power will motivate you to seek happiness rather than exist in and complain about an unpleasant situation. What may be good for someone else, however, may not be right for you. If the traditions that have shaped your life are stifling you, then you must draw on your personal power for inspiration so that you can create your own guidelines without guilt or the worry of offending others.

Before I recognized the strength of my personal power, I felt empty inside. Now that I have fully developed and exercised my power on a daily basis, I feel whole. I know now that I have no limitations, that life is a learning process, and mistakes are

Who Controls Your Life?

The following exercise relating to personal power can help you determine whether or not you are in control of your life. Think carefully, and answer each question honestly.

Please answer "yes" or "no" to each of these questions.

_____ Do you always follow the rules?

_____ Do you ever question the sensibility of rules?

_____ Is being viewed as obedient important to you?

_____ Do you feel guilty deviating from the rules?

_____ Do you find yourself engaging in soothing behavior when conflict arises?

_____ Are you unable to communicate your own frustrations or upset feelings directly?

_____ Do you feel you need to be in a romantic relationship to feel safe and secure?

_____ Do you have a low tolerance to being alone and enjoying your own company?

_____ Does having total financial and emotional responsibility for yourself frighten you?

_____ Do you feel you are *not* living your life to the fullest?

_____ Will you often do things you don't want to do in order to avoid disapproval?

_____ Do people's opinions about you concern you?

learning experiences. Most importantly, personal power has made me feel alive every day of my life.

TAKING BACK THE POWER THAT BELONGS TO US

If you answered "yes" to most of the questions in the box "Who Controls Your Life?," you are probably wondering how you lost your personal power or if you ever had any in the first place. No one took your power, because it cannot be stolen from you. Most of you have given it away to your families, your husband, and institutions without realizing you were doing so. If you had fully understood the value of your personal power, I guarantee you

_____ Do you have difficulty saying "no"?

_____ Is it very important that you do not disappoint others?

_____ Do you feel guilty when you disappoint someone?

_____ Are you persuaded easily?

_____ In a professional situation, do you have difficulty speaking out?

_____ Is it ever difficult for you to express a different point of view?

_____ Do you avoid being viewed as a wave-maker?

_____ Do you see being a wave-maker as being a troublemaker?

If you answered "yes" to three or more questions, you are probably allowing external factors to control your life (i.e., allowing people, places, and things to determine your life for you). If this is the case, you are not the master of your own life. It is said that no woman is free who is not master of herself. A person who is a master of her/himself is doing with their life exactly what they had wished for, including working a job that they truly love and having a mate who supports their choices. If these things do not apply to you, you are not the master of your life and not truly free.

would have never released it. Remember, it's never too late to regain your power; you just have to know how to go about getting it back.

Taking back the power that belongs to us means embracing the choices that directly or indirectly shape our lives. We can passively live our lives, accepting things as they come, doing nothing to change our situation, or we can be proactive, aggressively making decisions to develop and grow as human beings.

The passive approach ignores personal power. A passive person does not make decisions for herself and generally goes with the flow of life even if she is not happy with the direction. If we do not exercise our personal power, we become vulnerable to circumstances and to people. Passive people also tend to believe that they are not smart enough or strong enough to be in control of their lives.

Many Latinas take a passive approach to their lives. They have allowed themselves to be victimized by the belief that men will take care of them. Because of this belief, many Latinas have automatically handed their personal power and decision-making rights over to their boyfriends or husbands. This passivity creates feelings of inadequacy among many Latinas, who are then unable to make healthy decisions on their own.

In contrast, a proactive approach draws on personal power to help make daily choices, which may be as simple as deciding to go out for dinner, or as significant as whether to begin a new career. A proactive person aggressively pursues alternate directions in his or her life rather than going with the flow. Robert Anthony, Ph.D., a leading expert in the art of turning one's life around, describes in *How to Make the Impossible Possible* how choices affect our lives:

> In some way, either through conscious or unconscious choices, we set ourselves up for everything that comes into our life, good or bad, happy or sad, success or failure. This includes all facets of our life, be it business, relationships, health, or personal affairs. In addition, every choice has a natural result leading to further choices of a similar nature.

Every decision has an effect on your life and an impact on your general state of well-being. Latinas, you must realize it is not too late to take control of your lives. Start to develop and exercise your decision-making skills and adopt proactive attitudes. Stop passively complying with your spouse or boyfriend's wishes, stop being victims, and take back your personal power!

FAMILY POWER VERSUS PERSONAL POWER

How we perceive power, and our relationship to it, will determine how we interact with others throughout our lifetime. People who have been taught by their families to nurture their personal power grow into positive adults who demonstrate strength of character. These people make decisions from a position of power. Unfortunately, this is not the case for most Latinas, who have seen their mothers, aunts, or sisters abandon their personal power. These Latinas make decisions from a position of weakness, which will often generate an unhappy and unfulfilling life. Latinas must make a conscious effort to recognize their passivity, to change these learned patterns of weakness, and to gain self-confidence.

Family "secrets" can also negatively impact personal power. Many Latinas are taught not to discuss family issues with anyone who is not related to them, because that would disgrace the family name. To adhere to this code of silence, many Latinas have buried harmful secrets in their subconscious minds. In order for any of us to free ourselves from the burden of these secrets and to regain our power, we must expose and confront our family issues regardless of how painful they may be. This can be extremely serious; therefore, any delicate secrets should be discussed with a therapist or a close friend you can trust.

Our families have influenced us, but we cannot blame them for the outcome of our lives. We must recognize the obstacles they have created and take the necessary steps to get past them. We must heal the pain of the past; grieve, forgive, and move forward. Personal power is a tool for positive life enhancement that will gain strength when it is fueled by belief, desire, and hope. As you build your personal power, you will find it is much easier to take on new responsibilities and to tackle the important choices that life presents.

STEPS TO FREEDOM AND PERSONAL POWER

"Never rely on another person or anything other than yourself to determine how you live your life."

This statement is the basis of freedom and personal power, which go hand in hand. Freedom means living your life as you choose and having power over your own actions. Freedom is never handed to a person on a silver platter; it must be self-created for it to be true. People with true freedom and personal power are not enslaved by other people's expectations of them.

In order to begin the process of empowerment, you must believe the above statement and then adhere to the following five steps to freedom and personal power.

Step 1. Awareness   Become aware of who and what holds the most power over you. What kind of power do they have over you? How do they hold this power over you? Why do they have power over you? When do they exert this power over you the most?

Step 2. Understanding   In order to move on, you must understand why you allow others to have power over you. Remember that no one can have power over you unless you allow them to. Does being under their power make you feel safe and secure? Do you allow it so they do not get angry? Do you do it to feed their ego? To show them that you love them?

There is definitely a reward that you are benefiting from in allowing them to have power over you. Do you know what it is? The benefits could be anything from a feeling of safety to accepting the behavior in order to ensure that they love you. It is very important that you find the answer to this, so that this "reward" can be replaced with a healthy behavior trait. The benefit you are receiving for allowing someone to control your life is key to this process.

Step 3. Passion or Desire to Change   Unless you have the deep desire to take back your personal power, it will never happen. You will receive resistance from those who currently control you, which can make the process painful at times. Your passion for change is the only thing that will keep you moving forward.

Step 4. Strategic Empowerment Plan   Create a strategic plan for how you are going to take control of your life. A strategic plan exercise is demonstrated in the Resource section of this book.

Step 5. Implementation   Put your strategic plan into action. As you begin to take back your personal power, you will begin to feel more in control of your life. Eventually, your strategic plan will not be a plan anymore—it will have become your lifestyle.

Follow these five steps and feel the power that belongs to you!

Education Is Your Salvation

Education is a precious resource as well as one of the most important factors in leading a successful and fulfilling life. Not only does it open doors for better paying jobs, but it helps strengthen our emotions and prepares us to conquer life's challenges.

My mother claims that her life would have been different if she had received an education. When my mother was three months pregnant, she received a call from my father's mistress, informing her that she, too, was carrying my father's child. The news was devastating even though my mother was aware of my father's affairs. She had come to accept the fact that he was a womanizer, and she chose to ignore it.

I finally asked my mother in my sophomore year of college during a heart-to-heart conversation why she stayed with an unfaithful man. I could not understand why she did not leave him, especially in light of his illegitimate children.

"I couldn't leave him, because he was all I had," she said.

Disgusted, I said to my mother, "What do you mean he was all you had? What about you? You had yourself!"

"No I didn't, Yasmin," my mother answered. "When I married your father, he promised to take care of me, and I promised to take care of him and our future children. He said I had nothing to worry about, aside from the children, and I believed him. As the years went by, my life revolved around you and your sisters and your father. I believed he would take care of me forever, so I thought I didn't need an education. Then, I began to see a change in your father, and I knew his heart was no longer with me. I turned my back on his indiscretions because I didn't want to believe that this was my reality. I didn't want to believe that your father could hurt me. After the phone call from his mistress, I could no longer deny his lifestyle and infidelities. I wanted to leave him, but I couldn't. If I left your father, I could not provide my daughters with a good life. Staying with your father assured my daughters a top-notch education. Remember, Yasmin, I had no college education, no skills, and no money, and I did not know how to survive in this country without your father."

My mother took a deep breath and continued, "While growing up, I was taught that as long as a woman does her duties as a wife her husband will take care of her. What I did not learn was that the cost of this care would include having to swallow my pride, because I was dependent on an unfaithful man to feed me."

My mother's face looked so sad and distant as she continued her story, "Without an education, I could only work in a factory making minimum wage. How was I supposed to raise three girls on minimum wage? We would have ended up in a homeless shelter. I could not do that to my daughters. So I looked the other way and stayed with your father."

"*Mámi*, you mean to tell me that you tolerated fifteen years of infidelity and abuse because you did not have an education?" I asked.

"Yes, if I had been prepared, I would have left your father in an instant. But I was not educated, and I was forced to stay in an unhappy marriage because he paid the bills. So whatever you do, *mi hijita*, remember that a man is never your salvation. Your education is your salvation!"

My mother's heart-wrenching story has caused me to view education in a much different light. I realize today that an education is the foundation for intelligent life decisions as well as career decisions. It is imperative that children are given the opportunity to acquire the knowledge, skills, and values necessary to live rich and full lives as functioning, enlightened members of society.

We must start thinking about the future, because it is rapidly approaching. According to Lawrence Smith, by the year 2025, it is estimated that the average salary will be $176,000 per year. To earn a basic living salary, it is projected that a person will need to hold at least a bachelor's degree. Do not be overwhelmed by these statistics though. Every Latina has the opportunity to succeed and to secure her future if she takes a strong interest in her education, establishes a set of long-term goals, and develops a plan to accomplish those goals.

Short-term gratification or making decisions based on immediate results is a common deterrent of accomplishing future goals. Rather than looking ahead toward fulfilling an objective, many Latinas opt for instant rewards. For example, many Latinas choose to work full-time after high school graduation rather than continuing their education. The money from a full-time job is the short-term lure, but without higher education, long-term salaries can be much lower and even capped. Twenty years down the line, the opportunity to live a comfortable lifestyle may be impossible without a degree from a college or university, or technical training.

On the other hand, long-term gratification is geared toward accomplishing goals for the improvement of your future. Continuing your education directly after high school may leave you with no extra money for that trendy stereo system; it will, however, provide you with the education you need to obtain a much higher paying job in the future. With long-term gratification, your choices are limitless. As Sara Tucker, president of the Hispanic Scholarship Fund, says, "Education is the best way to give you choices in life. You want to be able to say, 'This is the life I choose,' rather than having your heritage determine your destiny."

We must have high expectations for ourselves and for our children in order to bring about higher achievement and success. Parents must support and encourage their daughters to further their education. Doing so will also help them achieve the level of respect they deserve. In 1999, during a "Latinas for Education" roundtable discussion held at Princeton University, White House Deputy Chief of Staff, Maria Echavaste stated:

> I get a certain level of respect, at least willingness to see what I'm capable of, whether it was in my corporate law practice or another setting, because I went to Stanford. I'm a minority woman, and the expectation, whether it's unspoken or subtle, is you're not quite as good. But, (if) you went to Stanford, you went to Berkeley, you practiced for a major New York law firm—you must have something there.

Now is the most opportune time for Latinas to attend college. America's top corporations, such as Microsoft, U.S. West, and the Gap, are actively reaching out to Hispanic college graduates due to the $348 billion purchasing power Latinos have in the United States. These corporations, as well as many others, recognize the need to market to Latinos. They want to hire Latinos who understand the needs of Latino consumers. As a result, many corporations are offering scholarships and programs to financially assist Latinos with their college education.

Finding the right college, university, or technical program takes a lot of research. *Hispanic* magazine published an article in March 2001 that lists the top twenty-five colleges and universities for Latinos. This list, along with contact information, can be found in an appendix at the back of this book.

Education is expensive, but there are organizations established to help with the financial burdens. The Hispanic Scholarship Fund, a national nonprofit organization that awards scholarships to Hispanic students, has created a Web site (www.hsf.net) that offers assistance to students. This site is designed to help people research universities to determine which one best suits their needs. It provides information regarding the university application process as well as the process for applying for financial aid.

It's never too late to go back to school. Utilize the references above to research the possibilities and investigate all angles of financial aid. Set goals, focus on achieving them, and choose your destiny. Psychologists believe that in order for a woman to have choices, she must believe she has alternatives. It is up to you to create your own alternatives, so that you never feel stagnant or stuck without a choice. Draw on your personal power to start making your own decisions. Let go of the past and look positively toward the future. If school is not appropriate for you, consider starting a new career or enhancing yourself in other ways. Write down your future goals and devise a plan to help reach your objectives. Look to your friends and family for support. Latinas, it's time to take back your power. Believe in yourself, and you can rule the world!

8

Every Child Wants an Empowered Mother

Evoking qualities, knowledge, insights, and inspiration . . .
empowering your child that way . . . is much better and stronger
than merely teaching them about something. Don't merely
teach—empower, from the inside, by example!

I met a young woman named Maria in May of 1999 at a leadership class I was teaching during a Latina conference at the University of San Diego. During the lunch break, I saw her in the quad, sitting alone under a tree. Engrossed in a letter, she was unaware of my presence as I approached her on that beautiful spring day. My voice startled her, and she jumped when I asked what she was reading. Maria swiftly folded up the pieces of paper, shoved them in her backpack, and answered timidly, "Nothing important." I knew from her reaction and the guilty look in her eyes that this letter meant much more than she was willing to talk about. Eager to have some company at lunch, I asked Maria to join me, and she agreed.

I was curious about the letter and kept thinking about it as we ate. Because of her reaction, I imagined it was something naughty or shameful. It had to be something extremely personal, so I was cautious about broaching the subject. Eventually, though, my curiosity got the best of me, so I asked her what was in the letter. She looked surprised and ashamed by my question, but slowly she began to talk about it. She said she had found the letter in a book she had checked out of the university library. The letter was written by a female college student to her mother, and it addressed various sensitive cultural concerns as well as mother/daughter issues. Maria said she felt guilty reading someone's intimate thoughts and emotions, like an intruder, but that she had to keep reading it since the content hit so close to home.

Maria really identified with the letter's author, and the words started to flow more quickly as she explained to me the parallels between her life and the life of the writer. Shocked to find another student who was experiencing the same exact issues she had with her own mother, Maria told me she had read the letter over and over again, hoping it would bring her the strength to write a similar letter of her own. Finally, Maria anxiously reached in her backpack and produced the letter for me to read.

Mámi,

I never ever want you to read this letter because I know it will hurt you. I wish I could tell you how much I admire your strength, your everlasting quality of always giving yourself to my sisters, my father, and all our relatives. You seem so content to always care for others, but how about yourself?

For me, *Mamá*, the story is different. I am engaged in "intellectual thought" that many times makes me feel good, yet sometimes guilty. I am afraid that this college education I have struggled so much to achieve will cause irreparable changes in my perceptions of womanhood. These new perceptions of womanhood are at odds with our traditions, and I am afraid that the differences in the way we express our femaleness may cause friction between you and me. I don't want to betray your teachings, but I feel that if I follow the female traditions of our culture I will perpetuate sexism by transmitting those notions of womanhood to my future sons and daughters. If I become like you, will I ignore all I have learned about patriarchy? Will I deny the monetary value of my household work once I get married? Will I serve my husband's needs without expecting the same of him towards me? Will my marriage work if I step out of the traditional wife role you taught me?

Mamá, at this point in my life, I wonder if marriage could exist without the servitude of the female. I sense that although legally it is a contract with equal responsibilities, in practice I have seen how you always give in. You were the only one who carried all the blame, as if it was a marriage where you were the only one that signed the papers and made the promises. Nobody ever condemns the man; it is always the wife, the one who needs to learn how to "trap" a man even when the contract of marriage has been signed by the man and the woman.

At the university, I have learned the definition of a contract, and when I get married, it will be a contract. That is, my husband will have equal blame if the marriage does not work out. *Mamá*, I am not willing to always be the one giving in and letting my needs be taken care of last. I am not afraid of breaking the traditions of marriage in our culture. I won't cook all the time, and I won't do the dishes or the laundry all the time. My husband will help me; the chores will be distributed equally, and the decisions will be joint decisions. As a result, I hope you won't remind me of the traditional ways or condemn the way I behave toward my husband. Most likely, you will be disappointed because I won't follow your example. *Mamá*, if I break the traditions, I will betray your teachings. You always cooked dinner; you always cleaned up the kitchen, did our laundry, and my father barely helped. When he did help, the work was never distributed equally. You were always the one who never stopped working.

Please do not think I am criticizing your marriage with Dad. It is just that I have watched you wear down and get wrinkles, watched your hair turn gray, while father looks fine. He has no gray hair, and he has time to exercise. I think that your laboring with the children, the dogs, and the chores has taken away your youth, beauty, and character. I don't want to look old and worn out at forty-two. *Mamá*, I have chosen the path of self-determination, and I hope you understand this once I establish my own household.

Mámi, when we discuss machismo in my class, I think about you. You were raised in a family that strongly emphasized the rights of the male. My grandfather never allowed you to go to college because he felt you were weak, *una mujer*. He argued that if in college somebody played a joke on you, he would have to defend your honor. *Abuelito* explained to you how problematic it would be for him to leave his office in order to defend you, but he never taught you to defend yourself or explained to you the value of an education. Since Grandpa never taught you how to defend yourself in a man's world, he either defended you, which he did not want to do, or you stayed home and learned how to mop the floors. Never did he give you the option of defending yourself, because of your gender.

You internalized the weakness they preached to you. You believed *Abuelito* and my uncles when they said people would disrespect you if you reared away from your role. You believed them when they lectured you about how a real lady's honor is protected by her father and her brothers. They never told you to pull it off by yourself; they did not want you to. You still believe you are stupid and weak. *Mamá*, you are not. It really hurts me when you say you are not intelligent but that you have experience. *Mamá*, you have experience, but because you are intelligent you can apply that experience. I get so upset in class when we talk about patriarchy, and it is so frustrating to know that you are a product of it.

Mamá, if I could change you, would you still be as sweet? You are sweet because you always took care of others first. I remember when times were bad, you would feed and clothe us first, and if there were any leftovers or extra cash, then you would eat or buy yourself the needed dress or shoes. *Mamá*, you always left your needs for last. I now realize that as your child it was to my advantage, but as a woman I know it was because you had no other avenues but motherhood to explore. Please do not think I despise motherhood. I think it is a hard and unsafe path, but I admire women like you who, with limited resources, bring up four or five children in the most loving way. Your sweetness was imposed on you; it is the only way you could be. Sweetness was your only defense and tool for survival. It is the only thing your parents taught you. They did not enhance your strength of character nor the aggressiveness you sometimes show. They curtailed these traits and forced you into being a subservient conformist, the dream wife for all your brother's friends! You did not have the options that I have now, and I resent myself because I was one of the beneficiaries of your womanhood. I resent myself, not only because I benefited from your self-denial, but also because I will never be able to make it up to you, to give you all the options your parents, your brothers, and society at large denied you.

Don't get me wrong; I really admire you, and believe me, I am proud of being of your blood. I just wish I could share with you my youth and strength and undo all the years of sexism you have experienced so as to show you my ways of womanhood. Going to college has given me the options and tools to define myself, to be myself. Education goes beyond mere monetary opportunities. These four years of college have taught me to be real, to believe in myself.

Sadly, oftentimes I feel that when a woman goes to college, she has to become part "male." It is almost impossible to finish college with your sexual identity intact. If you saw the competition and the treatment we receive! Not only are we sexual prey to most of the men, but we also have to become assertive and competitive. Many times, if you are a woman, you have to prove yourself to everyone because nobody believes you until you prove yourself. *Mamá*, you know how it is in our culture; women are not supposed to be outspoken!

Mamá, if I change in order to survive, will you still accept me as a woman, as your daughter? I promise you I will try to be sweet, to be understanding, to be caring and nurturing, just as you are. In this society, women have to become "masculine" to survive—or perhaps it's that survival strategies are considered masculine.

In college I have learned to be number one; I am the first priority to myself, and school is secondary. I am selfish and career-oriented, and this act of putting myself and my goals first is in conflict with your ways. I am split because I want to follow your example. I respect and admire you, but at the same time, school has made me so self-oriented that I realize I have learned to behave as my father does. I want to be like you, and at the same time, I don't. I want to care for my children as you took care of me, but I don't want to sacrifice myself as you did. I want to go to church, but I don't want the church to preach patriarchy to me. *Mamá*, I want a world where men and women are equal, where women can decide their own futures without having to worry about going to moral hell. I wish men could change their attitudes toward parenting, marriage, and religion in order to eliminate all the double standards that exist in our culture.

I realize I will never see the world as you do, so I will never be able to be like you, a saint. No, *Mamá*, men won't change, or they haven't, so the only way is for women to demand equality by using "male" strategies and learning to survive as "men." When I say to you that I am learning to be a "man," I really mean it, because I am learning to put myself first. Putting myself first is difficult because I have it engrained in my head that women should be like the Virgin Mary. However, being docile like Mary is impossible when you have to compete for grades.

I know that for you it was different; the circumstances were out of your control. Had you asserted your rights, your prestige, and your reputation as a woman, you would have been tainted, and one of the first insults would be *machona*. I don't condemn your abnegation; as I said earlier, as your child I benefited from it, but I wonder how much choice you had in deciding your ways. I think that only Latinas and perhaps Chinese women would understand what I am talking about when I say that school teaches us how to deny our cultural womanhood.

Mamá, please do not ask me to keep inside my feelings of anger and frustration when I see you degrade yourself because you are a woman. For example, when my father needs advice and you don't offer your advice because you know that he won't listen, it upsets me. It upsets me because you don't give validity to your ideas. Being a woman is more than what my *abuelito* taught you. It is true that part of being a woman might be bearing and rearing children, making tortillas, going to church, and carrying out the endless list of tasks assigned to us, by men, to please men.

Being a woman includes many other things, such as writing, singing, laughing, expressing our feelings in an open way, and saying what we think without feeling awkward. It is also about getting to know our bodies and accepting our femaleness, not as a tool to attract a nice-looking boy, but for ourselves. Being a woman is an integration of all these things; a woman is not complete until she can accept her feelings and herself wholly.

I know that to you, being deeply Catholic means being complete. This may sound like gibberish, but I wish I could convince you that the Catholic Church and almost all religions are sexist. Religion and, sadly, religious figures such as *la Virgen de Guadalupe*, have been used by priests (100 percent male) to seduce and manipulate the female psyche. I will respect your religion. I just wish we could talk about it without you thinking I am being blasphemous or, as you would say, *indigna*.

Mamá, I am not trying to change you. You are a wonderful person. I learned this when I was planning to leave home to go to college. It was in my senior year of high school when I saw your true colors. You were my ally, and you stood by me when my father tried to do to me what your father did to you; he was trying to keep me home because I am a woman, *una mujer*. It was great to see you talk back to him, scream at him that I had the right to pursue an education. It was invigorating! You were strong and powerful. You urged me to go away and continue my education.

You know, being away is hard, because I miss sharing with you. Still, *Mamá*, as I said before, I always think of you, especially when I am enjoying myself and my freedom. I wish you could be with me and learn with me. I wish I could bring you along as I grow up.

When we talk in class about family structure, familism, and especially motherhood, I think about you. I feel happy that I can incorporate whatever experiences we shared, as mother and daughter, into my "intellectual thought and development."

Mamá, I wish one day we could talk about my situation—that of constantly trying to redefine my womanhood according to society, our culture, the knowledge I have acquired, and your personal example. I am trying to be a woman in a "man's universe," and it is challenging. I hope that once I am out of school, we can share without fear of hurting each other what you feel about your womanhood, what I feel about mine, and together analyze the differences without you thinking that I am crazy, or an atheist, or amoral, or weird, or a "man." I hope that my college education never stops our flow of communication and understanding. I hope I never become antiseptic like some of the women I have seen around. I hope I can remain as sweet as you have always been without having to compromise my goals or my needs as a woman. You are a good person and a wonderful mother. I don't want these years of schooling to instill in me greed or the intense desire for money, success, fame, and all the other things for which many college-educated people struggle. I want to be as kind and caring as you are.

If Dad ever reads this letter, he will be hurt because of the way I portray him. Please tell him that I know he has been a victim of sexism as much as you have, because he himself never had the option of defying all his male friends and their code of behavior. Had he shown any compassion toward feminism, boy, would he have been called beautiful names!

Your daughter, who loves you very much,

Claudia

I finished reading the letter and sat quietly for a few moments, digesting the sentiments and the heartfelt emotions that Claudia had conveyed through her letter. I explained to Maria that she and Claudia were not alone. Hundreds of Latinas have expressed similar thoughts to me in focus groups and seminars across the country. I have also discussed similar situations with close friends and even experienced this with my own mother. So many Latinas view their mothers as role models, yet most would never want to be like them.

. The most common characteristic that emerged through conversations with Latinas, as exemplified by Claudia, is that they suffer watching their mothers in a subservient role while their fathers dominate the household. They do not understand why their mothers believe it is critical to keep their husbands happy, yet their fathers do not have the same concern for their wives.

In a recent focus group, a sixteen-year-old girl named Vanessa said that she had never seen her father working hard to make her mom happy, but her mom was constantly stressed out, making sure everything was right for her dad, so he wouldn't get mad. Vanessa said she had asked her mom why she was always scurring around the house straightening and cooking before her dad arrived from work, and her mom said, *"porque tu papá llega del trabajo cansado."* ("Because your dad gets home from work tired.") Vanessa asked, "What about you, *Mámi*? You work more than Dad, and you always look so tired. When you ask Dad to do something around the house, he gets to it when he wants and never stresses out about making sure you're happy." Sadly, Vanessa said her mother never answered her, and just told her to "shush" before her dad heard her.

Stories like these are common among Latinas all over the nation. Although many Latinas do not like their mothers' submissive behavior, they hold their mothers in high regard for their strength in loving and nurturing the family, for their endurance in keeping the family together, and for their courage to prevail in difficult times. They also respect their mothers for all of the sacrifices they have made and all that they have done for their children. I believe we all agree that Latina mothers can be the most loving women in the world.

Unfortunately, our mothers' internal strength is rarely used for self-improvement, and as a result, Latina mothers become victims of their families and of their husbands. Generally, young Latinas recognize the consequences of this excessive devotion to others, and they realize that, in the long run, nobody benefits. Statistics show, however, that, even if they are aware of these cultural precedents, they end up growing up to be just like their mothers.

Why does this happen? Why do we become our mothers when we can see that they embrace everything we are against? The answer is that we do not know any other way. Most Latina mothers say they want a better life for their daughters, but they can't show them what that life is. How are Latinas supposed to know how to create a better life for themselves when their only example is their mother? Unless we take an active role in changing our beliefs and our lives, we will inevitably continue the patterns of behavior we despise the most. The cycle will continue.

What Are We Teaching Our Mujercitas*?*

The most important time in a girl's life for developing a positive self-image and a positive view of the world is her childhood. Every *mujercita* (little woman) views the world through life experiences that are built on the foundation of her family. Experts generally agree that early intellectual and emotional development of our children plays a big role in their future success. Beliefs they accept as children are usually the beliefs they embrace as adults. The attitudes children form early in life become an intricate part of their development; therefore, it is difficult for adults to break away from the ideas and values of their parents. Mothers are generally their daughters' first role models; therefore, their influence is very powerful. I believe our *mujercitas* are born with unbiased views of the world and of how they should be treated in it. It is up to us, the mothers, to teach our little Latinas their significant place in this world. That truth should come before tradition.

Part of our obligation as mothers is helping our little Latinas find their identity and their inner strength. There is an adage that says a mother should not only be a person to lean on but a person to make leaning unnecessary. Mothers must realize that their *mujercitas* are not extensions of themselves but that they are individuals. They must be there to support their children and to shelter them from the destructive traditional beliefs of the Latino culture. They must foster a positive self-image and not impose gender roles on their children. They must give their children the freedom to stand on their own.

RETHINKING TRADITIONAL BELIEFS

Most mothers are unaware how stifling some traditional Latino beliefs are to their *mujercitas*. Let's take a look at a few of these beliefs, examining why they are destructive and how they can be corrected to help your *mujercita* become a healthy individual with her own set of values and beliefs.

Traditional Belief 1   *Mothers can take better care of children than fathers can.* Men are born with the same care-taking capabilities as women. The only thing that men cannot do, and women can, is breastfeed their children. This sexist myth is evident throughout the Latino culture and is exemplified by the letter from Claudia to her mother. Latino mothers take on full responsibility for the well-being of their children because they believe that their husbands by nature are not capable of helping. This myth places an enormous burden on the mother and causes a tremendous amount of stress. Child rearing should be shared equally between mother and father. If your husband does not know how to take care of the children, then teach him! Many men don't feel comfortable with children until they have had a lot of practice, so be sure to help them out on this point.

Traditional Belief 2   *It is good to take care of others before taking care of yourself.* It is unhealthy to ignore your own needs in order to care for others. This is one of the leading causes of depression among Latinas today, as discussed in Chapter 4. Ignoring your own needs can lead to mental and even physical illness. By teaching this myth to your daughter, you are sending the message that she is not worthy of receiving care from others. You are telling her that everyone else is more important than she is. You must recognize the importance of nurturing your own needs, along with those of your family. If you keep your mind and body healthy, you will be strong enough to attend to the needs of others.

Traditional Belief 3   *Loyalty to family should supercede loyalty to self.* Loyalty to one's self is necessary for an emotionally healthy life. By teaching your *mujercita* that she should be loyal to her family before herself, you are indicating that she is not worthy of loyalty. As discussed in Chapter 6, a person should consider practicality versus loyalty. She must determine whether loyalty to her family compromises her beliefs and whether it is practical in the long run. In order to be emotionally, physically, and spiritually capable of being there for her family, she must be loyal to herself.

Traditional Belief 4   *It is disrespectful to question authority.* Asking questions is essential in creating one's identity! It is not disrespectful to ask questions; it is an indication of independence and intelligence. An independent person does not rely on authority to define the world for her; she believes in defining the world for herself. She believes that what might be right for one person may not be right for another, so she questions what she does not know or understand in order to determine what is right for her. Encourage your children to ask questions. It will only help them grow.

Traditional Belief 5   *When you marry you must take your husband's last name; it's the law.* You do not have to take your husband's last name. You can keep your own name or combine the two and hyphenate them. Many young Latinas believe the law states that you must take a man's last name in marriage, and they never question this. A woman has a choice in this matter and in all matters of her life. Remind your daughters that every situation has at least two sides to choose from, even the choice of a last name.

Traditional Belief 6   *Children must carry their father's last name.* Children do not have to carry the father's last name. As a matter of fact, many children and husbands carry the wife's last name. When I ask single mothers who have been left without help from the children's father why they chose to give their children their father's last name, they usually respond, "Out of respect for the father." Respect? What kind of respect do men who walk out on the mothers of their children show? I don't think these deadbeat fathers are worthy of any respect. When a mother chooses to give her children the last name of a man who does not care about them, she is teaching her children that it is acceptable to respect a man who turned his back on his responsibility. She is teaching her children that although they barely knew their father, they should carry his last name because of his gender. Think about the negative connotations, and remember that you do have a choice.

Empowering Our Daughters to Embrace the World, Not to Fear It

Have you ever heard a mother say to her daughter, "*Adiós, mi hijita*, have a nice day, and be sure to take a lot of risks!" I haven't. Instead, it is always, "*Adiós, mi hijita*, have a nice day and be careful." It is human nature for mothers to want to protect their daughters from the world, and they will do everything in their power to assure their safety. When reasonably practiced, this inherent need to protect our *mujercitas* is healthy. Unfortunately, many Latinas as parents go to extremes, exaggerating the dangers of everyday life. They constantly tell their girls how terrible and dangerous the world is and, as a result, instill in them a deeply rooted fear of anything outside the confines of their community.

Fear is healthy in the sense that it keeps us alert to dangerous situations. It is our natural indicator, signifying when to exercise caution. If you are home alone at night, fear may cause you to take precautions such as locking the doors and windows. This type of fear is considered healthy and does not limit positive experiences. In the extreme, however, excessive fear can immobilize a person and keep her from living life to the fullest. If you are too afraid to stay home alone at night, then your fear is controlling you. This situation is very dangerous and causes people to become dependent on others to feel safe.

As Latina mothers, we are responsible for teaching our *mujercitas* how to conquer fear and how to protect themselves. We must provide enough support and strength of character for our children to feel confident to explore life freely. Naturally, this freedom will begin in moderation and will be determined by age and maturity level. But we must remember that if we shelter our daughters from the world too much, we will hurt them rather than help them. If our *mujercitas* are not wise to the ways of the world and are inexperienced before they go out on their own, they will suffer.

Girls who have had extremely sheltered upbringings are usually very naïve, and people are more likely to take advantage of them. Many of them will repeatedly suffer from broken hearts, and they will take very few risks. Although protective parents may vigorously try to shield their daughter out of love, in actuality, they have set her up to be a victim.

So how does a mother protect her *mujercita*, yet allow her to live freely? The answer is to teach children to embrace the world. We can either live in fear of the world, or we can embrace it. Living in fear limits you in every aspect of life. Fear will control every action and every decision you make. So often we hear people saying, "I should have done this" and "I should have done that." There are no should haves, would haves, or could haves. These people have limited themselves out of fear. If you let fear seize you, you will never truly experience freedom.

To embrace the world does not mean to be naïve about its dangers but rather to be aware of the negatives while experiencing all of the positive things life has to offer. Everybody has fears, but they should not stop you from moving forward. By embracing the world, you are embracing its challenges, losses, happiness, grief, joy, and pain. You begin to see challenges as opportunities, losses as lessons, grief as experience, and pain as growth. Your perception of the world will change and grow. By embracing the world, you will understand the true beauty of life—seeing, feeling, and experiencing love every day of your life. This is what we have to teach our children, our families, and our friends.

Twelve Ways to Teach Your Mujercita *How to Embrace the World, Not Fear It*

1. Enroll her in a self-defense program where she can learn how to physically defend herself. Feeling physically empowered is a very important element in a female's journey toward embracing the world.
2. Maintain complete and honest communication with her. Let her know that she can trust you with any questions or concerns she might have.
3. Strongly affirm that no one should ever touch her sexually or physically in a way that makes her feel unsafe—not even a family member. If they ever do, make sure she knows it is safe to tell you.
4. Give her all the confidence in the world. Tell her you love her ten times a day; tell her she is a good person and very lovable. Think of any positive characteristics she has and let her know about them on a daily basis.
5. Encourage her to take small risks, like running for class officer, being on a sports team, or trying a new hobby. Risk taking boosts confidence.
6. Give her strong spiritual guidance. It is very important that she believes in a higher power that will not judge her but support her at all times.
7. Teach her the value of education.
8. Explain to her the basic dangers of the world (those that apply to her age), and teach her how to avoid them.
9. If she steps into any of these dangers, assist her in dealing with the consequences. Do not take on the responsibility yourself; guide her through the learning process.
10. Teach her to believe that she is all-powerful, almighty, and able to conquer the world if need be.
11. Teach her to be empathetic to all people, irrespective of race, class, or gender.
12. Teach her that no one is better than she is, and that she is not better than anyone else.

9

The Courage to Change

Dramatic change can be attained if you risk more than others think is safe, dream more than others think is practical, and expect more than others think is possible.
—Anonymous

One cold and windy November day, I met up with some friends at a Carolina Panthers football game. My friend, Mike, had brought along his *compadre*, Carlos, who happened to be a U.S. federal judge. As we sat there and watched the game, Carlos and I began to talk. He asked me what I did for a living and what my future endeavors were. I was more than happy to share my goals, dreams, and vision for the future. He listened to me as I spoke, and at times he would nod his head as if to agree with what I was saying. When the game was over, we all went our separate ways. A week later, I met Mike for dinner, and once again the topic of dreams and goals came up. Mike asked me, "Do you really believe you can accomplish all those dreams you have?"

"Of course," I told him.

He mentioned that he and Carlos had gone out for a drink after the game and that my name had come up. Apparently, Carlos had made a comment to Mike about something I'd said. I could tell Mike wanted to tell me but was a bit hesitant. "All right, I'll tell you," he said after some prodding on my part.

"Carlos told me, 'Yasmin seems like a nice girl, but her ways of thinking are too idealistic. Her goals are unrealistic. She's young and doesn't know yet that many of the things she wants to do will never happen; she wants too much out of life.'"

I smiled when I heard what Carlos had said. This was not the first time I had heard these types of comments. Actually, I had been hearing them all my life. Mike looked at me and said, "Why are you smiling? I thought you would be mad."

"Why should I be mad?" I said. "There will always be people who will doubt my abilities to reach my dreams. Many people believe that when society says something is undoable, it is undoable. I don't allow that way of thinking to limit me. Just because something hasn't been done before doesn't mean that I can't do it."

"When did you start thinking that way?" asked Mike.

"I always have. When I was five years old, I established three life goals. Goal number one was to make history for women; goal number two was to save a life; and goal number three was to own my own corporation. At the age of twenty-five, my husband Norberto and I made history for women when he became the first NFL player to honor his wife's name as his own, putting it on his pro jersey. Out of tens of thousands of professional athletes, my husband and I are still the only couple who have honored women in this way. At the age of twenty-four, I saved a woman's life. Michelle, a sixteen-year-old girl, was addicted to drugs and had tried to kill herself twice. When she was brought to me, she had just been released from the hospital where they'd pumped her stomach, trying to save her from the overdose of pills she had taken in yet another suicide attempt. I took her into my home, flushed her drugs down the toilet, cleaned her up, and took legal custody of her. She lived with me until we found a good rehabilitation center that would admit her. She is now twenty-two, clean of drugs, and going to school. So, if you think about it, I have accomplished two of my three life goals, and I am only twenty-nine! My third goal will be completed when I start my own corporation, which should be within the next five years. Now you tell me, who is unrealistic?"

Quite surprised, Mike looked at me and asked, "How were you able to make these things happen?"

"I haven't *made* them happen," I answered. "They've just happened as a result of how I have chosen to live my life. I made a choice that, no matter how much it hurt deep down inside my soul, I was not going to live life through other people's expectations. It has been a huge commitment on my part to make that decision and then to live by it. I remember crying at times, thinking that my critics might be right about me. Maybe I *was* being unrealistic and too full of idealism. I used to ask myself, 'Could it be that these people know something about the world that I don't?' It wasn't until later that I realized that every time I wanted to do something that was out of the norm, I was criticized. I was confused. I wanted to live my life as I chose, but I also wanted desperately to be liked and accepted. So often, the way that I saw the world was in direct opposition to how a Latina is *supposed* to see the world. After a lot of thought, though, I decided that I needed to do what *I* needed to do—to live my life as I chose. I knew that I needed to connect with my courage, which would strengthen my heart and mind, helping to prevent other people's comments from determining my possibilities in life. Finally, I had to believe that I *deserved* to live my life as I chose."

Throughout the years, I have learned that if you take care of yourself and live in truth (rather than denial), opportunities to realize dreams and goals will come to you. It's just the way of the world. When you are truly ready to learn, the teacher will appear.

By definition, *courage* is having the strength to do what you know is right, despite fear, anxiety, worry, moments of indecision, weakness in the knees, and butterflies in the stomach. Courage is inside everyone, but sometimes we lack confidence; and although courage is an admirable characteristic, for Latinas it's a bit more complicated. In many cases, a Latina who takes the courageous stand to live her life as she chooses can be seen as being disrespectful—courage is supposed to be evident only in our men.

The new millennium is here, though, and many Latinas are becoming aware that the old ways are not working anymore. To some extent, these Latinas know they have courage, because they come from a long line of courageous women, women who have lived through terrible tragedies and pain. So what is it that holds Latinas back from exercising their courage in order to live more fulfilling lives? There are many reasons, but at the center of them all is fear. Fear of abandonment, fear of not being loved, and fear of being thought of as selfish or disrespectful; these are the core feelings that keep us bound. We are afraid to be judged as bad mothers, daughters, wives, and employees, so we hold on to a way of life that hurts us. Many times, we hold on to our husbands and adult children because if we let go, we wouldn't know how to feel. To be dedicated to oneself is not something Latinas are very familiar with. Therefore, our three most difficult challenges in changing our lives are (1) to truly believe that it is okay for us to love ourselves, (2) to heal our fears through a positive belief system, and (3) to let go of responsibilities that do not belong to us.

Women in general, and particularly Latinas, tend to take on everyone's problems as their own. It is important to understand that unless we let go of trying to fix problems that are not our own, we will never truly be free. Of course it is good and compassionate to be there for a family member or friend, to help someone through a problem or tough time. But it is another thing to make someone else's problem *your* problem. Unless we allow the people we love to work through their own problems, they will not learn the lessons that problems teach us. In every problem there is a lesson to be learned—let it be their lesson. Below is a poem that might help you understand what letting go really means.

> Let Go
>
> To "let go" does not mean to stop caring,
> it means I can't do it for someone else.
>
> To "let go" is not to cut myself off,
> it's the realization I can't control another.
>
> To "let go" is not to enable,
> but to allow learning from natural consequences.
>
> To "let go" is to admit powerlessness,
> which means the outcome is not in my hands.
>
> To "let go" is not to try to change or blame another,
> it's to make the most of myself.
>
> To "let go" is not to fix,
> but to be supportive.

To "let go" is not to judge,
but to allow another to be a human being.

To "let go" is not to be in the middle, arranging all the outcomes,
but to allow others to affect their destinies.

To "let go" is not to be protective,
it's to permit another to face reality.

To "let go" is not to deny,
but to accept.

To "let go" is not to nag, scold or argue, but instead,
to search out my own shortcomings and correct them.

To "let go" is not to adjust everything to my desires,
but to take each day as it comes, and cherish myself in it.

To "let go" is not to criticize and regulate anybody,
but to try to become what I dream I can be.

To "let go" is not to regret the past,
but to grow and live for the future.

To "let go" is to fear less,
and love more.

—Anonymous

Making the choice to change and making a commitment to stick to the process are the two fundamental principles in freeing yourself to live the life you want. If I had to sum up the secret formula of what it takes to change one's life, it could be explained in one phrase: *The willingness to do whatever it takes*. There you go, that's the secret formula. It sounds easy, but we all know it isn't. Having the willingness to do whatever it takes means not ever giving up in the quest for what you want. Of course, anything that is unethical or that may cause harm is out of the question.

Doing "whatever it takes" means that, even if your husband leaves you, you lose your job, your best friend dies, or you lose everything you have, you will not give up. Being sidetracked, lagging behind, or even taking a break is part of the equation; but doing "whatever it takes" is a mental attitude—one of commitment. When you realize that you deserve a better life, and you make a commitment to change, you will begin to attract the people and circumstances necessary to make that change. You will meet people who will encourage you to continue on your path, and you will notice circumstances that will affirm that what you are doing is right. For example, if you have made a commitment to break free of an abusive relationship, you may come across an ad in the newspaper for a support group for abusive relationships, or you might meet someone who has recently broken free from an abusive relationship. It's not as if these resources never existed before; it's just that your mind never focused on finding them. Once you commit yourself to something, you begin to visualize what it would be like to achieve it. If you visualize deeply enough, you can even imagine how good it feels! Your mind starts working, and you begin to attract people, places, and things that will help you to change your life.

Sue Patton Thoele, in her book *The Courage to Be Yourself*, suggests putting a three-by-five card on your fridge, mirror, or in your wallet that says:

> NOBODY SAID IT WOULD BE EASY! Too often, we hold the underlying assumption that things should be easy, that if we face difficult challenges, it means that we're somehow bad or the world is against us. With that victim attitude, we find it all too easy to crumble and never discover how strong and creative we really can be. Change isn't easy—ever. But if we avoid the difficulties in our lives, we never conquer fear. When we face challenges and win, or when we've overcome a fear, we experience wonderful feelings of accomplishment and mastery.

The greatest rewards in life come from taking risks and from taking on the challenge of being the best possible person you can be, for yourself first, and then for the rest of the world. Remember that you already have the courage inside yourself; you just need to connect with it. Try the following steps.

TEN STEPS FOR TAPPING INTO YOUR COURAGE

1. Think of a specific incident in your life in which you acted courageously, despite the fear you were feeling, or when you did something you had to do even though you lacked confidence in your ability. Write down that experience.

   _____

   _____

(Whether your experience was a success or not is irrelevant to this exercise. It is just the feeling of courage we are trying to connect with.)

2. It is extremely important that you recapture the incident in your mind. Take time to visualize the exact moment you acted, despite your fear. For the next three to five minutes, close your eyes and relive that moment of courage. Where are you? What does it look like? How do you feel?

_____

_____

3. Begin to identify what part of your body your courage originates from. Place both hands on this area.

4. Take two deep breaths and feel the power of your courage inside your body. Your courage might be powerful enough to make you want to cry or scream, or you may stay very silent. If possible, let yourself express whatever it is you are feeling. If you feel like crying, cry; if you feel like screaming, scream. Whatever your automatic reaction is from feeling your courage, let it come out.

5. Recall a time when you wanted to be courageous, but just couldn't. Why couldn't you? What were you afraid of?

_____

_____

In your deepest heart of hearts, you know exactly why you decided not to use your courage, and what you were afraid of. Take some time to think about it, and write it down.

_____

_____

6. What is the worst thing that could have happened if you had used your courage? What is the best thing that could have happened if you had used your courage?

_____

_____

Remember, sometimes the benefits of courage are not seen immediately; they become evident later. One thing I can guarantee: the more you use your courage, the better you will feel about yourself and the further you will be in your pursuit of happiness.

7. Close your eyes, and go back to the incident. See yourself and your courage giving you the strength to face your fear. What are you doing? How are you acting? How are you feeling?

_____

_____

8. Write down everything you feel about being connected to your courage.

_____

_____

9. Note how courage is truly part of who you are. Although it can appear when we least expect it, it also can be retrieved when we choose. Using our courage is a skill—when practiced, it becomes stronger and stronger.

10. By continuously working the steps above, you will strengthen your ability to act with courage. If you have a difficult time connecting with your courage, you may be experiencing an emotional blockage that is not allowing you to tap into your inner self. There are many different therapies to aid in this process.

Learning How to Love Yourself

I remember the first time a therapist asked me to look in the mirror and say, "I love myself." I told him, "I'll say it, but I won't mean it." I blurted the words out, and a tear came running down my face. I really didn't know how to feel, and it was a little bit scary.

Loving yourself doesn't have much to do with your outer appearance. I have known some very beautiful and glamorous women who hated themselves. To love oneself is to take care of oneself—emotionally, physically, and spiritually. Loving yourself means loving the self you are today, not yourself twenty pounds lighter or twenty pounds heavier. Most importantly, loving yourself means never, ever criticizing yourself, because self-criticism locks you into a pattern of self-destruction.

There are many different exercises you can embrace and practice in order to begin the process of self-love. The following is one that has been most effective in my own transformation.

INNER-CHILD WORK

I believe the true source of self-love is through your inner child. Many of us have an inner child who is hurting, frightened, and feels abandoned, and, sadly, often the only contact we have had with our inner child is to criticize her. We cannot abandon a part of ourselves and still be happy. Part of loving oneself is to heal inner wounds and fill inner voids so that we are whole and connected.

1. Find a photograph of yourself as a five- or six-year-old child. Look at the picture and try to remember what you were feeling when the picture was taken. Look closely into her eyes. What do you see? Happiness? Sorrow? Fear? Anger? Look at the "little you" and connect with her inner emotions. How does she feel? Write a few words about your inner child.

   _____

   _____

   _____

2. Looking at the picture, can you see yourself in her? How do you feel right now, looking at this picture of "little you"?

   _____

   _____

   _____

3. Close your eyes and envision the girl in the picture. Talk to her, and ask her any questions that come to you. If you listen carefully, she will answer you. Write down her answers. Some examples of questions to ask might be:

What do you like to do? _____

_____

What don't you like to do? _____

_____

What scares you? _____

_____

How can I help you feel safe?   _____

_____

Will you trust me to help you? _____

_____

If I promise to protect you, will you let me? _____

_____

Try your best, strange though it may seem, to have a deep conversation with your inner child. Be there for her and protect her. Love her with all your heart, and embrace her in your arms. Promise her that whoever hurt her in the past will never hurt her again, and make sure you keep that promise. Although you can never recreate your childhood happiness, you can create your adult happiness.

MY EXPERIENCE WITH INNER-CHILD WORK

When I began my own inner-child work, through the exercise above, I closed my eyes and saw a little five-year-old girl, sitting across the street from the house I grew up in. She was sitting on the curb, looking down at the ground. As I approached her, she looked up at me; sadness and grief overshadowed her beautiful eyes. I could see her pain, and I could feel her agony. As I tried to reach for her hand, she jumped up in fear. At first, she didn't want to come with me—she said her dad would get angry if she left and would later find her and hurt her. I told her that I was there to protect her and to make sure that he never hurt her again. She jumped into my arms, held me tight, and whispered in my ear, "Please don't let him hurt me, please!"

I broke down in tears and sank to the floor. For the first time in my life, I had met the "little me," the one who was holding all the pain, fear, and terror I had been feeling for so many years. There was a part of me that was dying, and I didn't even know it existed. From that day forward, there has never been a day that I've felt alone.

AFFIRMATIONS

For this next exercise, write down ten things you like about yourself. "I am caring" or "I am lovable" are examples. If you can't think of ten things, ask your family and friends what they feel is positive about you. Next, place this sheet of paper somewhere you can see it every day—in your bedroom, bathroom, car, or purse. Make sure you read these affirmations out loud at least once a day. The more you say them, the more you'll feel them, and the more you'll believe them.

Add the list of affirmations below to your own affirmation sheet. Read these affirmations every day until they become part of who you are. Do not memorize them; instead, try to really feel them when you read them to yourself.

1. No one can ever destroy my spirit, my soul, my being!
2. My true empowerment comes from the inside; I must be connected with it.
3. I can rise above any problems put before me.
4. I am in charge of my own life.
5. I make my own decisions and assume the responsibility for any mistakes. I learn and grow from my mistakes.
6. My emotional well-being is dependent, primarily, on how I love myself.
7. I deserve to be treated with consideration and respect.
8. I am as important as any person in the world.
9. As I change my thinking, I change my life.
10. Today I will be the master of my emotions.

11. My actions always speak louder than my words.
12. I carry myself with dignity.

Men Love Women Who Love Themselves

Until a woman has given herself permission to be spectacular, she will not find herself with partners who encourage her to be spectacular. As long as she tears herself down, she will attract others who tear her down; she will find people who agree that she is undeserving and lacking as long as that is how she thinks of herself.

If you remember one thing about men, remember this:

MEN WILL TREAT YOU THE WAY YOU ALLOW THEM TO TREAT YOU.

If you do not respect yourself, how can you expect a man to respect you? Why should he? You cannot ask someone to give you something, or do something for you, that you are not willing to do for yourself.

A woman who loves herself is an empowered woman; she can take care of herself, no matter what. An empowered woman chooses a man because she *wants* to be with him, not because she *needs* him. There is a big difference between the two. The woman who chooses to be with a man is a woman who knows she will be fine without him. That doesn't mean that she won't hurt if he leaves. (She might even be temporarily devastated.) It just means that after she grieves his loss, she will get right back up and continue making her life the best it can be. The empowered woman understands that if one man can't appreciate what she has to offer, then someone else will. She will see her relationships as a learning experience from which she can grow.

A woman who is with a man because she needs him is a woman who will suffer unnecessarily. She believes she'll never again be happy if he leaves, and because she feels this way, she will tolerate anything he puts her through. She will literally do anything to keep him. Usually, these women are used and abused by men.

A woman who loves herself is not a conceited woman. She doesn't believe she is better than anyone else or that she deserves certain privileges because of who she is. The truth is, conceited women usually act the way they do because of their insecurities, especially if they feel a need to put everyone else down to bring themselves up.

An empowered woman has a clear, indisputable sense of her power and her worth. She knows and understands what she brings to a relationship, and she knows what she deserves in return. She knows when to be gentle and when to be tough. The hard work she puts into her relationships is rewarded because she is getting back as much as she is putting into it. An empowered woman knows and respects who she is, and because of this inner knowledge she is in control of herself and her life.

The following is a list of things a self-loving, empowered woman knows about herself, her relationships, and men, from *Men Like Women Who Like Themselves* by Steven Carter and Julia Sokol:

AN EMPOWERED WOMAN KNOWS . . .

. . . if she wants a man to love her like crazy, she needs to love herself like crazy first.

. . . how to take care of herself without sacrificing her partnerships, and how to take care of her partnerships without sacrificing her soul.

. . . how to always keep at least one foot firmly planted on the ground.

. . . men like women who build bridges, not walls.

. . . when she receives a phone call from a man, that is exactly what it is, just a phone call.

. . . men like women who are so confident of what they have to offer, they never have to try too hard.

. . . she's not going anywhere if she leaves herself behind.

. . . she always wants to be remembered for who she is, not how she looks or what she's wearing.

. . . men like women who look like they have someplace to go.

. . . if she does not value who she is and what she has to offer, don't expect that anyone else will.

. . . if she is seriously prepared to give it all up for the man she loves, she's living in the wrong century.

. . . how to say "no," even when her body is screaming "yes."

. . . how to say "no," without saying "never."

. . . men like women who don't give mixed signals.

. . . men like women who are sensitive to their interests, their plans and their friends.

. . . men like women who don't audition for wife on the first date.

. . . when a man is pushing all her buttons, and she doesn't let it push her to the edge.

. . . neediness will often turn a good guy off and a bad guy on.

. . . she doesn't make herself available to the world when she needs to be taking care of herself.

. . . the difference between the man who likes women and the man who takes advantage of women.

. . . the difference between the man who wants her in his life and the man who wants her for the night.

. . . men like women who don't become obsessed with them.

. . . it's never smart to give away all her power, and it's never smart to usurp all his power, either.

. . . the only thing she can truly count on is that there is very little that she can count on.

. . . the difference between wanting to break up and wanting time alone.

. . . if she's a little bit jealous, a man can feel flattered. If she's excessively jealous, he may think it's time to call the witness protection program.

. . . men like women who aren't afraid of silence.

. . . she has the courage to draw a line in the sand without worrying about spoiling everyone's day at the beach.

. . . men like women they can't take advantage of.

. . . she doesn't have to answer the phone just because it rings.

. . . it's never smart to settle for less than she deserves.

. . . she is energy efficient; she saves her energy for the people who want to light up her life.

. . . it is good to give her man positive reinforcement.

. . . a man likes a woman who can tell him what's wrong without blaming it all on him.

. . . it's not smart to talk or act like a victim.

. . . the time to talk about problems is when she first notices them.

. . . she does not get what she wants by starting an argument.

. . . she must accept responsibility when she is wrong.

. . . just because her family did it doesn't mean it's fair; just because her family did it doesn't make it right.

. . . the difference between having a disagreement and tolerating abuse.

. . . trying to live with an uncommunicative man is like trying to live with a pet rock.

. . . how to make every decision an informed decision.

. . . there are only two times when she can issue an ultimatum to a man: when she is prepared to back it up, and when she is prepared to back it up.

. . . her worth is not measured by the size of her paycheck.

. . . bringing home the most money shouldn't make anyone the boss.

. . . commitment is a process, not a piece of paper.

My girlfriends are always telling me, "There are no good men out there," and my male friends are always telling me, "There are no good women out there." I believe that there is an abundance of good men and women in this world, but in order to attract a good man or woman, you need to be a good woman or man first. Being a good man or woman is simple, yet it's not easy. The most important rule is that you must only ask of your mate that which you are willing to offer—no more, no less. This shouldn't be taken in a totally literal sense—you can't, for example, ask your husband to become pregnant! Instead, he can promise, and fulfill the promise, to be supportive in the process of your pregnancy and delivery. It is a give-and-take situation; sometimes you give more to the relationship, and sometimes he gives more, but in the end it evens out.

A DECLARATION TO YOURSELF

Many times, when we want to change something about ourselves, we visualize in our minds how that change will look; rarely, though, do we visualize the process it will take to get us to the end result. Although the courage to visualize change is powerful, what we do to realize that change is where our power lies. Just as we declare our wedding vows to our mates and make commitments to our jobs and families, we need to declare a commitment to ourselves. We uphold our wedding vows because they are sacred to us; we also need to uphold our vows to ourselves because these are the foundation for all of the other vows we will make in our lifetime.

The first step is to write down the things you must do to create the change you want in your life. This might include a change in attitude, an assertiveness training class, more time alone, or any other thing that will contribute to the changing process. Every person has different ways to accomplish her goals. If you are not yet sure what you need to do to create change, write down what you think you must do, then make corrections as you think of them. My friend April wanted to become more assertive in saying "no." She was always overcommitting herself to people out of guilt. Her declaration to herself consisted of ways to help her connect with her courage—to say "no" without feeling guilty.

I understand and believe that I am the most important person in my life. I need to do things that make me happy because I deserve to be happy. I will learn to say "no" to things that I don't really want to do or choose not to do. I need to do this because if I don't I will be angry with myself and feel miserable about myself. I don't want to feel miserable or angry because these feelings rob me of feeling good about myself and about life. I will be honest with others about my feelings because if

I am not, it will cause me feelings of guilt, and guilt is pain. I will not be afraid of being honest, even if it might hurt someone's feelings, because as long as I am honest, I cannot be hurtful. It is when I am dishonest that I am truly being harmful because I am not being real; I'm being a fraud. I will practice my assertiveness and courage exercises every day, so that when the time comes for me to say "no," I will be ready. I will thank God every day for giving me the strength to conquer my fear of saying "no." I will love myself every day, and I will show my love by honoring this declaration.

Once you have created your own declaration, honor it every day. Remember, the first person you need to answer to is yourself. Everything else will fall into place if you live your life empowered with self-love. Take the time to look inside yourself; find the woman you want to be and help her come out. I guarantee that if you build your own life and truly believe in your own unique qualities, the good things in life (including the good men) will start coming your way. The way you feel about yourself radiates outward. And not only will you feel self-nurtured and loved, you will feel in control of your life and your destiny. Now who wouldn't want a woman like that?

10

Parallels Between the Latino Culture and the National Football League

There is only one success—to be able to spend your life in your own way.
—Anonymous

Life is rarely predictable—when I first began college at the University of Southern California, I vowed never to date a football player or a fraternity member. Then I learned never to judge a book by its cover; it happened that Norberto, my husband-to-be, was both!

We became acquainted in 1993, when we both lived within a few blocks of the university and rode University Transit to school. Quite a few people saw the potential before we did—Francisco, the transit driver, told each of us independently how wonderful the other was. He had been a USC driver for twenty-two years and claimed to know a love match when he saw one. Without our knowledge, Francisco told each of us that the other had expressed interest in exchanging telephone numbers. At first, each of us waited for the other to make the first call, despite the daily harassing by our friends. I guess we were both shy. After a few weeks, Norberto and I bumped into each other and finally began a conversation. We actually ended up teasing each other for not calling and promised to talk again soon. That very same night, Norberto called me and we spent six hours chatting, speaking as if we had known each other for years. During the next few months, we learned more about each other and realized how right Francisco had been.

In October 1994, my friends and I went to the Coliseum for the annual USC versus Oregon State football game. All week, my friends had been calling to make sure I would attend, something that was a bit odd since I rarely missed a game. On game day, just after the end of the fourth quarter, with 60,000 people in the stands, the USC marching band began to play the wedding march. Someone told me to look over at the scoreboard, where big, bright letters read: "Yasmin, I love you. Will you marry me?" There were fireworks exploding and, in a daze, my friends walked me down to the field where Norberto was waiting for me with my engagement ring. Security guided me to the center of the field; Norberto got down on one knee, told me how much he loved me, and asked me to spend the rest of my life with him. I was astonished. I looked up and saw thousands of people cheering us on, screaming, "Say yes! Say yes!" I looked over at the big stadium TV screens and saw my tear-streaked face. Never in my wildest dreams had I imagined that my marriage proposal would be like this. Norberto was too shy, or so I thought! I said "yes," and he slipped the ring on my finger.

Two years later, in 1996, the USC football team won the division championship and clobbered Northwestern University at the Rose Bowl. Having graduated the previous year, I was working for Philip Morris, Inc., and Norberto and I were very happy. Everything seemed perfect! Life was full of potential—Norberto had been drafted by the NFL; his dream had finally come true. I was very excited; friends of ours like Angie and Tony Boselli (Jacksonville Jaguars) and Felicia and Derrick Deese (San Francisco 49ers) were already living the NFL life, and they were still as sweet as they'd been in college. The fame and fortune had not changed them at all. I also felt comfort knowing that Norberto was not entering this new world of the NFL alone; two other USC football buddies of his—Keyshawn Johnson (Tampa Bay) and John Michels (former Green Bay Packer)—were also up for the draft. Norberto and I happily anticipated a new life of fame, fortune, and unforgettable moments.

However, it didn't take me long to find out that although the NFL does offer all of the above, it's at a very high price, a price I was not willing to pay. Instead of taking me forward in time, life as an NFL wife took me back to situations and ways of thinking that I had worked very hard to avoid. Everyone around me expected me to devote every moment of my time and every iota of my energy to my husband. I had never lived in anyone's shadow! Instead, I had struggled to conquer the limitations imposed on me. I thought I was now free to live the life I chose, but in the NFL there are no choices—either you're in or you're out. Players and their wives must play by team rules and by those rules alone. The truth is, if you don't like the rules, there is always someone dying to take your place. My husband needed my support; I knew how much this meant to him, so I had two choices: learn to play the role of an NFL wife or create a role for myself where I could offer support to Norberto without sacrificing my soul doing it.

The expectations of an NFL wife and the expectations of a traditional Latina wife mirror each other in an uncanny way. Wives in both arenas are expected to be very traditional. Contrary to what most people think, NFL wives rarely have nannies to take care of their children or a cleaning staff to take care of their home. It's not that the wives can't afford help; it's that, in the world of the NFL, value is placed on a wife who takes care of her own children and home. The mentality is that an NFL wife does not have to work; she does not have to do anything, so the least she can do is take care of her family.

Mentalities vary, of course, between teams and cities; each NFL team has its own culture. In Charlotte, North Carolina, the Carolina Panther wives were extremely conservative; in Phoenix, the Arizona Cardinal wives were very different: more down to earth, with more liberal views on everything from child raising to women's rights. Any way you look at it, the life of an

NFL wife has its privileges and its drawbacks, and although there was a time that I felt great anger towards the NFL, I am grateful for the experiences and the opportunities it has provided me.

My Life as an NFL Wife

Being an NFL wife has been one of the hardest jobs I have ever had. There are benefits, of course, to being part of the NFL sphere, including money, status, and access to "famous" people. Different wives might have different experiences, but one thing I am certain of is that we, the wives, are expected to live our lives completely around our husbands' careers. Many wives seem to be content with this kind of partnership; and, in truth, it's a great life for women who do not want careers of their own. In my five years as part of the NFL, I have never met another wife with her own professional career—although I've heard vague rumors about such things! In light of that fact, it's important to remember that the experiences I offer here are not typical of an NFL wife.

It all started on April 22, 1996, NFL draft day—the long-anticipated day that would determine my husband's future career. Little did I know that it would determine *my* future, or rather, it was *supposed* to dictate my future if I had followed the blueprint. We woke up early that morning and headed to Norberto's agent's house to watch the draft. The anxiety level around the house was high; everyone was nervous, and no one said a word. Before this very important day, I had made a conscious decision never to allow football to rule our lives, to dictate our happiness. I knew there were going to be many ups and downs in this business, and I was going to have to be the one to level out life for my husband when things got rough—like on draft day. Whatever was going to happen that day, I was ready.

As we arrived at the agent's house, along with Norberto's parents and my mother, we heard him speaking on the phone, making a deal with a team. A moment later, the agent announced the news: Norberto had been drafted by the Carolina Panthers. My mom and I rushed to the map to see exactly how far it was from Los Angeles: 2,225 miles—a forty-hour drive or a five-hour flight.

I had always been a very independent woman, always believing that I would create my own destiny. I never expected handouts; I never expected life to be easy, but I did always expect that I would live my life the way I wanted. I knew that once I got married I would have to compromise with my husband—we would come to agreements together. But with the NFL, there seemed to be very little room for compromise. Being part of the NFL meant that they dictated where we would live, where we would raise our children, where we would create our life. What's more, they had the right to change their minds any time they pleased. Team player contracts only work one way—a player cannot leave a team until his contract is up, but the team can cut a player any time it chooses. It reminded me of the *respeto* issue in the Latino culture—a one-way street. A player could be picked up by a team, he could sign a three-year contract, move his family cross-country, buy a home, put his kids in school, and then be cut a few weeks later. If this happened, he would become a free agent, and any other team could pick him up and do the same thing! There are never any guarantees in the NFL.

I arrived in Charlotte in August 1996. Since my husband was in football camp, I had brought my mother and a friend to help me move in and get settled. Somehow or other, I told myself, I was going to make this work. The first thing I noticed when we arrived at the airport was that there wasn't another Latino in sight; everyone was either Caucasian or African-American. Growing up in Los Angeles, I was used to great ethnic diversity, but in Charlotte there were no Indians, no Pakistanis, no Native Americans, no Koreans, just African-Americans and Caucasians. I had experienced culture shock before, but this was extreme; and although it wasn't long before I decided that Southern people were some of the nicest people I'd ever met, what I couldn't figure out was whether it was genuine, or if it was because my husband was a Panther.

My mother and I went to the grocery store looking for *tortillas de maíz y La Opinión* (corn tortillas and *The Opinion*)—or at least Carolina's version of *La Opinión*. We couldn't find anything even distantly related to our Latino culture—no tortillas, no *periódico* (newspaper), not even a Spanish television channel on cable! Given that my mother's native language is Spanish, I knew she was going to be terribly bored.

Two weeks later, my mother and friend left, and my husband came home. From that day forward, everything changed. He seemed different—distant and detached. I had no idea at the time that this was the norm for many NFL players. Just like our Latina mothers had told us ("Don't bother your dad; he's tired from work"), NFL wives were not supposed to "bother" their husbands during football season. Overwhelmed by the demands of professional football, I tried to blow off his behavior as stress from his new career.

The more time went by, however, the more distant my husband became. I tried to adjust to the lifestyle, going to the Panther's Wives Association meetings and to all the charity events the wives attended. The problem was, I felt empty and objectified. I was no longer perceived as Yasmin—the young woman with immense goals and aspirations. I was just a "Panther wife." No one seemed to be interested in my life and dreams; all they wanted to talk about was my husband and football. When I tried to reach out and create my own identity in this new town, I was ostracized and told that I wanted too much in life, that I just needed to have babies, and then all that energy I had for life would diminish. The more I tried to find commonalties between the other wives and myself, the more I realized how different we were. When we all got together, talk revolved only around our husbands. In fact, I got to know more about these women's husbands than about them!

"What about you?" I asked a few of the wives. "What plans do you have for your life?" Most of them said the same thing: "Well, it's too hard to do anything with the way my husband's career is and all." And this was the truth; it *is* extremely difficult for an NFL wife to have her own career, raise children, and live with her husband, because NFL life offers no stability. During the football season, players spend almost no time with their families. During the off-season, things change a bit; usually, a player and his family return to their permanent home and then move back when training camp begins again. If any player's wife wanted to have her own career, she would have to tell the company she worked for that she could only work six months out of the year!

Furthermore, she could not establish a career in one particular state, because the average NFL player moves at least two or three times during his career. What kind of company would want to hire someone like that?

In the four years that I lived within the Carolina Panthers' realm, there were only two wives that I can honestly say I felt a connection with. It wasn't that the wives weren't friendly, because many were; there was just a lack of commonalties. Sometimes I felt almost ashamed for wanting my own life. During Christmas of 1996, the team's offensive line coach had a Christmas party for the players and their wives. After dinner, the guys went outside to smoke cigars while the wives sat inside chatting around the kitchen table, talking about having more children. Every one of the women at the table spoke about following her husband, regardless of where or when, with pride. When it was my turn to speak, I had two options: to say something similar, or to say the truth. I chose the truth: "I plan to have my own corporation within the next few years. I plan to run for a local political office a few years after that, and then I'll probably run for Congress in about ten years, when my husband retires from football."

They all looked at me slack-jawed for a few moments until one woman asked, "What about children, don't you plan to have children?"

"Yes," I said. "I have that figured in also." No one said a word, and for a moment I regretted having told the truth—now they were really going to think I was a militant feminist. But I sat back and tried to convince myself that I was just different, not defective, just different.

As the season continued, my husband became more and more arrogant. The whole town praised these guys as if they were gods! This was only the Carolina Panthers' second season in existence; the team was being carried by a number of rookies, including Kerry Collins at quarterback, Norberto at starting right tackle, and a few other prominent players, and they were just a few games away from the Super Bowl. The better the team did, the more praise the players received everywhere they turned. Norberto would go grocery shopping, for example, and the clerks would ask, "You do your own grocery shopping? Why? We'll be happy to deliver anything you need, any time of the day or night!" Anything Norberto wanted, he got, and fast. Frankly, I was astonished by the supreme VIP service these guys received. The most important thing to remember, though, was that the team was winning.

I began to understand why so many young NFL players get themselves into serious trouble. When you take a twenty-one-year-old boy who hasn't yet established his own identity, and you give him a few million dollars and treat him like a god, sooner or later he starts to believe he's somehow more entitled, more special, than the average man. Unless a man has a strong sense of his identity before he enters the NFL, there is very little that encourages him to base his identity on who he is, rather than what he has. Then, when a player finds himself on a losing team, or gets injured, reality hits, and he sees how fast that feeling of invincibility goes away. Even my husband, who happens to be one of the most humble men I know, began to believe he was omnipotent, and he became more and more distant.

It wasn't long before I felt completely confused and alone. I couldn't find anyone to turn to for support because everyone thought I had it so good. When I tried to discuss my situation with friends and family, they just did not seem to understand. "Problems? You don't have problems. I wish I had your problems instead of mine," is what one friend told me. No one could see the situation through my eyes. It wasn't about the money; it was about my soul dying a little bit each day. I always had the choice to leave North Carolina, but I believed that the man I had fallen in love with still existed and that I would get him back, no matter what it took. Clearly, though, the price I was paying was taking an emotional toll on me. I had survived so much in my life, and I had obtained a good education in order to have a great career and live my dreams, but that didn't seem to matter anymore; there was no room for my dreams in the NFL. People would tell me, "You knew what you were getting yourself into, and you chose to do it." I would answer, "Yes, I knew that I was going to live a different life, but no one ever mentioned to me that I would have to give up everything. Somebody forgot to tell me that part!"

I told my friend Sara that I sometimes wished we had never received the NFL money, because all it seemed to do was cause problems. Everyone started asking for financial help from us. Our families expected it, and everyone else had a "great business idea" for us to invest in. Sara told me, "There are positives and negatives in a relationship; the positive is you've got real financial security now." She really did not understand what I was saying, though. It wasn't about the money; it was about my soul, my identity, myself. I didn't want the money if it was going to take away my freedom. What good was the money if I wasn't happy?

Although I tried to see the situation as a "trade-off," I couldn't; that was not who I was. I couldn't put up with that much crap, even if it meant that it would provide me with the money to eventually start my own company. That was exactly what so many of our mothers and grandmothers had done just to survive. I knew trade-offs had eaten up many souls and spirits. Most of our elder Latina relatives had never understood that they felt sick and lifeless because their trade-off had caught up with them, taking away their feelings of self-worth and power. Although this trade-off was different, my soul was not for sale. No career or financial security was worth the precious soul I had fought so hard to regain after my addiction. I supported my husband's decision to join the NFL, and I loved him for who he was, but if he was no longer going to be the man I knew before he entered the NFL, then he was no longer going to be my husband.

Before resorting to divorce, I decided that I would try everything in my power to make the marriage work. Then I would at least know that I had given my all, and I could live in peace. I decided to see a marriage counselor who had been recommended by the team. I should have known better. I sat across from her, feeling angry and depressed, and I told her my husband and I were having problems. I explained to her that Norberto had become distant and noncommunicative—how he would get home from work and not want to talk at all because he was so tired. I told her that he would walk through the door after practice, stop by the kitchen to grab something to eat, and then go to our bedroom and close the door. "Obviously," I told her, "he is not contributing to making this marriage work."

She looked at me and said, "Well, maybe you should wait until after the season to talk to him about this situation with your marriage. Right now he has football to think about, and the team is doing extremely well. Do you think they'll make it to the Super Bowl?"

I felt like I had just been slapped in the face. I was appalled by her suggestion. I could not believe that this "doctor" was telling me that football was a greater priority than our marriage. "I didn't know that I only had a husband six months out of the year," I told her. "Do I get to take six months off of our marriage, too, or is that just an exception for professional football players? I didn't know that being in the League meant that there was an on and off time for marriage. I thought the goal was to balance marriage and career."

"Yes," she said, "but some men don't know how to do that."

"Well," I said, "he's going to have to learn if he wants to stay married to me. If women are expected to learn how to balance motherhood, marriage, and a career, the least a husband can do is to learn how to balance two out of three."

Of course, I decided never to go back to her again, but she did cause me to question myself. "Maybe I *do* want too much," I thought. "Maybe she's right, and I shouldn't bother him during the season." For a minute I doubted myself and felt helpless, but it was only for a minute. Immediately afterward, I felt enough power and strength within myself to say, "No way. I deserve better than that. I deserve the same dedication and effort he puts into football. I deserve to have a husband three hundred and sixty-five days out of the year, maybe not physically, but certainly emotionally."

As the weeks went by, my husband became even more withdrawn and arrogant. When I asked him why he treated me with such a lack of courtesy, he would say, "Because I can. I'm a Panther; I can do whatever I want."

I looked at him and said, "When you walk through this door, you are my husband and only my husband. That Panther crap does not work with me." I couldn't believe what had happened to him. I didn't even know who he was anymore. As the season ended, I was becoming more and more desperate. I was hanging on to our marriage by the very last thread.

By March 1997, we were back in California, and I found a marriage counselor with a terrific reputation in Orange County. I thought that since we were in California, I might avoid the star treatment Norberto had received in Charlotte. I sat down with the counselor, and I told her the same story: "My husband is not contributing his share in making this marriage work." I felt like a broken record.

"Yes, he is," she said. "He added your last name to his. What else do you want?"

I literally thought I was losing my mind when I heard her say something so ridiculous. I told her, "I added his name to my name, too! Doesn't that mean anything?"

Again I was forced to listen to the same inane explanation I had heard so many times before. She had the nerve to say, "It's tradition for a woman to take her husband's last name. Obviously, by adding your last name to his, your husband is doing more than his share."

I was dumbfounded by her interpretation of what it meant to do your share in a marriage. "Tradition!" I said. "Slavery was a tradition, too. Does that make it right?"

As much as I loved my husband, I could not bear another football season in Charlotte like the one I had lived through in '96. Unless my husband changed back to the man that I knew before the NFL, I saw no future for us. I decided to pursue my life and go to graduate school. I needed to get away from him and the whole football scene in order to get my emotions and life back in order. I applied to a master's program in San Diego and was accepted. In the fall, I moved to San Diego and began the program. I was commuting between San Diego and Charlotte every other weekend, so that I could support Norberto during his home games. I found that when I tried to attend away games, I'd only get to spend an hour or two with him.

The 1997 season went south for the Panthers pretty early, and the coaches were not happy. Norberto's offensive line coach took him aside and said, "We know your wife is not here, and we think that's why your practices are suffering." Norberto denied the notion entirely, but it never failed—every time Norberto had an off game or practice, the coaches would say it was because I wasn't there. Norberto learned to blow them off because he knew, more than anybody else, that his performance had nothing do to with whether I was there or not; it had to do with his mental attitude toward the game.

In October, while I was studying in San Diego, one of the few Panther wives I could call a friend telephoned me from Charlotte to inform me that she had just heard the host of the sports-talk radio station, KCOP, in Charlotte call me a "bitch" on the air. Apparently the word had gotten out that Norberto had added my name to his and put it on his jersey. "What a bitch," the talk show host said. "Can you believe she made him take her last name and put it on his jersey? You know who wears the pants in that relationship."

I couldn't believe the whole machismo thing was starting all over again. This man didn't know me; he didn't know my husband; he didn't know anything about our marriage, yet he made the assumption that I controlled my husband because he added my last name to his. Not for a minute did he consider the fact that maybe my husband *wanted* to take my last name. When I heard the news, I was devastated. I didn't know the name situation was going to create such an ordeal, and, to my great surprise, that comment was just the beginning.

Soon everyone from sports commentators and newspaper reporters to NFL team players and fans had something to say about it. Both negative and positive comments were being made, but for every good comment there were twenty bad ones. In every interview Norberto had that year, the same question was asked, "Why? Why did you add her name to yours?" My husband's answer was always the same: "Because I respect her."

Players would never make negative comments in front of my husband (it might have something to do with the fact that he is 6'6" and 325 pounds.), but I would hear of remarks that players made, like, "She got what she wanted, and she left for California." One way or another, I was once again the "bad one." Not only were people making negative comments about the last-name issue, I was constantly criticized for not living with my husband full time while I attended graduate school. Just like the traditional Latina who lives for her husband's every need, nothing less is expected from an NFL wife.

One Saturday in October, the San Francisco 49ers flew into Charlotte to play the Panthers. A friend of ours, a 49ers offensive lineman, called to see what we were up to. As we chatted,

I mentioned how exhausted I was, having just flown in from San Diego to spend the weekend with Norberto. He sighed on the phone and said, "Girl, you are married now; you should be in Charlotte with your husband all the time. You need to be at home where you belong."

"I need to do what I need to do to prepare myself for my career, and graduate school is what I need to do right now," I told him.

"Why can't you put off this career until he's finished with football? Why can't you just wait eight or ten years until he's done?"

"So you think I should put my life on hold for ten years?" I asked.

"Well . . . yeah," he said.

"Sorry, but I'm not sticking to the NFL traditional wife lifestyle," I told him.

He took a deep breath and said, "What is wrong with the traditional way? It works perfectly fine for me and my family. I earn the money, and the wife's at home taking care of the children. Why are you trying to change all that? Why are you trying to ruin everything?"

"I just want to live my life as I choose! Everybody else has that privilege!" I answered.

"No, you are just putting a bunch of ideas into other women's heads."

We decided then and there not to broach the topic again. Even today we avoid it.

As the season went along, more players and wives found out that Norberto was alone during the week. "Poor Norberto," the other Panther wives would say to me, "he has no one to come home to and no one to cook him dinner." Norberto got dinner invitations from players and their wives nearly every night because they felt sorry for him. I lived alone at school, but no one ever thought of me as "poor Yasmin." I had no one to come home to every day, and no one to cook for me. No one ever invited me to dinner because they felt sorry for me.

In Charlotte, the wives would ask, "When are you coming home to be here with your husband, where you belong?"

"Wherever your husband is, that's where you should be." My standard response was: "Well, my husband doesn't seem to mind that I'm away at school. Why should anyone else mind?" I wasn't very popular.

By the end of the 1997 season, it was clear that the Carolina Panthers had bombed. Most significantly, Norberto had realized that he had been neglecting our marriage and was seeing what it would be like to live without me. We discussed the situation, and he understood the value of our marriage and the need to learn and grow from our experiences. We came to a compromise. We both agreed to do our part in our marriage and never to limit each other's opportunities to maximize our potentials, even if it meant living apart for a while. We both knew that the only way we could last a lifetime would be to allow each other to grow independently *and* together. Although playing football was his dream, Norberto realized that it didn't mean much if there was no one to share the dream with. He also realized that, if he wanted our marriage to work, he had to make our marriage a priority, right up there with football. He told me that he needed my love and my strength. After a losing season, he knew that the fans and coaches only loved the team when they were winning. Norberto was also beginning to understand what I had been telling him all along, that he couldn't determine his whole sense of worth through football and that playing in the NFL is what he did, not who he was. I had always let him know what I thought of the superficiality of NFL life; he was now beginning to see it with his own eyes, and he did not like what he saw or how he felt. It was his time to see the NFL for what it really was.

I was enormously touched by the fact that in all my husband's interviews, he would say that I, his wife, had been the biggest inspiration of his life. He would tell reporters that he had the ultimate respect for me because I was a strong woman whom he admired. He mentioned me in every single interview, and I knew how rare that was. The wives who dedicated their entire lives to their husbands were never mentioned in their husbands' interviews. It was always a coach or a teacher the player praised—never, ever a wife. Norberto was one of a kind.

Because he loved the game so much, Norberto was willing to take the ups with the downs, and that was fine with me—we had made a compromise. The NFL continued to provide everything he had dreamed of as a kid: fame, money, status, power, and a privileged lifestyle. No one ever promised happiness, though; it's what one does with the fame, money, status, and power that determines happiness. From the moment my husband understood this and experienced it himself, he turned back into the man I had fallen in love with and married.

Five years later, as a result of our compromise and Norberto's revelations, we have what I consider to be a wonderful marriage. I am a mother, wife, and career woman, but, most importantly, I am myself first. All these other roles add to who I am—they do not create who I am. Everyone is different; every woman's needs are different, and although people view situations differently, each woman needs to do what she feels is right for her and her family, regardless of what others may think. In order for us to live our lives as we choose, we must allow others to live their lives as they choose, without criticizing their choices. Many women are the first to criticize other women for their unique choices in life; yet, when we are criticized, we call foul. Remember this motto: "Treat others the way you would like to be treated."

Marriage is a partnership in which neither mate should limit the intellectual, emotional, or spiritual growth of the other. Each partner has two lives, one of their own and one with their partner, and it is through compromise that a true partnership will develop. Sometimes, one partner will need to take on more responsibility than the other, and vice versa. For example, during the football season, I am the primary caretaker of our daughter and our household. I make sure everything runs smoothly while Norberto dedicates himself to football. But during the off-season, Norberto is the primary caretaker while I take the necessary steps to enhance my own career. Before the off-season of 2001, Norberto mentioned to me that he would like to have another child right away. I asked him for a month so that we could carefully decide whether or not to pursue the idea. Meanwhile, I had a book to finish, and Norberto was taking full responsibility for our daughter. After two weeks of being home with our daughter every day and getting up with her every night, he came to me and admitted that it would probably be a better idea to wait a couple of years before having another child. It was only when he experienced raising a child full time that he realized how truly difficult it is.

However compromise within your family works, remember not to sacrifice your dreams and goals—Latinas have a habit of doing that. When you and your mate balance family responsibilities, you teach your children the true value of partnership.

Profiles of Courageous Latinas

Whatever course you decide upon, there is always someone to tell you that you are wrong. There are always difficulties arising, which tempt you to believe that your critics are right. To map out a course of action and follow it to an end requires courage.
—Ralph Waldo Emerson

Throughout my research, I have conducted focus groups with hundreds of Latinas. Throughout the process, I asked the women to write down what it is they would like to read about in a book written especially for Latinas. Hundreds of women responded similarly asking for profiles of courageous and successful Latinas; in particular, their lives, struggles, and accomplishments. Therefore, I chose to interview four Latinas who show remarkable perseverance, determination, and courage. These women have fought to survive emotionally, physically, and politically. In their respective fields, they have been challenged simply for being women. It is through their experiences that I learned how similar our lives are—every woman has her story, although we rarely talk about them with each other. For the sake of ourselves, and our souls, we need to begin sharing our pains, joys, and challenges with others. We need to stop being ashamed of our experiences, no matter how awful they may seem. It is by talking about them that we truly set ourselves free.

Therefore, I dedicate this chapter to the hundreds of women who asked to read about courageous Latinas. Through these women may you find inspiration to become your own courageous Latina!

Profiler of Courage

CONGRESSWOMAN HILDA SOLIS

Nationality: United States (Mexican and Nicaraguan heritage)
Born: October 20, 1957, California
Latina highlights: First Latina state senator of California; Eighth Latina in U.S. Congress

She has been described as the "highest expression of Latino politics in the new era." Some call her a "national star." Congresswoman Hilda Solis says her favorite description, though, is that of a "warrior." And a warrior she is, taking on the entrenched political network, comprised mainly of white males, on such controversial issues as the California minimum wage increase and environmental justice.

Congresswoman Solis won an Assembly seat in 1992 and two years later made history by becoming the first Latina to ever serve in the California State Senate. The affable, courageous Solis has been known for tenaciously pushing a progressive agenda and has championed labor causes, women's rights (especially in the area of domestic violence), environmental protection, education, and health care issues. In addition, her remarkable environmental efforts won Solis the Profile in Courage Award from the John F. Kennedy Library Foundation; she is the first woman to have been honored with this prestigious award.

Born on October 20, 1957, to Juana and Raul (immigrants from Nicaragua and Mexico, respectively, who met in citizenship class), she was the third of seven children and the first to go to college. Solis was elected to Congress in 2000, where she represents the San Gabriel Valley and an East Los Angeles district that has a Hispanic majority.

When I interviewed Congresswoman Solis, she was in the process of moving her office to Washington, D.C. As dedicated as she is to empowering Latinas, she took the time to talk with me.

YDG Tell me a little about how you saw the world growing up.

HS Well, I grew up in a small community, a small town in the San Gabriel Valley, La Puente. It was a working class community during the time when I was growing up. I was optimistic about my future and about our community and growing up there obviously was very different from other parts of L.A. County.

Once I started growing up and got into high school, I saw the differences in economic structures between the city that I grew up in and, say, downtown Los Angeles on the west side and other parts that were more economically sound. I grew up in a working class family, both parents were laborers. My father (for years) worked in a factory and had limited education. He is an immigrant from Mexico. My mother is also an immigrant; she's from Central America, from Nicaragua. She pretty much stayed at home . . . while raising five children. She didn't have to go to work until later on, and that really had an impact on our lives as children because at ten years of age I served as caretaker for my younger siblings, and my mother happened to have twins.

My older sister and I were the caretakers after she went to work. We would get out of school, come home, and help cook. We'd clean, we'd change diapers, wash; we would do everything. So I had it very different; it wasn't the normal everyday life where the young girl at ten is out playing with her friends or her dolls.

It was like being an adult, and it was being responsible, and it was something that we took on. We had to take on that responsibility. It made me mature much faster than, I think, other young girls at the time. And that has helped frame who I am. I think that's why a lot of people tell me, "Gee, Hilda, you're so young, and you've accomplished a lot of things." I think a lot of it had to do with my upbringing, how I was raised, and the kind of values that were instilled. It was very much working class, very close knit. My parents are very religious. Right now, in my life, I'm not as religious; however, I am a big believer. I have a lot of faith.

YDG   You mentioned that when you were young, you felt optimistic about life and about the world. In your opinion, what made you feel optimistic?

HS   I think a lot of it had to do with the way my parents raised us. They told us, "Be grateful that you have good schools, that you have the ability to get an education." They would tell us often how hard it was for them growing up, barely getting by with scraps, and barely even having . . . a roof over their heads, or being bounced around with different family members. The kinds of stories that they depicted were hard; we knew we were doing much better, and they often reminded us of that. So we could appreciate that.

[When I was] ten, and my sister was twelve, we were already like parents, taking on some major chores and responsibilities. And maybe that's not so different, because I've talked to a lot of people who are nonminorities who had problems or situations that forced them to also grow up sooner than most.

My parents were not of great means, so we had to share a lot with each other. So, whatever my sister didn't need one year, she grew out of, I got it. And we were very lucky that at the beginning of school, at least, we'd go down to the Sears department store and get two dresses each, and that was it.

YDG   And you had to wear them until you couldn't wear them anymore?

HS   Yeah, and that's the way it was. It was tough; it was a lot of sacrifice. My parents made a lot of sacrifices.

YDG   What kind of positive or negative messages about yourself did you receive growing up?

HS   Well, I think that the culture I grew up in is considered very traditional, so, generally, women helped to maintain all the traditional roles. A woman should be a mother, women should be the housekeepers, a woman should help support her family, her husband, spouse, and so on. Rarely did I see any Latina role model that went outside of that. I didn't know of very many

Latinas who went on to college. So when things started chang-ing, as I started to get more interested in college, I saw other opportunities and other Latinos encouraging me to excel.

YDG   Growing up, what was your biggest fear?

HS   Well, like anything, you wonder what career you're going to get into, how you're going to support yourself, what life is going to have to offer you. For me, it's not as though I knew all throughout my life that I wanted to be a politician. It was through a series of experiences, education, working in differ-ent areas and fields as an intern, working on campaigns and associating with people who were involved in politics that I became interested or attracted to public service. But it wasn't right off the bat that I said to myself, "Oh yeah, I want to be a congresswoman." In fact, if anything, I think I wanted to become a lawyer.

I remember taking classes in political science, but I didn't become a lawyer. And now, I tell people, "Look, it doesn't mat-ter, because I'm still writing laws." And I am still making an impact on public policy, and people assume I'm a lawyer.

To me, it doesn't take a rocket scientist. People can learn how to develop good public policy. And that, I think, is probably the message I would give to young people: that there is no mystery here. If you want to come into this arena, politics, or be a public servant, then there are ways of getting there. There are steps to take, people to meet, and opportunities to get involved with.

YDG   At many times in your political career, you've stood up for what you believed in even though influential people opposed you. Why did you do that?

HS   A lot of it was based on my personal values and beliefs. For example, the minimum wage campaign; there were a lot of busi-ness people, I remember, a lot of the Chamber of Commerces throughout the state, who were against me because of my tenac-ity in trying to get the minimum wage bill passed. And the ini-tiative finally did pass; it won by a large majority. Over 62 percent of the voters in California voted to increase the 1996 minimum wage of $5.75, which is higher, even right now, than the federal wage. The federal government offers you $5.15.

I took a lot of criticism from minority businesses, small businesses, who said, "Hilda, you're hurting us." But the fact of the matter is, the people that they employed deserved, in my opinion, an increase because they were supporting their families as well. And in most situations, minimum wage earners are women. They're usually single heads of household, holding two or three minimum wage jobs.

So it's not like they're asking for a handout; they're just asking for some pay equity, some recognition for their work, and even that, according to the federal statistics, is still below the poverty level. You're still talking about welfare wages as far as I'm concerned.

YDG   What do you believe gave you the courage to persevere, to stand up to all these people?

HS   I think a lot of it, again, goes back to my roots, family. They've had to persevere so much. They're a good example of overcoming a lot of obstacles. They came to this country, survived, and earned somewhat of a decent livelihood here. They had to surmount all kinds of racism, discrimination, and physical injury.

These are things that I think we have to share with others, especially because of the positions that we hold. People need to know that we're real. And that, to me, is probably the most important role that I can play, to try to make what I do easy for people to understand, to associate with. A lot of people tell me, "Gee, Hilda, you're not one of those fancy wishy-washy people who can't come down and talk to us little folks. You're with us, you're there, you're getting your hands dirty or walking precincts, or you're helping to feed the homeless." At Christmas season alone, we did a lot of things to help very needy families.

YDG   Have you ever doubted yourself in any major life decision?

HS   Oh yeah, always. Should I take that job; should I not take that job? Should I go on for a promotion? And you learn! Like anything, you learn from those experiences.

YDG   How did you make those decisions? Did you have some kind of strategy, or did you just jump into it?

HS   In some cases, it was gut reaction, and with some it was . . . planning. I wanted a better job than my parents had, but part of the planning was to get a college education and that took a lot of time. I was encouraged to go to graduate school, so I did. I spent a year and a half at the University of Southern California [USC] in their master's of public administration program. But with that program, I had work experience, an internship going along with it. I worked at the local level, and then the second semester I went to Washington [D.C.], and I ended up staying there for almost a year and a half and just completed my program there. I really had a good experience. I worked with the federal government, starting out as an intern; after that, I was hired on as a staffer at the White House for Esteban Torres when he was Special Assistant to [President] Carter for Hispanic Affairs. I got involved with writing, putting on special programs, and served as support staff. Later, I was able to get an analyst's position with the Office of Management and Budget.

YDG Growing up, did you ever carry a belief about something, only to realize later that that belief did not work for you anymore?

HS Well, I think as Latinas, if you're raised in a traditional family, you have a certain way that you're brought up. I think for me, as soon as I went on to college, a lot of things changed. I modified my beliefs because I was going through some different experiences. That had a lot to do with how I viewed the world and what I was going to do to go out and do what I needed to do. It even boiled down to moving away from home, living three thousand miles away, going to Washington, D.C. I remember my mother telling me, "Ay, *mi hija* you're going to go three thousand miles away; you don't know anybody, nobody is going to accept you; how are you going to take care of yourself?"

So she was disappointed at the thought of me moving away. But . . . other people were telling me, "No, no, this is right; this is positive; this is good, and you know you're going to have a good experience." Some of it was half-truth. I had to learn; it was a struggle. I was out there on my own; I didn't have family. I was on work-study; I was a student, but I made the most of it. And that's what you do. Give and take.

YDG How do you currently deal with adversity?

HS Well, it depends. Not everyone is going to agree with me on everything.

YDG   Is it important for you to be liked by a lot of people, or does it not matter?

HS   It's important. Yes, I think it is important for people to see who I am, the kinds of values, the kinds of responsibilities I have. And I think a lot of people really value what you do more than what you say. And I think that I've been able to prove that because, as you know, in these times right now, politicians aren't always viewed in a positive light. They want to paint us all the same way, and I really believe that, at least in my position, I've tried to let people know the kinds of things that I'm forced to deal with. So that makes them more tolerant and patient and understanding, and some people say, "You know, Hilda, I would never want to be in your shoes, and I give you credit because you're doing it." And I know that I probably don't have to do this, but I do. I choose to do it. I enjoy this job; I enjoy helping people and making government work better.

YDG   How do you deal with the pressures of politics?

HS   It takes time to adjust, especially if you're married. I mean, I don't have kids or anything, but I could imagine how hard it would be for other Latinas, because there aren't very many Latinas that do this. A lot of it, again, goes back to your upbringing. Some people say, "Hilda, you're selfish. You don't have any kids, you're selfish." You know, some of our own people say that! Far from it. They really don't understand what I'm doing. This is a personal choice. Men do not get criticized for doing exactly what they want.

YDG   Have you always felt that you've had control of your life?

HS   No. A lot of it was getting good advice from people. Steering my way through the maze. Even today, even now, a lot of it has to do with not having enough of my own personal time, because I have commitments, things I'm obligated to do, because of the position that I hold. So, it's not like I have total control.

YDG   Have you always known or felt your internal strength?

HS   No. Sometimes I doubt myself. I just set my mind: Okay, I've got to do this, I've got to complete this, I've got to see this through. I usually don't dwell on it much until I've gone through it. And then I say, "Gee, I did it. I can do it." People remind me, "God, you've done this, you've done that," and to me, I'm just going through these different passages.

YDG   Do you choose what traditions you live by? Do you disregard some traditions?

HS   Yes, whatever feels more comfortable for me, I accept.

YDG   What do you do when someone tells you that you can't do something when you know you can?

HS   I may not respond, but my actions will show that I will succeed or persevere. That's always kind of been my motto. Usually when people take me on and say, "No, you can't do this," and I know I can; I work even harder at it.

YDG   Do you believe that you had high self-esteem or low self-esteem while you were growing up?

HS   I was a very shy person. Growing up, in elementary, junior high, and high school, I was very shy. I think people who knew me would say that, too. Even when I started out in politics and ran for the school board, for Rio Hondo College, I remember a friend telling me, "Oh, gosh," she was telling someone else in front of me, "Hilda was so shy. She would come and stand next to me at an event or something because she didn't know that many people . . . now look at her!" It's about feeling self-confident and gaining confidence over the years.

YDG   Has there been a time in your life you have felt that the odds were against you?

HS   Yes! Sure. It wasn't a good feeling. I weathered it and moved on.

YDG   Do these feelings ever hold you back from doing what you feel is right?

HS   Sometimes. I'm sure everyone has self-doubt.

YDG   Do you believe in creating your own traditions?

HS   My own traditions? Well, I think that I do.

YDG   So you show it by actions. You just do things that haven't been done before, and they end up becoming new traditions.

HS   Right! Exactly!

YDG   What would you tell Latinas who feel they had no support from important people in their lives about doing something they want to do?

HS   I would just continue to ask them to reflect, and then figure out what it is they want to do and go after it. Go for it. And in spite of obstacles, sometimes there are people that are very close to you, telling you, "No, don't do this, don't do that," or whatever. But if you really believe you can do it, and it's a positive thing, then you should move with it. It might take you a little bit more time; it might take longer, but stick with it. Put all your energies and your heart in it. When you have your heart in something, chances are it will work out, because it's genuine. People will see that and appreciate you even more.

YDG   How do you balance all you have to do?

HS   You make adjustments, like anything else. It helps to have friends and family members you can talk to.

YDG   Is there any message you want to give to Latinas about life in general?

HS   I look at people like Dolores Huerta as someone who I really look up to very highly. Someone who has, through her whole life, been so nontraditional. Fighting for farm workers, for women's healthcare programs, for children in poverty, for world hunger, for women's freedom all over the world. She's a very humble person of little means. She's somebody that I've come to know as a good friend. But she's someone who hasn't changed in her approach. If anything, one day I'll see her with a group of young people on a college campus, and they're magnetized to her. On another occasion, I'll see her talking with *los viejitos*, and she can come in and out of those circles. To me, that's a special skill. I think we all have our talents and skills, and we can all do great things; they don't all have to be in the headlines. They can be great things that we do in our jobs, in our homes with our families, at the workplace, or something that we really have passion about. People need to have passion. There's nothing wrong with that, because we're very passionate people. We should use that as our strength. We should learn how to use that energy, because it's positive.

Her Courage to Prevail

CLAUDIA TREJOS
Sports anchor
Nationality: Colombian
Born: 1969, Colombia
Latina highlights: First Latina sports
    anchor in the United States

Claudia Trejos has been in the middle of controversy since her debut as a Los Angeles sports anchor in 1999. Criticized and ridiculed in top national newspapers such as the *Miami Herald*, the *New York Times*, and the *Los Angeles Times*, she has been fighting an uphill battle despite her profound professionalism, her extensive knowledge, and her impressive presentation skills. Claudia is a fighter, though, and says, "Hell will freeze over before I let them win."

Claudia began her broadcasting career at Fox Sports Americas in 1994 before moving on to KWHY, where she was a sports director/anchor six nights a week. In 1999, she joined Los Angeles' most popular news station, KTLA, and became the first Latina sports anchor in the United States. From the first day she appeared on the station, pronouncing Hispanic athletes' names correctly (with accents), she has been ripped apart by the media. Commentators all over Los Angeles were calling her debut "the worst in sports history." One commentator actually said, "She's a pretty woman, but she has a very thick Latino accent." Another compared her to Ricky Ricardo, commenting that the only difference was that Claudia Trejos was not funny.

In reality, Claudia is the first anchor to challenge the media's butchering of Latino names; she pronounces them as they should be, with as many *R*s as needed to make them sound right! Claudia is determined to rise above the criticism, and her courage to prevail over a very strong network of journalists is both admirable and astonishing.

Note: At the time of publication, Claudia Trejos had taken a new position as sports anchor for Telemundo's Channel 52.

YDG   As you know, I have chosen four courageous Latinas to profile in my book, and you are one of them, along with Congresswoman Hilda Solis.

CT   Wow! You're putting me in with a congresswoman? You're crazy!

YDG   Not at all! She's awesome, you're awesome.

CT   No. She's awesome . . . I'm just a little sports anchor.

YDG   It's not really about what you do, it's everything about you—who you are, what you stand for . . . not giving up.

CT   Well, thank you so much.

YDG   The reason I chose you is that you have an incredible amount of courage for standing up and not giving in to the criticism. The "good-old-boy" network can usually bring anybody down!

CT   Oh yeah! Oh, it can, and they would if you let them, if you allow them to. It's a losing battle, and the thing is, it comes down to . . . well, if I was a European anchor, they wouldn't have a problem with it. And you know what? If you look across the table, everybody has an accent in their own way. They don't only have a problem with me because of my Hispanic accent, but because, all of a sudden, there's a 5'2", 120-pound female Hispanic sports anchor. Then it becomes a big deal.

YDG   Are you Colombian?

CT   Yes, but I'm mixed racially. My dad's family is Turkish. My mom, she's also mixed, but she's basically Colombian—Indian Colombian—and there's some Italian in there somewhere. But she's a mestiza.

YDG   I heard that you have seventeen brothers and sisters, is this true?

CT   Yeah, but they're not all from the same mom. My dad was a very busy man.

YDG   Do you still talk to your dad?

CT   Oh yeah, my dad's still around. He's back home in Colombia, and we're very, very close.

YDG   And your mom? Is she still alive?

CT   No, my mom died three and a half years ago.

YDG   I heard that your mom became college educated after she raised her children. Is that true?

CT   Well, my mom quit school when she was thirteen because she comes from a family of six, and my grandpa couldn't make ends meet. He was the typical macho that wouldn't let the wife work. My grandma . . . was a midwife, so she would hide and work. My mom started working at a store keeping the books, and when she was forty-five, she decided to go back and get her high school diploma in Colombia, which was unheard of at the time. I mean this is an older lady, over the hill. So, it was very hard for her, especially competing with kids that had nothing else to do. My mom had her own business at the time, as a bookkeeper and accountant, and she became a C.P.A., equivalent to a C.P.A. here, through other ways like adult school and all that good stuff. She kept herself updated. She had her business to run. She had the family to run. And a very promiscuous husband.

YDG   She was still married to your father?

CT   Oh yeah. My mom did not get divorced from my dad . . . they never really got divorced. My dad did not leave the house up until ten years ago. My mom stayed with my dad because she believed in family, and she believed that there was only going to be one dad in our life, and she was going to keep the family, no matter what. And he had many women, forget about just three. I mean, we're talking about [women] in different cities, and he was married through the courts with the rest, not by the church. He was married by the church with my mom.

YDG   Did you ever resent him for that? For what he did to her?

CT   You know what? I was very clear about things. I was very aware of my dad's duty to me as a daughter. His duty was to give me the best education, provide a home, and I was very aware of that. My mom made sure that we knew that my dad was a good dad. Despite the fact that he was not a good husband did not take away from him being a good dad.

There were times when she called him every name in the book. And we were very aware of what was going on. I knew all my brothers and sisters would end up at my house. She knew that it wasn't their fault, and as long as these kids were being provided for, my dad was on the good side. She realized that even the women were not to blame for his doings. It was my dad, and in a way, my dad gave my mom a lot of freedom, because when my grandparents were raising her, those were the days when women were not even allowed to vote. The only thing my dad expected of my mom was that my sister and I, who are the only ones from the same marriage, would be taken care of. There was always a nanny; there was always a maid; there was always food on the table; there was always someone expecting us when we came home from school.

And I can't say my dad never spent a day with us, because he was always there. To this day, I still don't know how he managed. By forty-five, he had had three heart attacks. By the time he was fifty, he had a quadruple bypass. So that kind of shows the stress he was dealing with. So, I learned from very early on that that was my dad, and he did his best to provide for us, not only monetarily, but he was always there for a school picnic; he was always there for our little performances.

YDG   So, if your mom decided to stay with him, it was her choice?

CT   It was her choice. At one point in time, I did ask my mom why. I did question my mom's judgment. But it was more woman to woman rather than daughter to mother. Then I realized that my mom was doing it for *our* sake. As a mom, I could probably understand; but as a woman, I could not understand.

YDG   What did she tell you?

CT   That I would understand when I grew up. I'm thirty-two now, and I still don't understand.

YDG   Is it true that after you girls were grown up, your mother became a judge?

CT   Yes. She finished law school and . . . became a judge.

YDG   Were you living in Colombia at the time?

CT   Yeah, that was back in '80. I left Colombia in 1985, and I went to Europe. I was there for two and a half years, then I went back to Colombia, then I came here in 1990, and I've been here ever since.

YDG   Do you go back to visit?

CT   I haven't been back in a while. Since my mom died, it's very difficult for me to go back.

YDG   Did she die of natural causes?

CT   No. My mom was kidnapped and held for ransom. She was never to be found. She was one of the victims of violence in Colombia. They demanded *dinero* from my father, so he had to liquidate all his assets. Everything is gone, but my mom never showed up. My mom was actually kidnapped three times and had been returned the first two times. In her line of duty, that was just a labor hazard.

The third time they didn't return her, and she was never found. I feel she is dead; I don't know, but I feel it. It's one of those things you have to put closure to. You have to look at yourself in the mirror and realize you know, when you feel that emptiness, and I can't even start explaining how it feels. It's just something you have within you.

[At this point in the interview, Claudia answered a phone call.]

YDG   Was that your boyfriend?

CT   No. That's the executive sports producer, Joe Quasarano. He's a very good friend of mine.

YDG   He tells you he loves you! How cute!

CT   Yeah, he's like a dad. He's pretty much taken care of me ever since I started at KTLA.

YDG   Is that one of the reasons you kept your position here at Channel 5, because of your support systems?

CT   Very much so. KTLA has taken very good care of me. From something as simple as a phone call when the first couple of articles came out and my name was splattered all over the radio in LA. When my name was in the *Miami Herald* and the *New York Times*, they always called me. Every single time, they were calling just to make sure I was okay, if I was here. They wanted to make sure that I didn't read the newspaper. They were hiding the newspapers from me so I wouldn't see it. What they didn't realize was that, hello! I get the newspaper at home. Before they even looked at it, I had already seen it.

YDG   How did you deal with the harsh criticism?

CT   At first, I had that feeling of "What's going on here?" Then, all of a sudden, it made sense. I realized, "So that's why they are doing that." That's how it felt. You see, the criticism when I started here was not the beginning of it. When I started here is when it became public, but it started six months before when I was at Channel 22.

The *Los Angeles Times* was writing about me, and I didn't know why. I had no idea why. It was like, "All she knows about is soccer and boxing." I am at a Hispanic station, that's our bread and butter; you know what I'm saying?

And the Dodgers were not the priority. If I had time, then I would put in a piece on the Dodgers if they had a big win, or if they had a tremendous loss to some weaker team or something, but I'm not . . . and they would start writing about me and I didn't understand why. And then, when I got the offer from KTLA, I was thinking, well, I had the number one sports magazine show in Los Angeles, and I was having fun, because that's how I ended up doing sports, because I enjoy it, and it's fun. And it was an offer that I could not refuse. So when I started here, and the criticism got worse, then I understood . . . I'm a threat. I was a threat when I was at Channel 22, and I'm a threat now that I'm at KTLA. I'm the one person they do not know. Because if it would have been Fred Rogan or Carlos Del Valle coming in here, then it's somebody they know. I came out of left field, and they had no idea what to expect from me; so basically, for six months I endured the worst criticism because they didn't know me. After that, it was only for about three or four months that they kept writing and talking about me on air. But it was like those new pair of shoes that you love, and you know they look good, but they hurt like crazy. And you got to wear 'em and wear 'em until they finally contour to your foot. That's how it felt. But I understood.

YDG   So that's how you were able to tolerate it and deal with it?

CT   And, plus, KTLA helped me out a lot . . . I mean a lot. And it was definitely not just lip service. There were many people out there who were saying that it was lip service, that they were giving good face, but that they were really coming down on me and breathing down my neck. Not once. They never questioned me.

All they ever said was, "What do you need? You tell us what you need, and we will provide." And they have, they've provided for everything. Especially support. I have great people that work with me, and I have Tony Hernandez as my main anchor, and he's a great friend and a wonderful person to work with.

YDG Most Latinos would say "Tony Hernandez" with no accent, but you say "Tony Hernandez" with an accent, with pride. Do you get criticized for that?

CT Oh yeah. "Why can't you roll one less *R*?" is what they say. For example, when I say "Andre Gallaraga," they say, "Can't you roll one less *R*?" I go, "No, that's his name." Or, "Nomar Garcia Parra;" they tell me, "Girl, why do you have to say that?" And I go, "Ask him what his name is!"

What it is, is that they're not used to it. But guess what? You look, again, across the table—NFL, more Hispanics than ever; NHL, we finally have not just a player, but a star player; and, of course, baseball. Boxing has always been dominated, especially lightweights and middleweights, by Hispanics. So, finally, I get a chance to say the names right. You know, I respect French names; I respect Caucasian names; I respect Russian names; why am I not going to respect the Hispanic names? That would be playing double face! So why do we say "Limoh" and not "Lemieux?" That's how you spell it! We say "Mario Limoh." That's his French name. So why can't we say "Pedro Martinez?"

It's funny, because there's a tennis player; her name is Julie Halard Decuji. She's French, and she was playing here in Manhattan Beach, and nobody could say her name. It was funny, because everybody was asking, "how do you pronounce her name?" And it was such an issue. We want to make her feel okay, because it's such a complicated name. How come we don't do that with other players? Are they just expendable? Is it a "gimme"? Is that fair?

YDG It's not fair. And you're putting your foot down and saying, "Hey, this is the way it's going to be." And, sooner or later, you'll have all these anchors saying "Antonio Hernandez" with an accent.

CT See! And that's another thing: Tony, though he's from Hispanic descent and understands Spanish, he doesn't speak it, and his parents didn't speak it either. So when he introduces himself, his name is "Tony Hernandez." When I refer to him, I refer to him as "Tony Hernandez." But if it was, again, "Roland Galvan," that's his real name. But he says "Roland Galvan," so I keep it as "Roland Galvan." When I introduce myself, I say "Claudia Trejos." I know it throws a lot of people for a loop, and I try to slow it down. Sometimes, I just get caught in the action; I just go "Claudia Trejos" [fast], and people just go, "What?" I try to slow it down so people will get it. And I will not accept "Claudia Treyos." It drives me crazy. No, my name is not "Claudia Treyos," it's "Claudia Trejos."

YDG   So where do you think you got this courage? Where did it come from? Do you feel you were born with it? Did you learn it or acquire it? Did it just come naturally? Did you have to go through heartaches to be able to acquire it?

CT   I think it's a combination, but I think it's in the blood. My dad never finished grammar school, and I already talked to you about my mom a little bit. It's genetically engraved in my body. I think life throws you little curve balls that teach you how to deal with stuff. And you learn how to just get a hold of the bull by the horns.

YDG   But is that by taking risks or doing what? A lot of women get thrown a lot of stuff, and they just seem to stay down.

CT   It's a choice; it's a choice you make. And . . . the problem with women that might just choose to stay down is, maybe they're comfortable being down. See, I'm not comfortable being down. I would never take away courage from my mom for staying with my dad; I would never take courage from your mom for staying with your dad. I would never take courage from people that decide, "You know, this is what I want, and this is what I'm going to hold on to, even if my life is imperiled," because it takes a lot of courage. I don't think they're blind to whatever the outcome might be. In my case, I was not comfortable with not trying. I think my choice was, I'd rather find out if I could, than always wonder if I couldn't.

YDG   And that's something that you feel is in your blood? You never really learned that?

CT   Not really, I don't think. Because from a very young age, I was questioning, always, how far I could go, and I was always pushing the envelope and allowing myself to explore and, interestingly enough, I was a very shy, quiet little girl. Through my whole grammar school time, I was very introverted because I was dyslexic, because I had a lot of issues with learning. I tackled reading on a prompter; I enjoyed it, because I couldn't do it before.

YDG   So you like challenges?

CT   Yes. When I was five years old, they told my dad I was never going to learn how to read. At the time, they didn't know what dyslexia was. My dad said, "She's not stupid, so she's going to stay in a private bilingual school until I say she's not going to go." So not only did I learn how to read and write, I learned how to read and write in two different languages. I've been speaking English since I was four.

The big challenges when I was little were with my parents. When my mom or dad said "no" to me about something, I had to find out why; they had to give me a good enough reason why, and if it wasn't valid for me, I would question the fallacy of their statements, and then, you know, call them on it.

YDG   And you were allowed to do that? Wasn't it a sign of disrespect?

CT   I was not allowed to do that. I got my butt kicked many times. And, finally, you learn how to pick your fights, because it would have been hell for me. And I've got to say, there were some times when I realized, as I got older, I think I'm not fighting the right battles. You know? So you learn how to choose your fights and be very observant, and then I realized that it was a lot easier to say I'm sorry than to ask for permission.

I think one of the issues that made me become who I am today is the fact that my dad always expected the best of me. Nothing but the best, because he gave me nothing but the best.

YDG   But the best for him, was that the best for you, too? Given that he was a traditional male, as far as having women? Wouldn't the best for you be subservience to your man?

CT No, which was a dichotomy in his lifestyle. When we have conversations now, he says, "I was preparing you for a different era, because the world that I was living in was not what you were going to inherit." Yes, and he also realized that he could only hold on to me for so long, especially with my character; he knew that if he hung, if he held on too tight, I was going to slip away. I was always very inquisitive. He knew that my curiosity was going to take me very, very far.

YDG Would you recommend to today's woman that she do the same thing your mother did? If she had a man/husband here, and he had a few wives and children everywhere, would you tell her, "Stay for the sake of your family?"

CT You know, that is very, very hard advice to give. I think a woman should do what a woman feels more comfortable with. Because, again, I will never take away the merit from my mom. She was still a very educated woman. I cannot say she was uneducated, or she was stupid, because she wasn't.

YDG Was she happy?

CT In many ways she was. I learned from my mom that happiness is based on moments. You're never in a state of happiness. It's just very small and very short-lived moments in which you are happy.

Now, I think she was content and satisfied with the lifestyle that she led and the things that she got a chance to do, because she exceeded the expectations she had for her own life. Even though my dad was not the most faithful man on earth, he was still a very good provider, and she really didn't need him to provide for us, because she could do that, too. But she was satisfied with the fact that he was supportive when she needed support. When I look back at her life, I realize she did everything she ever wanted to. And she had two beautiful girls. My mother was great, because she knew the art of compromising.

YDG You don't feel you know how to compromise?

CT I don't think I have to compromise. But it's an issue, because life is about compromises. Because you don't have everything, you can't have everything. There's no way on earth. The more rational side of me says there's no way on earth I'm going to have everything I've ever wanted; there's no such thing.

So, somewhere along the line, I have to give. But the little girl in me says, "I'm not giving jack!" Because this is mine, you know what I'm saying? So it could be a tad bit of a problem. I don't think I could ever be half the woman my mom was. I can only hope that wherever she is right now, she's proud of me.

YDG   What kind of positive or negative messages about yourself did you receive growing up? Did you believe them?

CT   I think my dad always said, and my mom, they both said that I could do anything I wanted. And I believed it. And they always said there's no big task you cannot conquer.

YDG   Growing up, what did your parents teach you about fear?

CT   My parents taught me that you could only measure the power of your success by the number of times you tried to get there. And if you embarrass yourself in front of people, so what.

And I've embarrassed myself publicly many times [laughter], and then I go home and go, "How could I do this?" And then, at the end of the day, I'm thinking, "So?"

What I do here is a job. It's just that. Now, when I was going to medical school, I realized that a mistake like that could cost a person's life, and then you can't just say, "Oops, sorry." And that's how I measure the importance of what I'm doing now. Yes, I am on TV. Yes, it's the biggest independent station on the west side of the Mississippi. It is huge credibility.

YDG   So is it true that you are the first Latina sports anchor in America?

CT   Yes, I am. That sounds like a lot, but it is only a job. You can't get caught up in it. You can't let anything get to you, either good or bad. What happens is that you lose perspective of where you are coming from and where you are going. I mean, I've lived in my car before.

YDG   Do you live by many cultural traditions?

CT   No . . . Yes . . . No. Yes and no. I guess I take what works for me.

YDG   How do you feel about *respeto*? Do you believe that young Latinas should respect their elders, even when the elders don't respect them?

CT Hmmm, that's a huge issue. Now, if you respect your elders . . . and those role models are disrespectful of you, that could create low self-esteem and all the terrible things that come with that. That's a very, very interesting question.

If you have a sixteen-, seventeen-year-old who is assertive, most likely she will say something to her elders if disrespected. But at five or six, if you tell somebody that she's stupid or something, or underestimate her abilities or her future, the problem becomes that at sixteen or seventeen they're going to take that from everybody.

The problem lies in lack of education. Those elders are very uneducated, and they come from a country or a world where to be subservient was the only way to survive. Many were married off by the time they were thirteen, fourteen, to whomever would take them in order to be fed and have a roof over their heads. That was the only way their parents could assure their daughters or granddaughters that they were going to have a safe future.

YDG Has the criticism ever affected you to the point where you just want to quit your position?

CT Many times.

YDG What's kept you from quitting?

CT My pride. They weren't going to win. It would be a very cold day in hell. . . .

Also, my guys here are great. They feed my ego. My guys are like, "You're going to let them win? You flew all the way here from Colombia, your first language is not even English, you know more sports, more boxing, more soccer than most people that we know, and you're going to let these people beat you up?"

YDG Was it hard for you to come to terms with the fact that you weren't going to change their minds? Didn't you want to change their minds so badly?

CT Oh yeah, in the beginning I did. And it took some time. I had to put myself in that situation. So they don't like me for whatever reason, and I'm not even going to try to understand why they don't like me, but there's a point in time that I know, that I know how to do this. I don't care what he thinks or what she thinks; I know how to do this. And this is what pays my bills.

Not you, not her, not him, it's this. My station seems to like me, and they're the ones who sign the check.

So I don't want to say I have high self-esteem or low self-esteem, I just know what I can do. And I know what I can't do. I know I can't change anybody's mind; I know I'm not a golden coin to be liked by everybody, because the day I do become liked by everybody, the day everybody thinks I'm the hottest thing on earth since freakin' toilet paper, then there's something wrong with me.

YDG   Do you believe you learned that, and from where?

CT   Being bruised. Our culture teaches us to be crowd pleasers. We're definitely crowd pleasers. We're taught to say the right thing at the right time to the right people, and I always questioned why. I don't feel that way, so why am I supposed to say that?

I have become more politically correct. Something that I learned, too, with time, is that the only person that I have to live with for the rest of my life is me. And if I don't make myself comfortable, if I don't look after myself, nobody else will. Because I don't care how much my daddy loves me; I don't care how much my mommy loves me; I don't care how much my boyfriend loves me; they're people, too, and they've got needs, too, and sometimes their needs don't meet mine.

YDG   So that's the golden message more than anything?

CT   Yes. That is something I learned—hard knocks. I overextended myself; I spread myself out too thin, and I got sick. I got literally sick. I had to fight cancer, because of all the stress.

YDG   You had cancer? What kind of cancer?

CT   Cervical. I've been in remission for five years. It was about seven years ago.

I spread myself out too thin, because I was trying to do too much. People needed to have this and that, and they needed it now. And guess what? I wanted to please everybody. It did me bad. I went down to 95 pounds; I lost everything I ever had, and I didn't have much. The only thing that kept me going was school; because I was still going to school. And there were times where I couldn't even get up; I didn't even have enough money to buy . . . certain medications, so my stomach wouldn't react to the chemo. My stomach never settled, and I didn't have money for regular food either, so it beat me in more ways than one. So that I have a problem with. And though I want to say I beat it, you never know. With cancer, it's something that you never know. It could creep back in no time.

Latinas learn to be people pleasers all the time. And then, when I needed something, I didn't want to hold people to it because my situation was a little more complicated. It was emotional, and a lot of people have a hard time handling the "C word," you know? They couldn't overextend themselves for me. Not that I expected it. But once everything was said and done, it was me, myself, and I, and all three of us had a great time, and it was a hell of a team.

YDG   What is your greatest fear?

CT   Going back to where I was five years ago, living in my car, eating Fig Newtons and coffee, because that was the only thing that I could afford. That's my fear. And that's my drive, too. I don't want to go there again. Because even though I could do it, it was not fun, and it was a very, very rough time in my life. And then, when I lost my mom, I think that was the last thing I needed. But that's my greatest fear, to find myself again sleeping in my car, taking showers at work. I was fortunate enough to have people around me that would help me out.

I realize now that I needed to go through that to be a better person, to be a little bit more compassionate. But not even then did I compromise, and because I did not compromise, that's why I ended up where I am. And I got myself out of that without compromising.

You know why I didn't kill myself? Because I had too much pride. My thought at the time was, "What are they going to do with my body?" I had no friends; well, I had friends, but I didn't have friends that could send me back to Colombia. That's like $4,000 with a decent casket. And then, at the time, my mom was still around, and I couldn't do that to my mom. It was not only the grief but also letting her down.

We all have to fight our own demons; they come in different shapes, forms. And whatever we do, we cannot allow those demons to conquer and take over. We cannot. Where I come from, I was physically abused, sexually abused, mentally abused for long periods of time. I don't know how to compromise, because I feel that if I'm compromising, I'm allowing somebody to control me. And it's not easy to assume responsibility over that behavior, either, because it's also detrimental. I can wear myself out. I can work myself to death, because that's the only thing I know how to do, and I know how to do it right. And it took me thirty-two years to understand that about me.

YDG   I talk about sexual abuse in my book. It is a very touchy issue, but we cannot look the other way when one of four women is sexually abused in their own homes.

CT   Absolutely. It was my uncle. He sexually abused me when I was three until I was nine. I later learned that sexual abuse is not about sex. It's about control. And, unfortunately, they do have control over us when we are young. My uncle lived with us. And that was my mom's favorite brother. The baby boy in the house.

YDG   Did your mom ever know?

CT   Yes, I confronted my mom with it, and she denied it. And she said that that was not true and that I was making it up, because if that did happen, how come I never told her. I said [it was] because I was afraid. She never acknowledged my fear or my vulnerability at the time. And that's why, in many ways, I grew up to be almost cynical.

YDG   Why do you think a vast number of young Latinas are suffering from low self-esteem and depression?

CT   Again, because we are crowd pleasers. Our culture has confusing messages. We're expected to be whores in bed; we're expected to be virgins when we get married. We're expected to be chefs in the kitchen and assertive in the work force . . . and the perfect Mother Theresa! I mean, hello? There are only so many things we can conquer at one time.

And then we have the grandma that wants us to pray a gazillion "Hail Mary's" before we go to bed, and we have the boyfriends who want us to give it up; but if we give it up, then they won't marry us. What the hell is wrong with us? And then our dad is sending us to school to be independent, yet he is maintaining our mother in slavery, so talk about dichotomies!

YDG What would you tell Latinas who feel they have no support in doing something positive for themselves? What would be your message to them?

CT To believe in themselves, because eventually, the only person that will carry you through everything will be you. Yeah, you're going to have people cheering, but they're just cheering. Those cheers, like we know in the NFL, don't make players win games. And it's hard. At no point in time would I ever say it's easy. It's very hard. And that's why it's so important for us to find out what it is that we want to do in life, where we want to see ourselves in "x" number of years. The last thing I would like to say is that we all have courage; we need to use our courage to live the life we want and to carry us through the hard times. We will never know that courage until we call on it and use it.

Her Courage to Survive

IRENE IBARRA
CEO and President, O & I Inc.,
    Relocation Services
Nationality: United States (Mexican
    heritage)
Born: July 16, 1959, California
Latina highlights: CEO and President
    of a million-dollar corporation

At the age of sixteen, Irene Ibarra was pregnant and had been thrown out of her house; at eighteen, her fifteen-year-old brother died from a brain aneurysm. By the time she was twenty, she had three children, an abusive husband, and a second brother murdered in a drive-by shooting. Family and friends had written her off as "a lost cause." Irene had a gift, though; she had the foresight to see what would happen if she gave up, and she didn't like what she saw.

One evening, when Irene returned home, her husband was waiting to beat her into unconsciousness. As she entered the door, he slugged and kicked her, breaking three ribs, causing internal bleeding, breaking her nose, and disfiguring her face so severely that it took five months to heal. When she woke up the next morning, she found that her husband had kidnapped her three children, vowing to kill her if she tried to find them.

While desperately searching for her children, Irene came to the realization that unless she did something with her life she would not be able to provide for her children when they returned. She enrolled in junior college and began to work for the City of Santa Ana in California. Within three years, she went from making less than $12,000 a year to $42,000 a year. Eventually, she began her own business and is now the sole owner and president of O & I Inc., Relocation Services, a million-dollar corporation in Whittier, California.

From the moment I met Irene, a year prior to our interview, I knew she was an amazing Latina. In her presence, you can feel her strength and perseverance, but most importantly, you can feel how real she is.

YDG   Tell me a little bit about your life growing up.

II   I was born and raised in Santa Ana, California. Both my father and mother were born and raised in California. Both are of Mexican descent. Family roots on my mother's side go back to Guanajuato, Mexico, and my father's side goes back to Mexico City. Growing up, I had nine siblings—ten of us, six brothers and three sisters. I had two brothers that died. One was fifteen years old, and he had a brain aneurysm. The vein burst, and he hemorrhaged and ultimately went into a coma. My parents had to make a very difficult decision and that was to take him off life support. He died within minutes after the life support was removed. I was eighteen. Then, two years later, I had a brother who was murdered. He was twenty-one. It was a drive-by shooting, and it happened just around the corner from my parents' home. He wasn't a gangbanger; he wasn't involved in gang activity, but the people that killed him were.

YDG   How did you feel about that? Were you devastated?

II   I didn't have time to think or react. I had just given birth to my youngest son. I was twenty years old and married with three children.

My brother Steven died when I was eighteen, and when I was twenty, my brother Maurice died. I had a troubled marriage. It all happened so fast that I don't think I was prepared to grieve. In fact, two years later is when it finally touched me. There was just so much happening in my marriage that I tried very hard to conceal.

YDG   Growing up, did you have a typical family life?

II   Yes, my parents have never divorced, and there are no major family dysfunctions. My parents are homeowners. My dad is a Korean War veteran. My mom stayed home and raised ten children. My oldest brother served in the Marine Corps; everyone either worked or went to school; my father worked in construction—he was a grade checker. He would check the grade and the cut of the land when freeways or tracks of homes were built. He is a retired member of the International Union of Operating Engineers. Everyone is registered to vote, and to this day we still take our voting stubs to my dad to show him we voted on election day.

YDG   Was anybody in your family college educated?

II   No. I'm the one with the most college. The rest had high school diplomas and GEDs. My father's whole deal was, "If you aren't going to go to school, go to work." My mother thought I was wasting my time going to school. After I got pregnant with my oldest daughter, who's twenty-four now, my mother said to me, "Why are you wasting your time in school? You're only going to get on welfare." Not very encouraging. But it was important to me that I graduate from high school.

YDG   Why was it important? Where did you learn to value education?

II   I would like to say it was my parents who stressed education, but I have to admit that it came from my peers and my teachers in a "Mentally Gifted Minor" program that I participated in when I was in junior high. I entered that program when I was in seventh grade. My teacher, Mrs. Templeton, went to my counselor and suggested that I be tested for the MGM program, which is now called the GATE Program. GATE is an acronym for "Gifted and Talented Education." What I found most interesting was, in eighth grade, my peers in my classes had already selected the colleges they were going to apply to when they graduated from high school. They already knew where they were going to go to college.

YDG   At what age did you get pregnant?

II   At sixteen I got pregnant. I did not tell my parents. I was terrified. Actually, I wasn't worried that I was going to get in trouble as much as I was concerned about the disappointment that I would bring to my father. I started getting morning sickness, and I was embarrassed to go to school, so I started cutting classes. Everybody found out at school that I was pregnant. One day, my mother asked me, "Irene, are you pregnant?" I said, "Yes." She said, "Okay, tell your father when he gets home." I didn't tell him; she told him for me. She told him while he was eating dinner, and I was in my bedroom, which was at the rear of the house. He came to my bedroom and was really angry and yelling and screaming, and he wouldn't let me talk. He picked up the TV and threw it at me.

I remember dodging the TV, jumping off my bed, losing my footing, kind of crawling in the hallway, but getting back up and running out the front door. I was hiding by the side of the car with my legs where the tire was, so that my father, if he looked under the car, wouldn't see my legs. As I was running out the door, he was telling me to get out of the house, to leave, to not come back, and that's all I remember. My dad yelling at me to get out of the house, to leave and not come back.

I stayed with a friend for a couple of days and went on to another friend's house, and then another friend's house, and then, after talking with my baby's dad, my boyfriend at the time, his mother took me in. So I lived with them for a while, for a couple of months.

YDG   Were you in love?

II   I thought I was in love. We lived in Indio for a couple of months. It was summer vacation our junior year in high school, and I was in the last trimester of my pregnancy. His brother helped him get a summer job. He was abusive then; in fact, he was abusive before I got pregnant.

YDG   But you chose to stay with him?

II   Yes.

YDG   Why?

II   I was stupid! [Laughter.] You think you're in love, and you think you're going to change him. He really didn't mean it; he really loves me. [Laughter.] I can laugh now. It wasn't funny at the time.

YDG   So he was abusive emotionally and physically?

II   Emotionally and physically. He was verbally abusive. I talked to my mother, and she told me to come home. She was crying and asked me to have the baby in Santa Ana. So I went back home and had the baby.

YDG   What about your dad, was he receptive then?

II   I don't think that he was happy about it, but I was his daughter. I think that he felt compelled to put a roof over my head.

YDG   Did he talk to you, or was he very distant?

II   He was pretty distant. At seventeen, I had my first baby. I had entered a teen mother program at school and graduated with my class. Everyone was shocked to see me at graduation. Nobody thought I was going to come back. I stayed at my mother's for a couple of months, and it was real difficult. My siblings were not very supportive. We were not the touchy-feely type of family, so you were just kind of there. I was afraid I was going to disappoint my dad, because there was that promise, that future for Irene. Everyone would say, "She's so smart, and she's active in girls' athletics, student government, and she's an honor student; she is going to go far." And look what happened—I took a dive. At least in their eyes, I took a dive. So, I got back together with my boyfriend, and we lived together. His mother was with us for a while, and life was about as intolerable as it was at my parents' home, at least in terms of catty remarks, the sarcasm, the "It's the end of the world, you blew it, your life is over, you'll never accomplish anything in your life, look at the path you've chosen." It was so negative.

Once I graduated from high school, I began working for the state of California in the Workman's Comp office. I was a mail clerk, attending junior college at night. I would drop off the baby with my mother-in-law or my mother so I could go to school.

Before I married my baby's dad, I dated someone else for a short period of time. He was in college and was very nice, but he was getting a lot of flack from his friends for dating a girl with a baby. One day, we were going to a New Year's Eve wedding and he said to me, "You better make sure that you look your best because there's going to be a lot of competition there tonight." I said, "I'm not going," and I refused to go because, to me, that was such an insulting comment. We didn't talk any more after that. My daughter's father came around about a week later and said he wanted to get back together. He said he wanted to get married, and he promised to change. What I didn't know was that it was his family that was telling him, "You need to get married, and you need to be a family. Do the right thing; go marry that girl, and get your baby home." So we got married, and nine months later I had another baby. It wasn't planned.

While I worked for the State of California, he attended college. I was paying the rent, and I was buying the groceries. He was partying on the weekends. On our wedding day, he looked at me and said, "I don't know why I married you, I don't even love you." I was shocked. Because he was drinking, I thought, "Oh, he must be drunk. He didn't mean it." I never mentioned it to him, and I should have left him that day. I found out two weeks after we were married that he was having an affair with the woman he'd been seeing before he came to my door and asked me to marry him. He never stopped seeing her.

YDG   So what did you do?

II   Stayed married. When I was about five months pregnant, he would take me to my mother's on Saturday afternoon and pick me up late Saturday night. I thought he was doing it because he wanted me to spend time with my family. In reality, he was with his girl and his guy friends. They would party in my home and eat the food that I worked to put on the table. I paid the rent and I cleaned the house. When he'd pick me up, he'd smell like alcohol. I didn't think anything other than he must have been out drinking with the boys.

I didn't want to pick up on things. I was in total denial. I didn't want to know. I went home early one night. I had my mother drop me off because I wasn't feeling well. He had these people in my house. That's how I found out that he was partying. I threw everyone out. He was sick on the bed; he was lying on the bed, and he just rolled over and vomited all over the carpet. He told me to pick it up, and I said, "I'm not cleaning it up."

YDG   He didn't help you with anything?

II   He didn't do anything except go to school. The next morning, he nudged me and said, "Aren't you going to go to work?" I said, "No, I'm not going to work anymore." The day after, he said, "Irene, get up, you have to go to work." I said, "No. I'm not going to work anymore." The third day, he said, "Irene, you have to go to work!" I said, "I don't have to go to work because I'm getting fired today." It was my third day not showing up. I got fired, and I didn't go back to work. That was my way of rebelling.

YDG   So he had to go to work?

II   Yes. By then school was out, so he had to work that summer. In fact, he had to work every day after that because I never went back to work while I was married. When I was in high school, my senior year, I was going to school from 8:30 to 12:30, and then I had a job from 1:00 to 5:00, and then I had another job from 5:30 to 9:30. I was tired of working. I was just tired of working and trying to work towards something and not having my husband on the same track as I was. Then I got pregnant with the third baby.

YDG   Did you not believe in birth control?

II   I didn't take it because it used to make me sick. I was just stupid; I didn't think.

YDG   Did you believe in abortion?

II   No, I didn't allow it to be an option.

YDG   Did you grow up very Catholic?

II   Very strong Catholic family. We all went to Mass and catechism. There were First Holy Communions and Confirmations. I didn't get confirmed; at the time, I had my own rebellion against the church, at least the teaching. I would ask too many questions, and I was hushed all the time.

YDG   So you had your third child at twenty-one. Were you still married?

II Still married. My husband, throughout the marriage, flaunted his infidelity. He would come home with hickeys on his neck, hickeys on his chest. I don't know if I tried to repress everything or what. I remember arguing with him, and now I think, "Why did I argue, it didn't solve anything." I would yell at him and argue with him, and he would beat me and beat me until I shut up.

YDG Were the kids there?

II He would hit me in front of the kids, so I just learned to shut up. He would usually wait until the kids were asleep. He would come home late, smelling like he had had sex with other women. He was such a pig; he wouldn't even shower. I knew it wasn't me because he was not having sex with me.

I was tired by the third pregnancy. I was tired of the infidelity; I was tired of him flaunting it. I was tired of the beatings. When my brother Maurice died, the services were held at a funeral home. There was a rosary for him one night, and my husband knew I had to get to the funeral home. I told him to come home early, because I needed to go to the funeral home. Well, it was six, seven, eight o'clock, and he hadn't come home. He finally showed up at almost nine o'clock. I was the only family member missing at the rosary. He did that intentionally. The next day was the funeral, and he was supposed to stay home with the kids so that I could attend the funeral. He got up bright and early and went to work; he had never gone to work early before.

YDG So what happened?

II Gabriel was a week old; Sergio was a year and two months old, and Vanessa was three years old. I took them to the funeral with me. That's why I didn't react initially to my brother's death. I had all these other issues. By the third pregnancy, I was tired. I was tired of my life. I couldn't go home and tell my parents because then I would hear, "I told you so." It wasn't as though my parents were supportive anyway, because they disliked my ex-husband. My mother, to this day, is not close to my children and doesn't "like" my children. I say that freely because I know she doesn't like them. She doesn't like my children because she doesn't like their father. That's really a shame.

YDG Do they know that?

II   My children feel it. They sense it. They don't spend time with her. Why would you put yourself in a position where you're around people that don't like you?

YDG   Have you ever told her that?

II   No. She's seventy-four. I don't need to do that to her, I really don't.

She dislikes my ex-husband because of the way he treated me. When I was seven months pregnant with my third baby, I was at my obstetrician's office for a standard visit when the nurse tells me, "Irene, you need to take some test over; the results didn't come back right; something is wrong." The doctor needed another blood sample. The doctor said, "Irene, you need to come into my office right now." So I went into his office and the doctor said, "I hate saying this to you because I know you and your family, but you need to go to the county health department. Your blood test came back positive for syphilis. You have to go to the county and register yourself as a carrier of a sexually transmitted disease."

I walked into the county clinic, and I'm looking around me, and clearly I was among drug addicts, prostitutes, and I'm saying to myself, "I don't belong here." I was a married woman with two children and another one on the way. I was faithful to my husband. I wasn't supposed to be there anymore than I was supposed to get pregnant at sixteen; it wasn't supposed to happen.

So I found myself, again, in a situation where I didn't think I belonged, but nevertheless, I had to deal with it. A counselor called me into a room, and I'm sitting in this booth. The male counselor says to me, "Well, I need a list of names of all the people that you've slept with in the last five years." I looked at him and I said, "Well, I'm only twenty-one." He says, "Well, since you were sixteen, how many people have you slept with?" I said, "My husband, no one else." He said, "You want me to believe that you've not had sex with anyone but your husband for the last five years?" I said, "Yes, that's the truth." He said, "Well, I don't believe you, but I'll mark it down anyway." I couldn't believe what he was saying to me. I was crying. It was awful.

YDG   He totally shamed you for something that you didn't even do?

II   I didn't do anything except have sex with my husband, who passed a sexually transmitted disease to me. I went back to visit my doctor, and he told me that he wouldn't be able to participate in the birth of my baby. He said, "Well, as you know, your blood test came back positive for syphilis. We don't know how long you've had it. It was sometime after the birth of your second child, so somewhere in an eleven-month period you were infected." He said he had found another doctor that would be at the delivery, who would be aware of the situation. When I questioned him more, he said, "I won't participate in the delivery of your baby, because your baby is going to be blind." Syphilis affects the eyesight.

YDG But why would he not want to participate? Was it because of the baby's potential disability?

II Because the baby had a high probability of being mentally retarded. He didn't want to be there.

YDG But doctors are supposed to help you, not discriminate!

II Well, you learn a lot in life as you get older. He said my baby was going to be blind; he said that there was a high probability that my baby would be mentally retarded and a high probability there would be some physical deformities. I fainted. I could not believe what he was telling me. It could not happen to me.

YDG When your husband beat you all those times, did you ever go to the hospital? Did you ever report it?

II No, because I was ashamed. I didn't want people to know that I was getting beat. I wanted people to think that I had it together. If anybody found out, then my family would find out, and if my family found out, I would hear "I told you so." I didn't want to hear it from my parents.

YDG So what happened with the baby?

II I went to the hospital after that because I had to get penicillin shots. It's really awful how people look at you and judge you without knowing what really happened. They see your belly; there's a baby growing in you, and they look at your medical chart and it says you have syphilis. It was pretty humiliating. You could just read their faces . . . I'm sure they thought I was sexually promiscuous. When I got home, after about an hour, my back started stiffening . . . my whole body, I couldn't move. I called my mother to come and get me. I called the doctor, and they told me to get to the hospital immediately.

I was having severe muscle spasms, and I couldn't move. It was a result of the stress. Just all the drama. My mother had come to pick me up and take me to the hospital. I didn't want to call her; I didn't want to tell her, but I had no one else to call. As we were leaving the apartment, my husband came home. She told him, "You stay with the kids. I'm taking Irene to the hospital." We went to the hospital, and the doctor had to find out if the syphilis had traveled into my spine, so he did a lumbar puncture. They had to take fluid out of my spine. All I remember is sitting on the edge of the bed, holding onto the chair, and the doctor saying, "Don't move, because if you move, you can be paralyzed." So, I didn't move, and they gave me some zylocain to numb my back, so they could do the procedure. I was in the hospital for about five days.

YDG   Was the baby okay?

II   They didn't know. They could have done an ultrasound, but they didn't do it. I went home and cried every day.

YDG   But you still stayed with your husband?

II   I stayed with my husband and cried every day, praying every day that my child would be okay. I prayed to God and begged him to inflict upon me any deformity or loss of eyesight or brain damage, whatever, anything, but not my baby.

He was born fine. He was perfect. So that had a happy ending. But I really despised my husband at that point. I really despised him. After that, it was the same routine—he was out with other women, coming home reeking of sex, and hickeys, and not coming home, and just your worst nightmare. You never think it is going to happen to you.

One night we had some friends over. Actually, at the time, it was my best friend. Her sister had been over also; we were just adults getting together, and we were playing some music and having a couple of drinks, and my friend and her sister stayed over. In the morning, I gave her sister a ride home. When I came back, I was in for a surprise. My husband and my best friend were having sex on my bed. Apparently they didn't hear me. I walked in, and I distinctly remember being quiet because I didn't want to wake my three children. I thought she must have left, and I opened my bedroom door, and there she is, straddling my husband, and they're going to town, in front of my own eyes.

YDG   Had it ever occurred to you that she would do something like that?

II   Not from my best friend. So he pushes her off of him, and then he says, "I don't want that whore in my house!" I looked at him and said, "You're the whore!" and I remember getting hit. It was just not real; this could not be happening to me. There had been so much promise. How had I let myself get here?

YDG   You were feeling as if your life was over at the age of twenty-one.

II   Right. How did I get here? I'm twenty-one; my husband can't keep his penis in his pants; I've got three kids, my mom. I keep my distance from my mother and my father because I don't want to hear, "I told you so," and "see what your life is; it's a pile of shit," for lack of better words.

At that point, I said, "Okay, I need to make a decision. In what direction am I going to take my life?" I have no idea where I got the guts, but I called a friend and said, "You know what? My husband's not going to come home tonight. Why don't we go out, let's do something." I was twenty-one, and I had never been to a nightclub; I had never been anywhere. I was so green, so to speak. When I was in high school, I never got to go to any high school parties; I didn't get to go to school dances because my mother wouldn't let me go. In high school when I was in girls' athletics and we would travel to other schools, my mother didn't trust me and would follow the bus to make sure I wasn't lying to her. My mother just didn't have trust in anyone. So she followed us to the other schools and she'd wait for me to get off the bus to make sure that I really was there. My parents were overprotective.

YDG   So you didn't get to see a lot of reality.

II   No, I didn't get to see a lot of reality. I believed in the Catholic philosophy: you get married only once; this is your mate for life; you marry him, and you stay with him. I believed all that.

Getting back to my friend. She came over and picked me up that night. We didn't go anywhere but to her friend's house and had a few drinks. I just wanted to get out of the house; I didn't care what we did. I really didn't drink. I had a couple of shots of tequila and that was it. I decided to go home, and I was absolutely terrified because it was late. It must have been about

1:00 in the morning. I was thinking that I shouldn't have gone out. When we pulled up in front of my house and I saw my husband's car parked outside, I knew I was in trouble, and I was begging my friend to go inside with me, just begging her.

She didn't want to, and I said, "Please, please, please don't let me go in there alone; you don't know what he's going to do to me." That's when she found out that he was beating me. She went in with me. He was sitting on the floor with his back against the door. I opened the door and he started yelling at me, and I just went to the bathroom. I was praying and praying that he wouldn't beat me, but as soon as I walked out the door, boy, I got it.

YDG What about your friend?

II Well, she had gone into the room. She was scared. He had a nephew who was there with him. I think the nephew was eighteen, and the nephew just stood there and watched his uncle beat me. He was beating me and beating me. I don't remember the physical pain. I remember him hitting me in the head, and I remember seeing flashes. He was hitting me so severely that I could just . . . it was almost like I could see these little electrical charges. He was beating me on the head, and he had these steel toed shoes on. He was kicking me. I remember counting the kicks from the hallway to the living room. He kicked me ten times. He ended up breaking three ribs, my nose, and I was bleeding internally. I didn't know I was bleeding until the next day. I couldn't breathe. He was beating me because I went out, and his wife wasn't going to do that. He could do it, but I wasn't going to do that.

My friend was trying to climb out of the window when he grabbed her. She said to me later, "I don't know where he came from, Irene; he grabbed me, and he said, 'If you get out, you're next,'" and she froze. He told his nephew to watch her and to make sure she didn't get away. He didn't want her to run and call the police. Somebody had already called the police because they heard my screaming. My husband, like my father, opened the front door and told me to get out. My husband literally grabbed me by the back of my clothes and said, "If you're going to act like a whore, then go live amongst whores," and he threw me out of the house.

I went to a neighbor's house. The police had come and talked to him. He had this very innocent look about him. He was sitting with the kids, and he told the police, "Look, she scratched me. She came home drunk; she does it all the time." They came over to talk to me at the neighbor's house. I couldn't breathe. I didn't know I had three broken ribs, and my eyes were already swollen; my lips were cut, and my nose was bleeding. So they could see, clearly, that I had been beaten. But they also thought I beat him, and I attacked him; therefore, I deserved what I got. They said, "We're hearing two stories; we're hearing one story from him and one from you. Which is it?" I looked at them and said, "If you believe his story, then you need to leave." So they left. The next day I called home and told him I wanted to come and get my kids. He told me that if I went near the house he was going to kill me. I waited another day. I was terrified.

I called a friend from high school, and she came and got me. She was horrified at what she saw. Horrified. She said, "We need to hide you; you need to get away. That man's going to kill you." I called him again and said, "I just want to come and get the kids. I just want to get my clothes and get the kids. You can stay there; I just want the kids and the clothes." He said, "If you come near this house, I'm going to kill you and take the kids to Mexico." It was a very real threat. I was scared. People were telling me, "Your husband is looking for you; you better be careful or he's going to kill you." I didn't know what to do. I didn't call my parents or any of my siblings because I knew if they saw me . . . I was more afraid of what my brothers might do to him. I didn't want my brothers to go to jail. I was afraid of what my parents would do if they saw me. I looked horrible. I went to the hospital the second day because I couldn't breathe, and that's when they took the X rays and told me I had three broken ribs.

I tried calling him again, and he just kept making his threats, and then he moved. He just got up and left with my kids. I didn't know where they moved. I was looking for them, but I didn't have any money. I had nothing. I had nobody to help me. I didn't even have a car.

YDG   Were you fully dependent on him?

II   Totally, 100 percent dependent on him. I had nothing. No money. I had nowhere to go. And there weren't battered women's homes; there weren't any kind of support systems like there are today. I ended up staying with my friend, Alma, for quite awhile, three or four months, and I just said, "Okay, what am I going to do? Where am I going to go? What is my plan? I don't know where he moved. How do I find out where he moved? How do I do that when I don't have any money?" I needed to get a job; I needed to do something. So I enrolled in school. I went to Santa Ana College and took some classes.

YDG   And all the while you didn't know where your children were?

II   No. First, I thought they had gone to Mexico. But then I thought, no they didn't go to Mexico; they're here. So I would drive by where I knew his brother had rental property to see if they were in one of those units. I didn't find them.

It took five months for me to heal; it took five months for all the deformities in the face to go away. The bruising, my lip, the swelling was so severe. My nose was crooked for a long time. It was crooked from being broken.

I enrolled in junior college, and I met somebody. I ended up moving in with him. He said that I could go to school and work on my college education and live with him and just work part-time, that he would take care of everything else, which was great. Two years later, I got pregnant, and that's my youngest child's dad.

I used to cry every day for my kids, because I didn't know where they were; I didn't know anything. And my boyfriend said to me, after about a year and a half, "Irene, you need to go find your kids." He gave me money to go talk to a lawyer. I went to see a family friend that was a lawyer, and she started all the paperwork, the entire tracing, everything that had to be done. I didn't know how to do it. I could do it today, but I couldn't do it back then. So, from public records, she found them. Someone in her office found them, and then we served him. Actually, he was in Santa Ana. We had him served, and we were going to court. I also found out I was divorced. I didn't know he had divorced me. I wanted to fight him for full custody, but the attorney told me, "Irene, you've been gone too long. You've been gone for two years, and I'm going to tell you right now, you're not going to get custody of your children."

YDG   Even though he left you and hid the kids from you?

II It didn't matter. That's not the way courts work. It's very black and white; they don't want to hear the story behind it. My attorney said, "To the courts, you basically abandoned them; it doesn't matter what the circumstances were. You've been gone. Let's just work on getting some visitation." And that's what we worked on.

I got visitation rights, and then he sued me for child support. At one point in 1995, I received notice that I owed $13,000 in welfare reimbursement, and the state of California was going to garnish it from my wages. They did. He collected welfare, and I had to pay it back. Getting back to the visitation of my children, I got to see them every other weekend and once during the week. By this time, the kids were six, four, and three, and the baby did not know me at all. Oh, it was awful, it was awful. He didn't want to come with me at all. My daughter remembered me vaguely, and my son, the middle one, was just coming along to see what he could get. That's what he tells me. It was not easy getting to see the kids, because his mother would say, "No, you're not taking the baby," and then he would block the doorway. Then his sister would block the doorway and [say], "You're not going to get the kids," and I would go to the corner and call the cops, and show them my court order. I had to call the police to get my children! Finally, after four times that the police were called, I called my lawyer, and she sent them a letter stating that if they continued to interfere with my visitation rights, we were going to request a change of custody. They stopped. My ex-husband remarried and had four children with the second wife.

I was working for the city of Santa Ana at the time, and then I got a job offer in San Jose to work in the real estate department as a relocation specialist. Prior to that, I had been a receptionist in personnel with the city of Santa Ana. I had taken some building inspection courses, hoping to become a code enforcement inspector, because that would get me out of the clerical field. I was now looking for the quickest way out of clerical without a degree.

I knew I was capable of doing more. I wasn't satisfied with answering phones, typing envelopes, that type of stuff. I could do more. I compared the different departments and tracked them on my own—where the best opportunity for women was, and where the best opportunity for Latinos was. That was the

Planning Department, and that was the code enforcement program. They lacked Spanish speakers. I'm bilingual.

I had talked to the Code Enforcement Coordinator prior to applying, and I said to her, "You know, Rita, I've been tracking your department, and the planning department offers the most opportunity to Latinos and, more importantly, to women. You have the number one department in the city. You have the best team. I'm a star, and I'm ready to join." She said, "Go put your transfer in." So I transferred departments and quickly promoted from a Typist Clerk IIIn Personnel to Code Enforcement Officer in Santa Ana. There was some protest to my being hired because there were men in the trades that scored higher and felt that they should be hired over me.

YDG   Why do you think you were hired?

II   Well, I had the technical knowledge. I had the book knowledge because I had just come out of class. Number two: I was hired off the bilingual list. More importantly, I already understood a little bit about municipal government. At least the process. . . . In addition to that, I was an honor student at Santa Ana College. So this woman, Rita Hardin, really went to bat for me. That's what I've learned. I used to attribute my success to myself. I did it on my own! Nobody helped me! The truth is, there were lots of people that were helping me. My ex-boyfriend gave me the money to go to the lawyer to at least get to see my kids. There was this woman, my mentor, who gave me the opportunity to transfer to her department and become an inspector.

YDG   How long were you an inspector?

II   I was with the city of Santa Ana for four years. Then, Rita called me from San Jose and said, "Irene, I've got this relocation project, and I want you to handle it. You can shine like a star, and you can shine my star. Come up and turn this project around." I said, "Rita, I am so flattered that you have so much confidence in me, but I don't know a thing about relocation." She said, "Don't worry about that. I need your people skills. Get up here." I actually started on contract, and then subsequently took the civil service exam and became a city employee. I worked for the city of San Jose for three years. Then I took a leave of absence. My youngest was starting kindergarten.

YDG   So the youngest child was with you in San Jose?

II   Well, the youngest one was. Her father and I split up when she was about five months old, and we had her an equal amount of time. She wasn't in school, so it wasn't a big issue. She would spend two weeks with me, two weeks with him, one week with him, one week with me, like that. She had an American Airlines frequent flyer card.

I took a sudden leave of absence because I missed the opportunity with my other children, and I didn't want to do it with her. Then, I got a call from an engineering firm in Louisiana. They had a project in Petersburg, Virginia, and they wanted me to do the relocation work. We negotiated a contract over the phone. They said it would only be two weeks, so I took the job. When I got to the project in Virginia I realized it was a six-month project. Nobody could complete it in two weeks. We renegotiated. I talked to Desi's dad, and he said she would be fine: "She'll just start school here instead of up north. Don't worry about it, I got her." I'd come to California once a month and visit my daughter.

YDG   Did you see your other three children?

II   No, I didn't see them as much because now their dad had remarried, and they had children, and his wife didn't like me coming to their house; she didn't like me coming to the door . . . she wanted to erase me is what she wanted to have happen. It wasn't going to happen, but she would have liked me to have been gone. Then the fighting just got to be too much. I'd see the kids sometimes but not as much as I had wanted to.

When I came back from Petersburg, Desi's dad sued me for child custody. In court he lied, just flat out lied. I'm cordial and I'm kind to him now because he is the father of my child, and I don't want her to lose any respect for him. I don't want her to be thirty years old and say, "You used to say these things about my dad." It was about a six-month process; I spent about eight thousand dollars, and he probably spent an equal amount. In the end, we went to the court and told the judge our solution: fifty/fifty, no child support, and we'll keep her covered with medical insurance.

YDG   What happened then?

II   I was staying with a friend. She was renting a condo, and I was staying with her because I had to be in Orange County for court. I had to show that I had a residence. Now, instead of coming down here and spending a week with Desiree and then going back home to Aptos, I stayed here and flew up to San Jose to do my work and then came back the same day. What I didn't know was that the friend I was giving half the rent to was pocketing the rent, not paying it. She got evicted while I was going through this custody battle.

I relocated here to Orange County in 1989. I was staying at my parents. I took a year off and took my daughter to school, kept her over every other week. Then I had to go back to work. I started thinking of other consulting opportunities, but most of my work was up north. I was working up north, and coming down, spending a week here at my mom's and then going home to Aptos for a week, coming back for a week, going home for a week, and that's what I did throughout Desi's second-grade year, until she was seven.

One day she woke up—and this is something I've been crucified for in the past, but it was a decision I made, and I think it was the right decision—she woke up one morning, and she was lost. She didn't know where she was. I had to remind her that she was at grandma's house. I felt so horrible for doing that to my child. How could she not know where she lived? She's at her dad's; she has a room there; she's here with me, and we're sharing a room. Two different lifestyles, totally. I would drop her off Monday morning at school, and then I wouldn't see her until the following Monday after school. He would pick her up. Her father and I weren't talking. After that morning I told him, "You know what? You win. I can't do this to her anymore. I don't want her ever to wake up again and not know where she is. She needs stability. She needs to be in the same environment; she needs routine, and she's not getting it this way. You win; she's yours during the week; I'll pick her up on the weekends." We didn't need a court order for that.

YDG   So how long did that go on?

II   It still goes on today; she's now seventeen.

YDG   When did you decide to start your own business?

II   I was doing independent consulting work, but in 1992, I went to work for an engineering and planning firm in Orange

County. They were a company that I had subcontracted to for a lot of work in northern California. I took a significant cut in pay, almost half, and I went from having my own contracts to working for them. But that afforded me the opportunity to see how a larger corporation worked, how they packaged proposals, how they interviewed. And I was looking at the benefits of coming home and being closer to my children and not having to travel so much. I ended up benefiting from watching their operation. I didn't go to business school; I don't have an M.B.A. or a B.A., and so I just kind of learned on the job.

One afternoon I went to a prebid conference for the M.T.A. (Metropolitan Transportation Authority) and saw another Latina relocation consultant, Vila, and I said to her, "Hey, these guys have made a lot of money off of us, what do you say about teaming up? Let's go out there and get some of that money ourselves." So that's what I did. I was working full-time, and in the evenings, I was writing two proposals that we barely got in on time. We won both contracts from the M.T.A. After that, we picked up the Los Angeles Unified School District, and then the city of Garden Grove, the city of Glendale, Paramount Unified, San Jose Redevelopment, Santa Clara Water District, Alhambra, city of Carson, and so on.

YDG   Through all the difficult times in your life, why do you believe you never gave up?

II   I think that I had the foresight to know what would happen if I did give up, and I didn't like what I saw. If I was satisfied with being a receptionist, then that would be my life for the next forty years. I also saw that I would have less to offer my children. My own personal growth had a lot to do with my children. Even though they weren't living with me, I knew at some time in their life they would be back.

I don't think that some women realize their potential. I think for some women it's easy to find someone to get married to and be taken care of. I think that our culture dictates that, and I think that they accept it. And once you accept it as final, that's it. There is no option. There are no choices. The choices have been made for you.

YDG   What were the messages you received growing up?

II   Well, I think my family stressed family first. Take care of your own. I think that my father, especially, instilled in us that we had to be responsible for our actions. My father instilled a really hard work ethic and watching him leave for work early in the morning, coming home late at night, working six days a week, ten hours a day to support his family, those are the values that we grew up with. You know, "You're going to stay out of trouble; you're going to go to school, at least graduate from high school." For my dad it was, "If you could just get a job and join the union, you're going to be okay." My dad used to always tell us that we were capable of doing the best job, and I believed that. I still believe it today.

YDG   What has been your biggest fear in life?

II   To be mediocre. There are still some areas of my life that I think I'm still working on not being mediocre.

YDG   Growing up, did you ever carry a belief about something, only to find later that the belief did not work for you anymore?

II   I grew up believing that if you worked hard, you're going to be successful. But the truth is that you need help from others. You need to make professional contacts. You need to work smart; you need to delegate to others. You can't do it alone.

YDG   Factory workers probably work harder than anyone.

II   That's right. And how successful are they? Look at the people that work in the sweatshops. Look at how hard they work. Look at how hard machinists work, or look how hard the factory workers or furniture movers work.

YDG   How did you learn that?

II   I think I learned it early in my career when I was a receptionist in personnel. Without anyone in the department realizing it, it gave me an opportunity to see people get promoted. People take civil service exams, but I saw exceptions being made, and then I realized that this isn't about how hard I work or how efficient I am at what I do, it's about having contacts, and it's about working smart. It's about recognizing opportunities and taking advantage of those opportunities, because they don't come around all the time. I learned that you have to take risks. You have to be willing to fail. You have to try. Because if you try, you don't fail. But if you don't try, then you have failed.

YDG   Do you live by many cultural traditions?

II   I used to live by very oppressive traditions. I believed what my mother-in-law used to tell me about how I was supposed to take everything my husband put me through. One time, I remember going to her in tears because my husband was being unfaithful. She said to me, "You know, Irene, that's the way men are. *Tienes que aguantarle.* (You have to put up with him.)" I wanted to die; I wanted to run out of her home. I wanted to scream. I couldn't believe I was hearing that. So those are traditions that clearly had to have been set by men.

I would like to think that I have kept good traditions and passed those on to my children, because I really believe that our culture is the glue that holds our families together. We have to know where we came from in order to know where we want to go. Now, the negative traditions, I'm not going to teach those to my children because I don't want them to go where I've been. I want them to go in another direction.

YDG   How do you feel about *respeto*?

II   I believe very strongly that respect is earned and is not a given with age. I don't believe elders can say whatever they want to you, and that's okay because they're older than you are. It's not okay. In fact, my oldest daughter needed a ride to work this morning. I picked her up, and she said, "Mom, when did I start being disrespectful to my dad's family?" I said to her, "You're not disrespectful. They're disrespectful, because they say nasty things to you. They think it's okay, because they're older than you, because they're your *tiós*, your *tiás*, your grandma, and that makes it okay. The truth is, it's not okay. You're not disrespectful; they're disrespectful, and all you're doing is calling them on it. When your grandma said, 'Ay, Vanessa, *estás gorda* (Vanessa, you're fat),' and you say to her, 'Why do you say that, grandma?' It's not being disrespectful. It's calling her on her rude comment." My daughter then says, "That makes so much sense." So I find it incumbent upon myself to make the change, to make changes for my children.

YDG   Have you ever felt like you just wanted to give up?

II   Yes, often I want to give up. Sometimes I say, "That's it. I've had it. I don't want to do this anymore!" But oftentimes, it's because of frustration. You know, it's "I've got to meet payroll, or my taxes are up, or something is coming up," and I get frustrated sometimes; or my clients aren't paying me the way they're supposed to; they're delaying payment. So I get frustrated in a business sense.

YDG   How about in life?

II   I think in life I wanted to give up when I couldn't do enough for my oldest daughter, to make her realize that the lifestyle she was living was one that she wasn't raised to live, and that in the life that she had chosen she was living on the edge, and there was nothing I could do to save her. Either she was going to persevere and snap out of it, or she would take a deep fall. That's when I really wanted to give up on life. My ex-husband had portrayed me as the devil, and she saw me as one, and I had feelings of "I can't do any more; I can't save my children from the evils of the world," and that's when I wanted to give up.

YDG   How do you think you acquired your courage to prevail?

II   I think that I developed the courage through the adversity in my life, going back to when I was sixteen when my dad threw me out. I think that tough times make tough people. I know that sounds corny, but I think it's true.

YDG   Growing up, did you believe you had a strong self-esteem or low self-esteem?

II   I always had strong self-esteem. I think that came from my grandfather. I was about six years old, and he was dying of throat and lung cancer. I didn't know at the time that he was dying, but my mother would visit him often and I would go with her, and I would sit next to my grandfather while he was eating. It was milk with mashed bananas, and that was all he could eat. I would sit next to him, and he would share his milk and bananas with me, and he would tell me in his hoarse voice that I was very special and that I was very smart, and he said, "You're going to do a lot with your life." I have believed it ever since.

YDG   Have you ever doubted yourself in any major life decision?

II   Oh, my God, almost every day, all the time! You know when I really just doubted myself? I don't know if it was so much a major life decision, but in 1987 I had to have my gallbladder removed. I remember sitting with my father in my parents' backyard, and I was telling my dad that I was going to have surgery. My dad said, "How's work?" and I explained to him how successful I was in San Jose, and he said, "How's your family?" I said, "My family is good." So he said, "Well, Irene, if you don't come out of the surgery, if you were to die tomorrow, are you satisfied with what you've done for your children? Are you satisfied that you know your children well? Are you satisfied that they know you well?" That really made me think about my relationship with my children. That's when I doubted; I started to doubt my relationship with them.

YDG   Have you always known or felt your internal strength?

II   I think I did. I think that strength was nurtured by my grand-father. He always said I was special.

YDG   Why do you think a vast number of Latinas are suffering from low self-esteem and depression?

II   We live in a dual society. On one hand, our families are telling us that we have to devote all our time to our families, otherwise we're not good daughters or mothers. Then, on the other hand, we're told to pursue higher education and leave our families if we have to. I think that those messages conflict with each other, and I think that it's very difficult for Latinas to find a balance. You have to find a balance.

YDG   Do you believe you are the hope for your children?

II   Yes, my children comment to me often, "How do you do it? How do you handle everything?" I say to them, "I don't have a choice. It has to get done. What's my alternative?" My son will call, and sometimes I'll be in the office, and he'll say, "Mom, what are you doing in the office?" "Well, honey, I have to get this stuff done." "Go home right now, Mom, go home; turn off the computer, get your purse, get out of the office. I'm going to call in twenty minutes, and if you answer the phone, I'm going to bug you, and bug you, and bug you until you leave." I tell him I just won't answer the phone! So they know . . . they know that while there may be days that I have to work late, there are also days that I just work from home.

There has to be a balance, and I think part of learning to bal-ance is to dispose of the bad. If you keep the negative and the bad, it will repress you, or oppress you, and you'll find guilt, and life is too short.

YDG That's true. Many Latinas don't realize it's bad for them. That's the only way of life they've known. They haven't explored the world; they're already married and have kids. They just feel like, well, I'm already in here, so what can I do now?

II That's right. Look what happened to me. At twenty, I've got three children. At twenty-one, I'm asking myself, "Is this my life? This is it? For the next twenty years? I'm going to get beat up for the rest of my life? I'm going to have a husband that's going to give me sexually transmitted diseases? I got a husband that's going to come home and beat me because I don't cook for him? For twenty years? I might as well be dead!"

Both of my daughters, especially my oldest one, when she dates a guy, she'll tell him, "You know, I really like you; you're a nice guy, but I really don't want this relationship to go any further. I like you, but I really don't see us spending the rest of our lives together." And she moves on. Well, they call her "white girl"; they call her Marsha Brady. It's not that she's a "white girl," but she chooses not to pursue a relationship that has no future. I instill positive cultural traditions; she has learned that certain behavior, not just on a man's part, but on her part as well, is either going to make her happy or unhappy.

YDG What would you tell Latinas that have had children at a young age and feel trapped?

II Boy, I've been there. I thought about that, and I was going to tell them to tie their tubes. [Laughter.] I had a tubal ligation, because after my fourth daughter I was pregnant again. My relationship was not very good with her father and I chose to have an abortion. I don't think it's right, but I don't think that it's right to tell a woman that she can't have one either. As I get older, I think that if one of my daughters got pregnant, I don't think I would want her to have an abortion. I think that I can give them the support that I didn't have when I had my children. After I had that abortion, I was so remorseful that I had a tubal ligation. I said, "I'll never do this again." I said I would never get pregnant again.

YDG Are you okay with that now, or do you still have issues with it?

II No, I don't have any issues with it. I think that what issues I did have I've come to terms with them. I needed to be forgiven, and I believe I have been. I'm okay with that now. Going back to the Catholic tradition, you know, you do that. You feel guilty, because it's a sin; it's a mortal sin. I felt that I had the sword of Damocles hanging over my head, just waiting to fall and hit me. I felt my soul was in danger of going to hell.

What I want to tell Latinas who have children at a young age and feel trapped, I would tell them, "You're eyes are on the front of your head, so always look forward! Don't be afraid to take risks." I would tell them, "You're not a failure if you try, but if you don't try, then you have failed. Don't ever give up."

YDG What would you tell Latinas who felt a lack of support (from those closest to them) when they wanted to do something positive for themselves?

II I would tell them to find a mentor, not a *menso* [silly person]. It's true. What happens when your family doesn't support you? Your man, your boyfriend, your husband is right there. And he could be a *menso* in the sense that you don't have the support from him anymore than you do from your family or friends. You're really not going to get support from a *menso*, so all you've done is hop from one frying pan to another. What they really need to do is to find a support group that they can open up to and share and bounce their ideas off of and get a reality check. A lot of our young Latinas, let's face it, they live soap opera lives. I say this because I employ so many young Latinas that live soap opera lives. I have to sit down and tell them, "Okay, now that works on *One Life to Live* and *All My Children*, but in life it doesn't work like that, *mi hijita*, and let me tell you the way it really is," and I give them a reality check. The other thing I would tell them is that it's tough being alone, but if you believe in yourself, you're halfway to meeting your goals. If I didn't believe in myself, that I was capable of doing the things that I've done, I wouldn't be where I am today.

YDG So how do you believe in yourself?

II Again, my grandfather told me that I was special. I had so many teachers that made so many positive impressions on me, and that's why I have so much respect for the teaching profession. I had this one teacher; I was a freshman, and I was in a geometry class, and I hated the class because I was the only freshman, and the rest of the students were juniors and seniors. I was cutting class a lot, and the teacher came up to me, and she said, "You don't care about this class, do you?" I just gave her this tough look. She said, "You don't care about your life, do you?" I just looked at her like "you're crazy!" Then she said, "But you know what? I feel sorry for you. You see that boy over there? He works on his homework two to three hours a night, and the best grade he'll ever get is a C. You waltz into my classroom, and you take tests you haven't studied for, and you're going to get an A, and I'm sorry that God gave you the brain that he did because you don't appreciate it. I wish he had your brain." It hit home, although my first reaction was to be defensive.

I thought about it throughout the day and for a couple of days after, and I went to her and said, "Well, what do I have to do to catch up in this class?" She said, "You've missed half the book; you need to do half the book." In two weeks, I completed all the assignments, which would have been a half of a semester. I completed all the assignments, and I walked out with an A in her class.

I really take to heart what people say to me except for the negative. The negative, I just let it slide off of me because people say negative things out of envy. They try to project their own low self-esteem on you.

YDG Any message you want to give to Latinas about life in general?

II Well, life isn't fair, and you make your own breaks. Don't dwell on the negative or the past. By being proactive, you can make things happen. Finally, get an etiquette book. We are usually taught manners at home, and as you move up professionally and socially there are social graces that you are expected to have in addition to your education.

Fifteen years ago, I went to the Ambassador Ball in Santa Ana, and I sat at a table with people that I didn't know. I waited to see which fork everyone else picked up at the table before I picked one up. There were so many forks and spoons I didn't know which one to grab! From that day, I said I would never let this happen again. I went and got an etiquette book out of the library. In fact, I have a business etiquette book, too. I think that's important, because we're judged outside of our cultural circle. We're judged as we move up professionally; we're not only working with Latinos, we're working with other groups of people.

Latinas have the power to create their own lives. That's what's so wonderful about this country. You can go as far as you want to go. You can make excuses; you can cop out and say that people are against you, but the truth is you have to be for yourself to make yourself.

Contractor with a Conscience

MARTHA DIAZ-ASZKENAZY

CEO and President, Pueblo Contracting
   Services
Nationality: United States (Mexican heritage)
Born: 1958, United States
Latina highlights: CEO and President of a $20-million corporation

She has been condescendingly referred to as a "decorator" and repeatedly questioned about her qualifications as a general contractor, but when you talk to Martha Diaz-Aszkenazy she says, "I don't know why people think it's such a big deal. I'm just doing what I love—building and real estate development!" People who work with Martha say she's a "tough cookie" because, although she stands 5'2" and weighs only about 115 pounds, she negotiates her contracts until she gets what she wants.

Martha and her husband, Severyn, began Pueblo Contracting Services in 1984. They are partners in the business, and Martha holds the title of president, although she says, "Most people assume that my husband is the president, and I'm not. If I had to pick a group of people who are the most critical, I would have to say it is Latino men, even more than white men."

Growing up in the 1960s, Martha remembers her mother preparing her for the "men in green cars" (i.e., immigration). "She would tell me that if they ever pulled me over to let them know I was a U.S. citizen. I don't know many kids that had to think about being randomly pulled over by a green car." Discrimination was everywhere in Martha's neighborhood in the San Fernando Valley, so much so that Martha would feel embarrassed about taking burritos to school for lunch. She was afraid of being viewed as different or weird. "And now, people have made billions of dollars off of these burritos I was embarrassed to take to school!" Living through discrimination, Martha was determined to get a good education and to eventually become wealthy.

With a deep belief that what you put out there is what you get back, Pueblo Contracting Services refuses to build prisons or any property that they cannot drive by. Her motto is, "If I can't drive by it, I don't buy it." With a powerful team like Martha and Severyn, there isn't much they can't accomplish. Both are firm believers in education as the key to accessing opportunity. So, in keeping with their values, they recently developed and built Library Plaza, which is a real estate development that uses a public library as an anchor for the plaza.

Martha has the undeniable courage to do what she loves, along with an uncanny ability to make it look easy.

YDG Tell me a little bit about how you saw the world growing up.

MDA I always saw myself as smart, and I remember, I think it was in the fifth grade, there would be honors programs and the gifted program, and I asked the teacher, "You know, I could do the work that those kids are doing." I think she was a little prejudiced, because she said, "No, I don't think you can." So, when I was in junior high, there was a Latino teacher who was my counselor, and he noticed that I had been getting straight A's on my report card, and he said, "Why don't we have you tested to see if you can get into the gifted program?" I took the test, and I got into the gifted program, and from that point on I had different classes, with smart kids; I was with great teachers, and the world was wonderful! We were diversified in school; there were Japanese and white kids. I saw the world as good. There were some fearful times, uncertain times, but I think they might have been caused more by growing up than just being Latina.

Within our own community, there was some stress with the kids if you were too dark. Being light was always better, and that was within our own community. That was stressful. In elementary school, it was a little bit weird because my mom would make burritos for me, and people would say, "Ugh, what are you eating?" I kind of had to hide what I was eating because I didn't want people to ask me. When you're a kid, you don't want to stand out. And now, people have made billions of dollars off of people saying, "Ugh, what is that?"

Immigration was a big deal, because in San Fernando there was a large immigrant community, many of whom were undocumented, and immigration officials would take people away. They would actually patrol the streets, and they would ask you, if you looked Mexican, if you had a green card.

YDG   Did they ever ask you?

MDA   No, but I remember my mother preparing me for it. She said, "If they ever pull you over, you're a U.S. citizen. Don't forget to tell them." My sister and I were both U.S. citizens. When we moved into San Fernando, it was in a transition period. It used to be a white community of professionals, actually: lawyers, doctors, teachers, and so forth. Then, all of a sudden, it started turning. So, when we came in, I remember Mr. Otto used to live next door. He didn't know what to make of us, so immediately he put up a little row of thorny rosebushes so that we wouldn't jump over to his yard. Then, when he befriended my dad a little better, he said, "Okay, you've gotten into the neighborhood, but you have to promise that you'll never sell your house to a black person."

I did notice that my dad, when he got pulled over by the police, they never gave him any breaks. He would always get tickets. I mean, there was some racism there, but I think probably the thing that confused me the most while I was a kid was that my dad told me that the church we used to worship at was filled, because the white church didn't want the Mexicans to go to church with them. That kind of turned my world upside down because I thought, "Why, if they're supposed to be good Catholics and good Christians, and all men are equal, and we're all brothers and sisters, why can't we go to their church?" I felt like there was a lot of hypocrisy.

YDG   Did you ever ask your dad that question?

MDA   You know what? Not really. But I think it hurt my dad, too, because he remembers even way back when the landlord would open all his mail before it got to him. Yeah, because his mail would go to Mexico, or his mail would come from Mexico, and at the time they had just finished World War II, and they were still concerned about spies, and so it was encouraged for people to open other people's mail. Even at the post office, they would open your mail, too. And my dad remembers that.

It's like you're a second-class citizen. I remember when we were growing up, my dad always used to say, "You were born in the U.S.A., but they may never accept you as a true citizen, so don't ever forget that."

I think that my culture is an unending kind of peace, in that there's always hope, and it keeps me going; it keeps my blood pressure down. It helps me understand that there's a reason why things happen. I choose to look and say, "Hey, I was misguided," and that was a subtle way of guiding me in the right direction. I learned, as a kid, that things you fear would disappear if you faced them, which still is my mantra in business. I think, "What happens if I get to the other side, am I going to fall off a cliff?" No. It's the fogginess of not knowing that's scarier than what is really on the other side.

So my culture, I think, helped me deal with it, because my parents would say, *"Si Diós quiere."* (If God wants.) That used to irritate me, because I thought, *"No, si yo quiero."* (No, if I want.) But I think growing up as an American kid with Mexican parents, we had to reconcile two worlds. But, like I said, we were brought up to think we could do anything. My dad told me, "Just don't take shit from anybody at school. If anybody ever pushes you around, you push them back; and if they kick you out of school, I'll take you back."

YDG   Growing up, what kind of positive or negative messages did you receive about yourself?

MDA   Well, I got messages from my grandmother at a very young age.

YDG   Was that very powerful in your life?

MDA   Oh yeah. She died when I was at Loyola Marymount University. I cried for days because she was just like this rock and this source of inspiration and support that I knew I had lost forever. If there was anybody who was influential in my life, it was my grandmother and her positive messages. I'm stubborn; I don't always believe what people tell me. I mean, I say "okay," and then I think about it, and I say, "No, no, they're wrong. I'm right. I'm going to do it again, and I'm right." I got negative messages along the way that I was ugly, because I was too dark.

YDG   Did you believe them?

MDA   Sometimes I did. When people tell you that, what are you going to do? In our culture, being light is better. It's so deep seated, and it goes back so far that I don't think anybody really remembers where it even started. It's the ultimate to be light. It's kind of like a self-hate thing. It kind of had a life of its own and grew on its own. So I think those were some of the messages that were . . . a part of growing.

YDG   So you came from a traditional family?

MDA   Oh, hell yeah! My mom and dad are both immigrants from Mexico. My dad came here on the Bracero Program and worked up in Stockton on the railroads, and he came down here because he heard the union was paying well. He joined the Laborer's Union and retired from the Laborer's Union. He met my mother here in the city of San Fernando, and they went back to Mexico and got married; and then my sister and I were born here, and then they shipped my mother and us to Mexico, and we lived there for three or four years. I remember we had a store. I have vague memories of living in Mexico. When we came back to the United States, I went into the first grade.

YDG   Did you know English when you came back?

MDA   No. I hadn't even seen a TV set!

YDG   So how did you learn English?

MDA   I went to a white school in Sylmar. I still remember the first day of school: they asked me if this was how I spelled my name, and I answered, "Yeah, I guess." I had no idea what they were saying to me. So they had these tutoring classes for remedial kids in the morning. They stuck me in those tutoring classes to bring me up to speed in reading and writing, and then they graduated me from the program within a short period of time. That was the extent of ESL [English as a second language]—it was all done in English. They didn't speak to you in Spanish.

YDG   Where did you grow up?

MDA   I grew up in the city of San Fernando; my parents bought a house, and we settled, and they're still there in the same house.

YDG   Did your mom work?

MDA   My mom worked when I was in the fifth or sixth grade; she worked as a seamstress. I have two sisters and two brothers. I'm the oldest of five.

YDG   Were you smart in school?

MDA   I was a nerd. On the weekends, I would take loads of books home, so that I could read. I liked to read, and I liked to read articles, whereas my sister used to ditch school.

YDG   I know that you went on to Loyola and that your dad was reluctant about you going to college. Is that because he thought you should just get married?

MDA   No. I think he was more concerned about my virginity, to be honest, and I think that he was concerned about me moving away. He didn't think that I shouldn't get an education. I think he was more concerned about my safety, how he wasn't going to be there to protect me, and then, of course, the ever present issue of sexuality. My parents took us to church every weekend; we went to Catholic Church every Sunday, never missed any of the celebrations during Lent. I mean, we were Catholics. So that was a big deal. Of course, getting pregnant would have been out of the question, but my mom was enlightened to a certain extent. I think she saw some of her friends that were in marriages, and they weren't that happy, but they had to stay because of the financial situation they were in. I remember my mother told me that I needed to go to school, and I needed to get an education and become independent because I shouldn't be dependent on any man for my livelihood. I should be able to support myself. You see, my dad wanted boys, so I was kind of a tomboy anyway. I loved sports. They wouldn't let me play in leagues and stuff, because they didn't think that was a ladylike thing to do. But I have always had that drive to compete, you know. I played on a volleyball team, as short as I am! I remember when we used to lose; I would try so hard, and sometimes I would cry after the game. I lived at Loyola, but I'd come home on the weekends. My dad was working at a job site nearby, and I'd go home with him, and he'd pick up my roommate and I, or we'd go home with somebody. We'd always find a ride home on the weekends. I never stayed the weekend (at school).

YDG   And were you okay with that?

MDA   Yeah, I was okay with it. I didn't have a problem with it, really. I kind of thought, I'm doing what I need to do.

YDG   Was sexuality taught to you as something that was bad?

MDA   Yeah. The church had a very strong grip on us. I want to make sure that I make it clear: all of the experiences that I had, regardless of whether they were negative or positive, I choose to believe that they all have helped to make me who I am. So in the end, I don't judge those experiences as really being bad or good. It's just that, experiences.

For example, I look at my parents and I see proud, brave people who left their entire families to come to a foreign country because they wanted to do better for themselves. I think my mom and dad tried as hard as they could to keep us safe, and with their experience, they did the best job that they could for us. So I'm thankful for that. I've learned from my dad to be proud of who I am, to work, to never think I am any less than anybody else. We just said [to ourselves], "You're smart; you can do it; you can compete." My dad was very proud. He was unemployed for a while, but he would not go on welfare or anything like that. We had beans instead, and no meat. He was that proud. I learned from him to pay my bills on time, to be orderly about things, to take pride in what I owned, and to be responsible. At an early age, when I was like fifteen or sixteen, I wanted to work because I wanted to have my own money to buy my own clothes. I didn't want to be a burden on my family, because I saw that my parents worked hard. I saw my mom get ripped off a few times when she took in work as a seamstress. People would leave and never pay her, and that would hurt. As a kid, you see that, and it hurts you. So I said to myself, "I don't want to be a burden on my parents." I had this drive to be independent early on, and when I was in college, I worked as a teller, and I would work in the summer, and I would work any break I got, and I would save my money, and then I would budget my money to last me throughout the whole year, you know. I didn't ask my parents for money.

I had scholarships. I couldn't have gone to college without my scholarships. I am thankful for that, and I think that this program should continue because I think that's the key to people making it in this world. I don't know where I got that from, but that was my drive. I learned to budget, and I learned to live within a budget, and I was poor because the school I went to, it had a lot of rich kids that had a lot more than I had. I wore the kind of clothes I could afford; I ate the kind of food I could eat, and I did the kind of activities I could afford. I stayed within my budget. If the money was gone, it was time for me to go back to work, and it worked out really well. I bought a car, my dad cosigned for me, and I made sure that no payment was ever late, because I figured I didn't want to ruin my dad's credit.

YDG   Where do you think you got that sense of responsibility?

MDA   I think I got that, to a certain extent, from my parents, and from my grandmother in Mexico who owned a business. She would sell *leche*. She had a farm, and she would sell milk to people, and she would give massages and do a number of things. She always used to tell me that I was smart, that she saw me as a successful woman, and that I would drive a car. To her, that was a big thing. She lived in a small village in Mexico. So I'd come back from our visits with grandma, which were about a month long, and even if people were to think I was dumb, or a dork, or stupid, I'd remember that my grandma thinks I'm wonderful, and she thinks I'm beautiful, and she thinks that I'm going to be somebody, so I had this inside of me. If she said so, then it must be so. I think it was a combination of a number of things. I'm kind of feisty. I've always been a bit of a fighter all my life.

YDG   You are the president of a real estate development and construction company named Pueblo Contracting?

MDA   Yes, my husband Sev and I are partners, but I am the president.

YDG   Tell me about your company. What are your company's yearly revenues?

MDA   We make from about $14.5 to $20 million a year. We have a tightly knit organization. Our employees have been with us, many of them, for over five years, so that's good. It doesn't happen everywhere. We have a good core and everybody gets along. You have to surround yourself with good people. You can't be intimidated by people who are smarter than you. You have to have some confidence in yourself.

YDG   So are you very selective in your purchase of properties?

MDA   Yeah, one of the theories that I agree with completely is that we don't buy anything that we can't drive by. Like, we have a building in Hollywood that's in an area that's turning, which is really good, because it's in an area that's appreciated a lot. It's fully leased out; we don't have any vacancies whatsoever. We got a façade grant, and that fixed the exterior of it, and we remodeled the whole interior, and it's like night and day; it's wonderful, a wonderful building. Then we put in a coffeehouse that's run by Latinos. They were featured on TV as an L.A. Latino hot spot. They've been featured all over the place.

We're really happy to have been involved in that. We pride ourselves in doing things better than anyone else—being true to the past of that particular building, having nice, simple, clean lines. We hire good architects who tell us what they feel is the right color for the building. We don't pretend to know the right color. Some of these companies come up with really brilliant ideas, and so we say, "Hey, this is cool!" In the summertime, the gang members get wild in any community, and they tag our buildings. We paint it that same day.

YDG   How did you meet your husband?

MDA   We're high school sweethearts, and we've kind of grown together, both as people and in business. In a way, it's kind of cool that we never really had anything to worry about. We married each other, because we love each other.

YDG   Did you two go to college together?

MDA   We went to college together, too.

YDG   Did you both apply to the same college in order to be together?

MDA   I went to Loyola because that was the closest thing to my house. I think we talked a little bit about our culture, and the fact that because of my dad it was difficult for me to leave home. My dad understood that I should go to college, but he had a real difficult time that I would be living on my own. I'm the oldest. I had offers to go to other schools, but the happy compromise for all of us was Loyola. My mother went to bat for me and said, "Look, let her go. She needs to go to college," and my dad was thinking I was staying with my boyfriend, sleeping with him, and I was going to lose my virginity.

YDG   Growing up, did you ever carry a belief about something, only to find later that that belief did not work for you any more?

MDA   Well, maybe there was a belief that I was supposed to help my family forever, because, remember, in the Latino community, providing for your parents is what you're raised to do. We're there to help, and I always kind of felt bad because I didn't give my check to my parents. I never did that. I thought, "I need to take care of myself; I have needs." Then I thought, "Oh shit, I'm a real jerk of a daughter." I realized later that I had to be independent at some point and that it was okay for me to want to have the money.

I try to be generous with them, but I don't sit down and write checks for their bills or anything like that. I try to be generous with my nieces and nephews. I had a car that I sold to a family member at a real low rate, but I sold it to him; I didn't give it away. I have tried to benefit my family. If we build affordable housing . . . I have a young lady that my brother had a child with a while back, and I love my niece . . . we say, "Hey, why don't you rent one of the apartments here." I employ my two brothers, but they know construction, so it's not like I'm doing them any favors. I employ my niece's mother as a receptionist, and she's wonderful, you know. So I try to give in that way.

I don't believe I should just pay for stuff, just because I have more than they do. I get my ass kicked every day doing what I do. It stresses you out; you have to deal with it. It wakes you up at night, and you think, "How could I have done that better?" You always try to improve yourself. So I think that to a certain extent you just don't worry about it. You're taking a chance; you're a family; you and your husband are doing well, and you shouldn't feel guilty about it, because you made it.

It's liberating. I think, "Hey, I'm a businesswoman; I get my butt kicked everyday, and that's why I earn the money that I earn." The more money you make, the more risk you take. There is more pressure, more stress, and everything. There's a price to pay for everything. People need to know that it doesn't come that easily. We made the sacrifices, and that's why we're being rewarded. We all make choices. We make choices one way or the other, and some of our choices sometimes work out.

YDG Do you live by many cultural traditions regarding women?

MDA No. I don't even think I live by "white" standards, because my husband and I are equal. . . . He doesn't subordinate to me, and I don't subordinate to him. I'm not better than he is, and he's not better than I am. We respect each other. We duke it out like equals whenever we disagree on stuff, and in the end, we respect one another because we both complete each other as far as our personalities. We're two different people, but together it works for us. Even though it's not always smooth, and we fight, we're just two people who are independent, and because of that, it's going to cause friction sometimes.

YDG How do you feel about *respeto*? Do you believe young Latinas should allow their elder relatives to disrespect them?

MDA Well, I think . . . that's a tough one because, I mean, it's so engrained that you respect your elders, no matter what. But when you look back on things, you're right, some elders maybe don't respect you. I think you have to be very careful there, because unless your foot is completely in the "new world," so to speak, you can get your mouth slapped.

I don't think you should allow anybody to disrespect you, but I think when you're a kid, sometimes you don't even know you're being disrespected. It's kind of a tough one. If you recognize it, you should probably get away from the situation, avoid situations of conflict.

YDG   But do you think that it hurts young Latinas as far as assertiveness when they grow up?

MDA   I think that the disrespect, if you don't see it as such, could be a way to be demotivated, and it could instill some kind of insecurities that you'll never be able to get rid of. I was telling you that my role models were very good because they were telling me good things about me. If my role models had been telling me that I was not good, and I would never amount to anything, that's totally disrespecting me, right? But I wouldn't have known the difference; they're raising me.

I would have just thought it was true, and you kind of live up to people's expectations. I would say, if you realize you're being disrespected, depending on the situation, if you're home, and you depend on these people, find a way to deal with it, and get yourself independent as soon as possible.

I do think we make a mistake when we make our children kiss their relatives even though they don't want to. I raised Aaron, my son, to be respectful of people, but not beyond the point where he felt comfortable. If he didn't want to kiss somebody, I'd never push him.

I definitely believe that if relatives are giving you negative feedback, absolutely it's going to affect you. It does affect young Latinas, and if you're expected to grow up and get married and have kids, and that's all you're supposed to do is be a good wife, then unless you're really rebellious or something, it's going to affect you. I know some Latinas' self-esteem is pretty low, and that's why I think we have such a high incidence of teen pregnancy, because, first of all, they may be giving in to sex sooner than they should, because they don't want to say "no" because this guy won't come around anymore. There's insecurity there. Or, secondly, they want something to call their own, so that they can feel grown up and have respect.

You don't get respect in our culture, many times, for being the wife if the mother-in-law is still alive. In our culture, the only way to get the ultimate respect is by having children, because they are supposed to make you worthy. You need to watch what you say to these little girls; they're sponges, and everything you tell them, they're going to believe. I think that we are perpetuating the problem.

YDG You have been very successful in a male-dominated field. How have you accomplished that, and what have you had to deal with in terms of this type of career?

MDA Of course, many times, when you're in this career, and I'm the president of the company, they just assume that any man that's with me is the president, and I'm not. Or they always assume that the male is the superior between the two of us. They always assume that if your husband's involved that he does all the work. They assume that you don't do anything, and you have nothing to contribute. They assume that there's no way that you could know this business. I don't know why they think it's such a big deal. So those are some of the things that you come across. Some people have thought, "Oh, you guys are just a front for affirmative action and minority opportunities." People who say that don't know anything about affirmative action, because there's nothing out there that says, "Just because I'm Latina, I'm going to get all this business." I've got to scrape for everything I get. I have to bid it, and I have to make it profitable. I get the most raised eyebrows from Latino men. Even more so than white men. But . . . women are even worse: "You're a general contractor? Oh, are you licensed?" So you kind of just learn how to ignore people.

When I first started in the business, people thought I was a decorator when I came to a job site. Many times, I'm the only woman there. Sometimes I'll be the second woman at our job site because our operations manager happens to be a woman. But you know what? Men cannot handle us, you know. They don't know how to deal with us. I know that there have been clients that, if our operations manager were a man, they'd be golfing with him; they'd be going to the bar, whatever; but because she's a woman, although they respect her because she knows what she's doing, it's not the same. But there's a lot of raised eyebrows, many times, just because they have a mind-set that women don't go into construction. They'll ask me, "So you're out there over-looking your men all the time?" I'm not a superintendent; I'm the president of the company, you know. I'm not out there on the job site every day. That's why I have superintendents, and that's why I have an operations manager. If it was reversed and there was a man in my position, they'd never ask him if he were out there supervising his men.

YDG So you've gotten to the point where you don't even care anymore?

MDA It used to bother me, but it doesn't bother me anymore. You get to the point where you say, "That's your problem. It's not my problem, and I'm not going to lower myself to your level and explain anything to you. You're obviously a narrow-minded person." I think you need to have that kind of confidence after a while. I've always been a tomboy, and I've always competed against boys. When I was younger, I used to run and have races against my cousins, and I'd beat them all. I was a good runner. We'd get our bikes, and we'd go bike racing, and we'd race boys. I never thought anything of racing boys; it was no big deal to me. I never really thought that I couldn't do it. I was sometimes a little bit afraid, but I said, "This is what I want to do, and this is what I'll do."

When I went into sales, right out of college, and I didn't know what I wanted to do, I went into 100 percent commission sales, and I wasn't afraid I wasn't going to make any money; I wasn't afraid I was going to starve, none of that. All I could think of is that I wanted to make a lot of money. To a certain extent, I've always been a risk taker, but I've never really sat and thought about it. I choose to focus on my strengths rather than my weaknesses, because if I played into my weaknesses, I wouldn't get anywhere in life. I remember my dad, when we were young, he would pass by bridges and buildings, and he would say, "I built that," and "I built that," and he was just one of the team. It seemed like a cool thing, so when the opportunity came up, I took it. I started a little bit at a time and didn't make any money at first. I mean, you don't hit the ground running; you have to learn; it's a learning process. But after a while you get focused, and you do your thing.

It is very important that you feel confident and carry yourself with confidence. I think that people who aren't afraid and really don't care what people think are the ones that can break through. Sometimes, when you think too much, you kind of screw it up, and you never take action. So you've got to have a little bit of "get up and go." When the time comes for action, you've got to take action and not worry about it. If you always wait for the ultimate situation, you will never know it was the ultimate situation. You need to get prepared, do your homework, and then it's time to take action. And if you fall on your face, you fall on your face. You get up and try it again. I would say that's a hard lesson, and some people fail and then don't try again. But you've got to keep trying until you get it, until you find something that you're happy with. I'm happy doing what I do. I like what I do every day, even with the ups and downs.

YDG   Has there ever been a time when you thought, "I can't take this anymore, I want to quit?"

MDA   No, because if I ever feel that way, I'll quit. If I ever get to that point where I think it's overwhelming for me and I just can't do it, I'll quit. Because I'm not going to do something that I don't want to do.

YDG   Where do you think you got that kind of courage?

MDA   Well, I'm perceived sometimes as a bitch. Even my husband sometimes thinks I'm a bitch!

YDG   I haven't seen that side of you!

MDA   Well, that's because you never have had to deal with me when I think I'm right! Some people think I'm a bitch; some people think I have been arrogant, that I'm not nice. I've heard things people say, "Oh, don't talk to her; she's so arrogant; she thinks she's all that." I never really thought about it, but I don't care. That's just me. I know how I am. I'm friendly to everybody. I can be nice and everything, but I don't necessarily go out of my way for everybody, you know what I'm saying? I like to choose my friends carefully, and I think people read into it because I've gotten a lot of awards in the past, and I guess people think, "Oh, look at her, who does she think she is?" It's probably something within them.

YDG   Has being a woman in this field worked against you?

MDA   It's done both, helped me and hurt me. It's hard, because sometimes you have to do the unpopular things that, at the time, are uncomfortable, and you have to be willing to live with that, because most of us, as human beings, want to be accepted and liked by everybody. Nobody wants to go out there and not be liked, and you say, "I think I'm doing the right thing, and I think it will play out right because I think I'm on the right side."

YDG Do you go with your intuition a lot?

MDA Your gut feeling is something that's very real, but for some reason we kind of take it for granted or overlook it, or dismiss it as being butterflies or something. But your gut feeling can usually tell you a lot. Every time I've ever gone against my gut feeling, I've lived to regret it. So now I say, "No, I've got to go with that gut feeling. I'll stick with it." You've got to trust it. If you feel like something's pretty good, and you've done your homework, I wouldn't say, "Oh, gee, let me go invest my money in this one stock, because I have this gut feeling." That could be indigestion! But after a while, in your business, if you've got a sense for what's out there, and I think as you grow older you kind of become more set in your ways, and then you kind of hone your skills a little bit more, it becomes a little sharper and a little better.

After a while, if you don't learn from your mistakes, from the lessons that you get, then you're not going to keep going, and I think you learn that you have to stick up for yourself, and it's okay to stick up for yourself, because if you don't, nobody else is going to do it. So you hang in there, and you make your case, and you tell it like it is, and you just kind of go, and that's it. So, that's kind of the way that has worked for me, and if I come off as a bitch, fine. If I were a man, I'd probably be deemed assertive and shrewd. But if you're a woman, you're a bitch.

They'll tear you up the way you look, too. Like Florida's secretary of state. I mean, come on. Whether you like the turnout of the vote or not, to talk about her makeup, her red lipstick, I mean, they just had a field day with this woman. They don't say those things about men. They never say, "Look at that potbelly." But for women, they're quick to criticize how we look, and we seem to allow it. If you go in looking like shit, they say, "What the hell's wrong with you?" If you're too pretty, they think, "Oh, she's just a little sex kitten."

I don't really stop and think about the fact that I'm a woman in a man's field. I didn't even think about it when I went into it for the first time, when I first started in construction. There were people pointing it out to me who kind of brought it to my consciousness, but I know where I am in this world, and I don't mind. I kind of like it.

YDG   Have you always felt your internal strength?

MDA   Well, I think it's probably through a series of things that happen in life, that you kind of know that you're on the right path, whether you call it inner strength or whatever you want to call it. Being valedictorian was a good thing for me. It said, "You're on the right path," and then graduating from Loyola. I really made a mistake in my first job that I ever took, but I learned some lifetime skills that I never would have received had I not gone through that baptism by fire, you know. So even though it was a nasty, negative experience, it was good. With patience, you see things work out. You make decisions that, at first, are very painful and unpopular with people, and then, when they work out, and it was the right decision, you say, "You know what, I was right." It encourages you to make those decisions again in the future. So I think that you have to, first of all, venture into the unknown, make a decision, and when it works out correctly, or even if it doesn't, find that silver lining. Then it kind of encourages you to go on and do what you need to do. You kind of build on that a little bit at a time and take baby steps, and I think, at some point, the major thing is getting over some of the cultural stuff and realizing that wanting to be wealthy is really okay.

YDG   What do you think we need to teach our young Latinas?

MDA   Well, there's a teacher at San Fernando High, where I went to school, and he invited me back to speak to his class to shed some light, specifically to the young ladies, because he felt that the future of the community lies in these young Latinas. He felt that Latinas should be demanding and expecting more of the men that they date and marry because when young Latinas think it's okay to have a boyfriend in jail, because he's nice, we're really in trouble. He says, "You women have the power to make us do more than we think we can achieve, and so if you, as young women, decide that it's not good enough to date a loser, guys are going to start applying themselves a little bit more." I thought that he had a good perspective on that, and he feels that Latinas are the key to changing our society and a lot of our community. I think that he's very enlightened in that sense, and he says it in a very matter of fact way—he says, "That's why I concentrate on these young women. I want to see them become successful." He has them in his computer lab, and they are just as involved as guys because they can do it. He thinks that through their involvement and their success and their demand for success from their boyfriends that it just helps everybody out. We've set our standards too low.

I did this one conference for young Latinas, and I told them, "You can ask me whatever you want, I'm here to answer your questions." One of the girls asked me what my husband thought about my working, and it kind of gave me a quick glimpse into where her world was.

I was talking to one of my employees—we had a meeting downtown—and we drove down together, and we were talking about her parents, how her mother waits on her stepdad hand and foot. If he needs to eat, she gets him his plate and she brings it to him, and then when he's done, she takes it and buses it and cleans it and everything else. Whatever he needs, she's at his beck and call. If he needs a tortilla, she gets up and warms it for him. But now that she's got arthritis, it's a little more difficult. She said, "Now she expects us to wait on him." I said, "You know, they come from the Old World. My mother waits on my father hand and foot. My dad sits down at the table—and I used to get angry about this when I was younger, but I know now I'm getting older because I kind of let go—my dad sits down at the table and says, *"¿Vieja, qué hay para comer?"* ("What is there to eat?") And then my mom serves him his food. Then it's *"Vieja, I need a tortilla,"* or *"Vieja, tráeme una cerveza."* ("Bring me a beer.") My dad doesn't get up from the table at all. When he's done, he says, *"Vieja, I'm done,"* so my mom comes and picks it up, and then he goes outside. But as far as that, my mother is like hand and foot with him. It used to piss me off because I would think, "Mom, he could get up." But then I realized that it works for them. My dad respects her, he really does. But this is what she thinks is okay.

YDG   And we wonder why these young girls think the way they do.

MDA   Well, my sister and I had all the chores in the house, pretty much. My brothers were treated like kings. They didn't have to do anything. I think they got shortchanged, because they didn't have the responsibility that we had growing up. We were being taught how to wash dishes, how to iron. I never was taught how to cook, really, but all of the other domestic things. It was probably that way so I could be a better wife or whatever. But my brothers were never asked to wash, iron, wash dishes, none of that. They never had to, just because they were men. That's part of our culture.

YDG   If you had to name three things that oppress young Latinas today, what would they be?

MDA   Well, number one, I'd say that they have to take control of their own bodies and not get pregnant. Don't fall into that. Number two, I think they need to concentrate on their education—find a way to get themselves through college, whether it's through scholarships or whether it's through junior college and then college. They need to go through that because I think that's another thing that keeps us down. And then the third thing is believing that they are disadvantaged, that for some reason something happened to us along the way, and we don't have the same value as everybody else.

This is kind of weird, because sometimes when you get into the affirmative action thing it's kind of like a double-edged sword, and you can get negative feedback. The most disadvantaged people are the ones that need affirmative action. People say that if you get affirmative action, you get some kind of help, and so you say, "I've got to be disadvantaged, right?" So, if you don't act disadvantaged, you don't get the help. Maybe you say, "I don't care if I have that or not, because in affirmative action the pie is so little." You want to look at the big pie instead, and if you have to give up that small slice, then fine, go somewhere else. I think that with our community, the way that it's excelling and becoming wealthy, I think there will be more opportunities for Latinos to come. But I think that, as Latinas, I think the main thing is to get control of your body, and your sexuality, and get an education. I think the third thing, perhaps, is the issue of poverty and socioeconomic status; but if you stick with the education, I think you'll make it. I think, though, with Latino kids in general, I think our education system, especially our public education system, is oppressing them. I don't think that they're getting the educations they need to really survive in this world.

YDG   I agree. Today you really need to be educated and technologically savvy in order to be competitive.

MDA   Right. So you need to know that if you are in that kind of situation, that's kind of a tough one. That's an external threat. But even so, I think there are other threats, too—the need to have that boyfriend early, and then, of course, sex, and the whole issue of "should I have sex or not?" You end up having children, and it's very difficult to recover after you've had a child. It's possible, but it's a life-changing decision. Think about it. When you're young, boys are at that stage when they're all horny and everything, and to be accepted, if you sleep with your boyfriend, you could get pregnant. Especially when we have that whole thing to reconcile with the church that says you shouldn't be having sex at all. Of course, you're not going to look for anything to protect yourself, because then it would be premeditated. I mean, it all comes together, and I think, as far as oppression, I think it would be not getting an education and having a child too early.

YDG   What would you tell Latinas who felt a lack of support— from those closest to them—whenever they wanted to pursue something positive for themselves?

MDA   Well, first of all, they don't need support. The support needs to come from themselves. You have to believe in yourself, and do it. Don't do it because you feel that somebody else is going to support you or not. If you're saying your mother is not supporting you, or whatever, maybe she can't support you because she doesn't have the ability to, or she's too tired, or whatever. If you know you're doing the right thing, just do it. It doesn't take much to say, "I want to excel in school." You need to study a little bit more; you find time to do it. I think you have to have confidence in yourself. Don't look externally for total validation. When I was going through school, my parents, because they had limited educations, similar to most other people, couldn't help me with my homework. Yet I wanted to do well. That didn't mean they didn't support me. They didn't have the money to get me a tutor; that was unheard of. It was just like

I had to work it out, and so I worked it out myself. You don't necessarily need support; I used to study in the kitchen on a little table. I didn't have my own desk. It doesn't always have to be perfect for you to do it; you just do it. Just do it. I think that's what you need to remember, that you are in control of yourself. I would say that to take responsibility for your actions is probably one of the biggest things that people can do. If you take responsibility for your own actions, then you don't have to worry about saying, "So and so didn't support me, so that's why I failed." You're responsible for yourself. You're the one that chose not to open your books, or you're the one that decided to ditch class, or you're the one that decided to be late, or get yourself educated, or study. You're the one that's responsible. Bottom line. That's your job. So I think that you may not always get the support, you just need to do it.

YDG   Any message you would like to give Latinas about life?

MDA   Well, I think as far as life is concerned, it's very short. It's over before we know it. I think that many times we lose sight of that brevity and get caught up in things or worry about things that in the end never really will matter. I think that if you stay focused, become truly responsible for yourself, and you know that you're the one that can make things happen, even though it may seem at the time that other people are going against you, you're the one that can make things happen. I think that in the end, you will be successful at whatever it is that you want to be. Whether you want to be the best mother to your children, and that's success in and of itself, or whether you want to be the CEO of a corporation, or a writer, whatever it is that you want to do. Know that choosing something and being happy is true success, and money is secondary. You're always going to need a certain amount so you're comfortable, but as far as happiness, it's about ultimately finding what makes you happy and where you feel the most comfortable. Some people with all the money in the world are unhappy. I think being focused and responsible and having courage and the determination to do things when things look like they're tough, I think that's what can make the difference in life.

On Your Way to Empowerment

During my time in the recovery program, we were required to attend at least two Alcoholics Anonymous meetings a week. These meetings, which were attended by individuals struggling with mind-altering substances, were filled with people waiting to get their chips. Different chips were passed out to individuals who had gone for thirty, sixty, or ninety days clean and sober; one individual acquired a chip that represented thirty years of sobriety. At first I didn't understand why these chips were so important to these people, and why most would cry at meetings when they were called up to receive their honorees chip. It wasn't until I learned the principles of the twelve-step program that I understood the importance of that little piece of metal—it represented hope, freedom, and truth. These chips symbolize the process of recovery, which consists of taking one day at a time, living in truth, confronting your fears, and releasing your shame. While my healing progressed, the pain, anger, shame, and guilt intensified so deeply that at times I wondered if it was all worth it—was I going to make it through this thing they called healing and self-empowerment? Although my faith kept me alive, I found myself running to Alcoholics Anonymous meetings in order to feel safe. When I received my thirty-day chip I cried—I knew at this time I was going to make it because I believed in the process of the program. I carried my chip with me wherever I went, from the boardroom to the shower. Every time life seemed unbearable, I would pull out this little piece of metal, hold it tight, close my eyes, and say, "Let go and let God." I knew I was doing everything in my power to live a good and healthy life; whatever else happened in my life I knew I had no power or control over, and I had to let it go.

I want this book to be your chip. Every time you feel weak about something that you know is not right for you, grab this book, wrap your arms around it, and know you are not alone. Many Latinas are experiencing the very same feelings you are at exactly the same moment. Close your eyes and feel the power within yourself to stay strong. Children need teddy bears to feel safe—it is okay for us to have something too. In order for you to prosper, you need to truly believe in the process of self-empowerment. You are a worthy, loving, beautiful Latina Queen who deserves to protect herself from the things, people, and places that will hurt her.

You would be surprised at the incredible response *Empowering Latinas* has received throughout the nation. The power of consciousness within the media, radio, and press is evidence that the world is ready for us; we are vital for the betterment of the nation. Yes, our numbers are staggering when it comes to education and other issues pertaining to the challenges Latinas face, but *Empowering Latinas* provides the power of knowledge, the tools to implement the strategies, and the *ganas* to succeed. There is no stopping us.

Adelante, mujer!

Resources

Domestic Violence

Alternative to Domestic Violence
(800) 339-7233
Emergency shelter for battered women. Outreach counseling, advocacy, and community education.

Domestic Violence Hotline
Chicano Service Action Center
(800) 339-3940

Drug/Alcohol Addiction

1-800-9HEROIN
Information and referral to support groups and treatment for all types of drug and alcohol abuse, including heroin.

1-800-COCAINE
24-hour hotline for information and referral to cocaine treatment programs and any other drug or alcohol treatment programs throughout the United States.

1-888-MARIJUANA
Information and referral for support groups and treatment for marijuana and any other drug or alcohol abuse.

Ala-Non & Ala-Teen
(760) 242-9292
Support groups for friends or family of those abusing drugs or alcohol.

National Association/ Children/Alcoholics
(888) 554-2627
Provides prevention and reduction of alcoholism and related problems in children of alcoholics.

Homeless Support/ Shelters

Casa Youth Shelter
(800) 914-2272
Emergency shelter for runaway youths in crisis.

East Los Angeles Hotline/ Shelter
Chicana Service/Action Center
(800) 548-2722
24-hour hotline and shelter for women and children.

Free Spirit Shelter
Chicana Service Action Center
(323) 937-1312
Shelter for battered women and children.

Legal Aid

Inland Empire Latino Lawyers
(909) 369-3009
One-on-one consultation with attorneys, and preparation of court documents. Assists low-income families on such issues as minor custody, divorce, civil summons, restraining orders, and so on.

Legal Protection for Women
(323) 721-9882
Paralegal services, preparation of family law forms for divorce, legal separation, nullity, temporary restraining orders, support, civil harassment, modification of child custody, and so on.

Mexican American Legal Defense and Education
(213) 629-2512
Promotes and protects the civil rights of Latinos in the United States in the areas of employment, education, immigration, political access, and language.

Mental Health

Bilingual Family Counseling
(909) 986-7111
Provides a range of drug and alcohol abuse prevention and treatment programs. Outpatient drug and alcohol treatment and child abuse treatment.

Caritas Counseling
(909) 370-1293
Individual, family, group counseling, parent education, anger management, and substance abuse groups.

Co-Dependents Anonymous
(602) 277-7991
International organization created for spiritual and emotional assistance in dysfunctional personal relationships through the application of the 12 Steps.

Depression Awareness
(800) 421-4211
Call to request up to three free brochures on the general symptoms of depression.

National Alliance for the Mentally Ill
(800) 950-6264
Provides information about mental illness and referrals to community resources.

Nueva Vida Counseling Center
(909) 825-6188
County Mental Health Services: individual, group, marital, crisis intervention.

Turning Point Counseling
(800) 998-6329
Christian outpatient counseling for individuals, marital and pre-marital couples, and children.

Rape/Sexual Abuse

Incest Survivors Anonymous
(562) 428-5599
Literature for survivors of incest as well as information on groups meeting in the area.

Rape/Sexual Abuse Hotline
(800) 842-8467
Information and referral service for crime victims.

Rape/Sexual Abuse
Project Sister
(909) 626-4357
24-hour sexual assault crisis hotline. Support groups for rape and incest survivors.

Survivors of Incest Anonymous
(562) 806-7270
Self-help group of women and men age eighteen and older who are survivors of incest.

Safe Sex Practices

AIDS Project Inform
(800) 822-7422
National information referral for AIDS resources.

Birth Control Information Line
(800) 722-4777
One-stop family planning health services for men and women age twenty-one and under.

CDC National STD Hotline
(800) 227-8922
Information and referral to health clinics. Crisis intervention regarding sexually transmitted diseases.

California Family Planning
(800) 942-1054
Recorded information and referral to local birth control and family planning services.

Choices/Teen Awareness, Inc.
(714) 525-5997
Abstinence and resource education targeted for youth, parents, and families. Promotes support that is needed to make healthy, wise decisions for future success.

Planned Parenthood
(800) 230-7526
This number automatically connects the caller with the Planned Parenthood office in their area. These offices offer reproductive health services, the WIC Program, and educational services. Birth control, STI, GYN, colposcopy, prenatal care, cancer screening, pregnancy testing.

Teens Teaching AIDS Prevention
(800) 234-8336
National information and referral hotline. Answers any questions regarding AIDS or any STD. Referrals to testing sites support groups in your area.

Suicide Hotlines

(800) 843-5200
(800) 914-2272
(800) 570-4673

Women's Support

La Leche League International
(800) 525-3243
Worldwide organization providing support to pregnant and breastfeeding women.

Pregnancy Hotline National
(800) 843-5683
24-hour hotline with live response every day for pregnant women in crisis. Resources for pregnancy tests, clothing, housing.

Project Cuddle
(888) 628-3353
24-hour hotline for pregnant women or women who are contemplating abandoning their children.

Women Helping Women Services
(877) 655-3807
Provides free phone counseling, emotional support, and practical information on any issue.

Youth Support

California Youth Crisis Line
(800) 843-5200
24-hour crisis line, intervention-counseling youth-to-parent message services.

Hit Home Youth Crisis Hotline
(800) 448-4663
24-hour hotline for kids age eighteen and younger to call when in crisis. Caring listeners talk with youth about their problems.

National Runaway Switchboard
(800) 621-4000
24-hour hotline for runaway and homeless youth and their families, provides crisis intervention.

Teen Line
(800) 852-8336
Teen-to-teen hotline. Referrals given to community agencies as needed.

The Twenty-five Best Universities for Latinos

Because it has such an impact on an individual's standard of living, getting a college education is critical for young Latinos. *Hispanic* magazine published the following list in the March 2001 issue to help guide college-bound students.

University of California, Berkeley
110 Sproul Hall
Berkeley, CA 94720
Phone (510) 642-3175
http://www.berkeley.edu

Rice University
6100 Main Street
Houston, TX 77005
Phone (713) 527-4036
http://www.rice.edu

Florida International University
University Park
Miami, FL 33199
Phone (305) 348-2363
http://www.fiu.edu

Massachusetts Institute of
Technology
77 Massachusetts Avenue
Room 5-111, News Office
Cambridge, MA 02139
Phone (617) 253-4791
http://web.mit.edu

Stanford University
Stanford, CA 94305
Phone (650) 723-2091
http://www.stanford.edu

San Francisco State University
1600 Holloway Avenue
San Francisco, CA 94132
Phone: (415) 338-1113
http://www.sfsu.edu

University of New Mexico
Student Services Center #150
Albuquerque, NM 87131
Phone (505) 277-2446
http://www.unm.edu

University of California,
Los Angeles
405 Hilgard Avenue
Los Angeles, CA 90095
Phone (310) 825-3101
http://www.ucla.edu

New Mexico State University
(Main Campus)
Box 30001 Dept. 3A
Las Cruces, NM 88003
Phone (505) 646-3121
http://www.nmsu.edu

Rutgers, Newark
249 University Avenue
Newark, NJ 07102-1896
Phone (973) 353-5205
http://www.rutgers.edu

The University of Florida
201 Criser Hall
Gainesville, FL 32611
Phone (352) 392-1365
http://www.ufl.edu

University of Texas at El Paso
500 W. University Avenue
El Paso, TX 79968
Phone (915) 747-5576
http://www.utep.edu

California State University,
Los Angeles
5151 State University Drive
Los Angeles, CA 90032
http://www.calstatela.edu

Texas A&M University
College Station, TX 77843
Phone (409) 845-3741
http://www.tamu.edu

The University of Texas at Austin
Main Building, Room 7
Austin, TX 78712
Phone (512) 475-7440
http://www.utexas.edu

University of Miami
P.O. Box 248025
Coral Gables, FL 33124
Phone (305) 284-4323
http://www.miami.edu

DePaul University
One E. Jackson Boulevard
Chicago, IL 60604
Phone (312) 382-8300
http://www.depaul.edu

St. Edward's University
3001 S. Congress Avenue
Austin, TX 78704-6489
Phone (512) 448-8500
http://www.stedwards.edu

Our Lady of the Lake University
411 S.W. 24th Street
San Antonio, TX 78207-4689
Phone (210) 434-6711
http://www.ollusa.edu

University of Houston,
Downtown
One Main Street
Houston, TX 77002
Phone (713) 221-8522
http://www.uh.edu

University of Southern Colorado
2200 Bonforte Boulevard
Pueblo, CO 81001
Phone (877) 872-9653
http://www.uscolo.edu

San Diego State University
5500 Campanile Drive
San Diego, CA 92182
(619) 594-7800
http://www.sdsu.edu

Northeastern Illinois University
5500 N. St. Louis Avenue
Chicago, IL 60625
Phone (773) 794-2600
http://www.neiu.edu

The University of Texas, Pan
American
1201 W. University Drive
Edinburg, TX 78539-2999
Phone (956) 381-2206
http://www.panam.edu

CUNY City College
160 Convent Avenue
New York, NY 10031
Phone (212) 650-6977
http://www.ccny.cuny.edu

References

Alarcón, Norma, Ana Castillo, and Cherríe Morago. 1993. *The Sexuality of Latinas*. Berkeley: Third Woman Press.

Allen Zieger, Carol, and Stephanie Allen. 1993. *Doing It All Isn't Everything*. Austin: New Perspective Press.

Anonymous. 1994. Living with Depression. *Self*, 8 (June): 36–41.

Anthony, Dr. Robert. 1996. *How to Make the Impossible Possible*. New York: The Berkeley Publishing Group.

Canfield, Jack, Mark Victor Hansen, and Bud Gardner, eds. 2000. *Chicken Soup for the Writer's Soul*. Deerfield, FL: Health Communications.

Canfield, Jack, Mark Victor Hansen, Marci Shimoff, and Jennifer Hawthorne, eds. 1996. *Chicken Soup for the Woman's Soul*. Deerfield Beach, FL: Health Communications, Inc.: 73.

Coalition of Hispanic Health and Human Services Organizations (COSSMHO). 1999. *The State of Hispanic Girls*. Washington, D.C.: The National Alliance for Hispanic Health.

Dolgoff, Stephanie. 2000. Feeling sad, feeling bad. *Psychology Today*, 12 (August): 87–92.

Dyer, Dr. Wayne. 1977. *Pulling Your Own Strings*. New York: HarperCollins Publishers.

Espín, Olivia M. 1997. *Latina Realities*. Boulder: Westview Press.

Flores, Bettina R. 1990. *Chiquita's Cocoon*. Granite Bay, CA: Pepper Vine Press, Inc.

Garcia, Maria. 1997. Being your niña's biggest booster. *Latina*, 3 (April-May): 51–54.

Gawain, Shakti. 1998. *The Living in the Light Workbook*. Novato, CA: Nataraj Publishing.

Gil, Rosa Maria, and Carmen Inoa Vasquez. 1996. *The Maria Paradox*. New York: The Berkeley Publishing Group.

Gilligan, Carol. 1982. *In a Different Voice*. Boston: Harvard University Press.

Hay, Louise L. 1990. *Love Yourself, Heal Your Life*. Carlsbad, CA: Hay House, Inc.

Jeffers, Susan. 1987. *Feel the Fear and Do It Anyway*. New York: Ballatine Books.

Kolotkin, Richard A. 1996. The shame. *Weight Watchers*, 5 (August): 11–15.

Leserman, Linda J. 1997. Impact of negative self-esteem on physical and emotional health. *Psychosomatic Medicine,* 59 (2): 152–160.

Marotta, Priscilla V. 1990. *Power and Wisdom: The New Path for Women.* Plantation, FL: Women of Wisdom, Inc.

Martinez, Sonya. 1996. Examining ethnic differences and commonalities. *Evaluation Review,* 20 (2): 123–145.

Mason, Marilyn J. 1991. *Making Our Lives Our Own.* San Francisco: Harper San Francisco.

Mirandé, Alfredo. 1997. *Hombres y Machos.* Boulder: Westview Press.

Northrup, Christiane. 1998. *Women's Bodies, Women's Wisdom.* New York: Bantam Books.

Patton Thoele, Sue. 1991. *The Courage to Be Yourself.* Berkeley: Conari Press.

Phelps, Stanlee, and Nancy Austin. 1997. *The Assertive Woman.* San Luis Obispo, CA: Impact Publishers.

Philips, Dr. Debora. 1998. The power of positive reinforcement. *Psychology Today,* 15 (March 2000): 23–29.

Rutledge, Tom. 1998. *Earning Your Own Respect.* Oakland, CA: New Harbinger Publications, Inc.

Ryar, Sonya, Ph.D. 1997. Culture and Hispanic girls. *Hispanic Journal of Behavioral Sciences,* 2 (3): 199–217.

Sigundo, Jose Luis. 1978. The Theological Discourse about Marriage, Family and the Church. In *Seminario de Historia de las Mentalidades.* Mexico: Joaquin Mortiz/Instituto National de Antropologia e Historia: 17–78.

Tamez, Elsa. 1987. *Against Machismo.* Costa Rica: Meyer Stone Books: 8.

Tschirhart Sanford, Linda and Mary Ellen Donovan. 1984. *Women and Self-Esteem.* New York: Penguin Books.

U.S. Department of Health and Human Services. 1998. *Children and Sexual Abuse: Reports from the States of the National Child Abuse and Neglect Data System.* Washington, D.C.: GPO.

Valdez, Carmen. Personal interview. November 10, 2000. San Diego, California.

Vanzant, Iyanla. 1999. *Don't Give It Away!* New York: Fireside.

Williamson, Marianne. 1993. *A Woman's Worth.* New York: Ballantine Books.

Internet Articles

Bogart, Cathy. 1997. The price of growing up female. *Forum,* 3 (Spring): 13–19. Available at: www.avila.edu/departments/womensstudies/newslett/1997/spring/s97p5.htm

Napolitano, Grace F. 2000. Napolitano becries lack of mental health and substance abuse care for Latinos. Press Release. April 13, 2000. Available at: www.house.gov/apps/list/press/ca34_napolitano/decrylatinoMH.html

Perez, Cristina. 2000. It's not all in your head. Available at: www.latinola.com/mental_health.htm

Ramirez, Veronica. 1998. The case for diversity. Available at: www.hisp.com/dec98/diversity.html

Sarracent, Mari Carmen. 1999. Latinas speak out at Princeton University roundtable. *Hispanic Outlook in Higher Education,* 10 (20): 24–27. Available at: www.hsf.net/whatsnew/LatinasSpeak.htm

Smith, Lawrence. 1998. The economic value of education. Available at: www.hawaii.gov/dbedt/hell-98/value.html

Top 25 Colleges for Hispanics. Available at: www.hsf.cybercampus/collegeguide/04.html

Zate, Maria. 1999. Putting the money where her heart is. *Latingirl Magazine*, 4 (April/May): 16–18. Available at: www.hsf.net/whatsnew/Puttingthemoney.htm

Index